TENANT MANAGEMENT
Findings from a Three-Year
Experiment in Public Housing

MANPOWER DEMONSTRATION
RESEARCH CORPORATION

BALLINGER PUBLISHING COMPANY
Cambridge, Massachusetts
A Subsidiary of Harper & Row, Publishers, Inc.

This book was prepared by the staff and Board of Directors of MDRC, in connection with its work in carrying out and evaluating a National Tenant Management Demonstration under the following grants or contracts:

> U.S. Department of Housing and Urban Development
> Office of Policy Development and Research
> (Contract No. H-2543)
> Office of Housing—Federal Housing Commissioner

> The Ford Foundation
> Division of National Affairs
> (Grant No. 760-0045)

The points of view, opinions, and conclusions stated in this book are not intended to represent the official position or policy of the sponsoring funding agencies.

International Standard Book Number: 0-88410-694-2 (Cloth)
0-88410-696-9 (Paper)

Library of Congress Catalog Card Number: 80-28637

Library of Congress Cataloging in Publication Data
Manpower Demonstration Research Corporation.
  Tenant management.

  Principal authors: M.A. Queeley, J. Quint,
S. Trazoff.
  Includes index.
  1. Public housing—United States—Management.
2. Real estate management—United States.
I. Queeley, Mary A. II. Quint, Janet. III. Trazoff,
Suzanne. IV. Title.
HD7288.78.U5M37 1981   363.5'8   80-28637
ISBN 0-88410-694-2
ISBN 0-88410-696-9 (pbk.)

TENANT MANAGEMENT

CONTENTS

List of Figures ix

List of Tables xi

Acknowledgments xv

Basic Conclusions on the National
Tenant Management Demonstration 1

Nature of the Demonstration 1
Nature of This Book 4
Major Findings and Conclusions 5

Chapter 1
The Origins of the Demonstration 11

The Historical Setting: Highlights and Issues 12
Predemonstration Experiments in Tenant Management 16
The Need to Test the Model 20

Chapter 2
The Demonstration Idea:
Content, Organization, and Planning   21

Tenant Management Model and Process   21
Organization and Management of the Demonstration   26
MDRC's Role: Managing the Demonstration   29

Chapter 3
Status of Tenant Management
at the Demonstration Sites   37

A. Harry Moore TMC   37
Curries Woods TMC   41
Iroquois Homes RMC   43
Que–View TMC   46
Calliope Development TMC   48
Sunrise Acres TMC   51
Ashanti TMC   53

Chapter 4
The Tenant Participants   57

The Tenant Management Board of Directors   57
The Tenant Management Staff   72

Chapter 5
The Housing Authority—Tenant Management
Corporation Relationship   89

Predemonstration Relationships   91
Attitudes of Housing Authority Personnel   92
The Management Contract   101
The Housing Authorities View the Demonstration   103

Chapter 6
Training and Technical Assistance   111

Modification in the Program Model   112
Technical Assistance   114
Training   122

Chapter 7
Achievement of Demonstration Goals   127

Real Estate Management   127
Physical Improvements   163
Tenant Employment   180
Tenants' Satisfaction and Assessment: Tenant
  Management and the Resident Community   196

Chapter 8
Costs of Tenant Management   209

The Methodology of the Cost Analysis   210
The Incremental Cost of Establishing the TMC   214
The Annual Incremental Cost of an Operating Tenant
  Management Corporation   230

Conclusion   239

Appendixes   245

A — Research Methodology for the National Tenant
      Management Demonstration Program   247
B — Projected Rental Income and Net Incremental Operating
      Expenses of Tenant Management under Three Alternative
      Assumptions about Inflation   259
C — MDRC Documents on Tenant Management   261

Index   263

LIST OF FIGURES

2–1   Organization of the National Tenant Management
      Demonstration Program   27

7–1   Performance Indicators in the Tenant Management
      Demonstration by Site and Calendar Quarter,
      Average Monthly Rent Due   136

7–2   Performance Indicators in the Tenant Management
      Demonstration by Site and Calendar Quarter,
      Average Monthly Rent Collected   140

7–3   Performance Indicators in the Tenant Management
      Demonstration by Site and Calendar Quarter,
      Rent Collection Rate   141

7–4   Performance Indicators in the Tenant Management
      Demonstration by Site and Calendar Quarter,
      Units Owing Over One Month's Rent   146

7–5   Performance Indicators in the Tenant Management
      Demonstration by Site and Calendar Quarter,
      Vacancy Rate   152

7–6   Performance Indicators in the Tenant Management
      Demonstration by Site and Calendar Quarter,
      Vacant Unit Preparation Rate   155

7–7   Performance Indicators in the Tenant Management
      Demonstration by Site and Calendar Quarter,
      Routine Maintenance Job Completion Rate   159

LIST OF TABLES

2-1   Division of Responsibility Under Tenant Management
Demonstration Prototype   24

2-2   Funding Sources, Amounts, and Recipients: National
Tenant Management Demonstration Program   28

2-3   MOD and TPP Allocations to Participating Sites:
National Tenant Management Demonstration Program   28

4-1   Characteristics of Tenant Management Corporation
Boards, June 1979   64

4-2   Characteristics of Tenant Management Staff,
June 1979   74

6-1   Technical Assistance and Training at the Tenant
Management Sites   116

7-1   Performance Indicators in the Tenant Management
Demonstration by Site and Calendar Quarter,
Average Monthly Rent Due per Unit   134

7-2   Performance Indicators in the Tenant Management
Demonstration by Site and Calendar Quarter,
Average Monthly Rent Collected per Unit   138

7-3   Performance Indicators in the Tenant Management
Demonstration by Site and Calendar Quarter,
Rent Collection Rate   142

7-4   Performance Indicators in the Tenant Management
       Demonstration by Site and Calendar Quarter
       Units Owing Over One Month's Rent   144
7-5   Performance Indicators in the Tenant Management
       Demonstration by Site and Calendar Quarter,
       Vacancy Rate   150
7-6   Performance Indicators in the Tenant Management
       Demonstration by Site and Calendar Quarter,
       Vacant Unit Preparation Rate   156
7-7   Performance Indicators in the Tenant Management
       Demonstration by Site and Calendar Quarter,
       Routine Job Completion Rate   160
7-8   Summary of Management Performance Measures
       by Site   164
7-9   Modernization Projects and Status of Activities
       at the Tenant Management Sites   170
7-10   Modernization Projects: Summary of Activity
       at End of Demonstration   174
7-11   Analysis of Tenant Employment During the Tenant
       Management Demonstration by Site and Calendar
       Quarter   182
7-12   Distribution of Employment Categories by Tenant
       Management Site   185
7-13   Parameters of Tenant Employment   186
7-14   Tenant Employment: Utilization of MOD and CETA   194
7-15   Residents' Experiences and Perceptions of
       Management   198
7-16   Tenants' Perception of Improvement in the
       Performance of Management Functions   201
7-17   Resident Satisfaction with Project Conditions   203
7-18   TMC Tenants' Evaluation of the TMC   206

8-1   Comparison of Estimated Cost of PHA Management
       and Actual Cost of Tenant Management, 1976-1979,
       Jersey City—A. Harry Moore   215
8-2   Comparison of Estimated Cost of PHA Management
       and Actual Cost of Tenant Management, 1976-1979,
       Jersey City—Curries Woods   218
8-3   Comparison of Estimated Cost of PHA Management
       and Actual Cost of Tenant Management, 1976-1979,
       Rochester—Ashanti   221

8-4 Comparison of Estimated Cost of PHA Management
and Actual Cost of Tenant Management, 1976-1979,
New Haven—Que-View   224

8-5 Comparison of Estimated Cost of PHA Management
and Actual Cost of Tenant Management, 1976-1979,
New Orleans—Calliope   227

8-6 Comparison of Estimated Cost of PHA Management
and Actual Cost of Tenant Management, 1976-1979,
Louisville—Iroquois Homes   229

8-7 Comparison of Estimated Cost of PHA Management
and Actual Cost of Tenant Management, 1976-1978,
Oklahoma City—Sunrise Acres   231

8-8 Comparison of Estimated Cost of PHA Management
and Actual Cost of Tenant Management, Contract
Period Annualized, Jersey City—A. Harry Moore   233

8-9 Comparison of Estimated Cost of PHA Management
and Actual Cost of Tenant Management, Contract
Period Annualized, Rochester—Ashanti   235

8-10 Comparison of Estimated Cost of PHA Management
and Actual Cost of Tenant Management, Contract
Period Annualized, New Orleans—Calliope   236

8-11 Net Incremental Costs of Tenant Management   237

A-1 Data Sources: Tenant Management Demonstration
Research   250

A-2 Urban Institute Survey: Sample Sizes by Respondent
Category   254

ACKNOWLEDGMENTS

In the preparation of this book the Board of Directors of Manpower Demonstration Research Corporation concentrated on its first section, Basic Conclusions. They were led in that effort by Mr. Anthony Downs, as chairman of the board's Tenant Management Committee. The body of the work was written by members of the MDRC staff. The principal authors of the book were Mary A. Queeley, Janet Quint, and Suzanne Trazoff. Background writing, data compilation, and analysis were provided by Margaret Boykin, Alvia Branch, Stephen Grayson, Susan Motley, and Sallie Shuping-Russell. Robert Sadacca and Suzanne B. Loux of the Urban Institute were the principal investigators for the survey component of the impact analysis. Grace Critton, Judith Gueron, and Vivian Manning contributed critical reviews of the work during its various stages, as did staff members of the program's funding agencies—the Department of Housing and Urban Development (HUD) and the Ford Foundation. The editorial and production processes were coordinated by Sheila Mandel and Suzanne Trazoff. Mary Queeley was in charge of the research effort for MDRC through the life of the demonstration, and William Grinker was responsible for coordinating and overseeing the preparation of the final text. Finally, appreciation must be expressed to the tenants who participated in the demonstration and to the housing authority staff members who supported that effort.

PARTICIPATING PUBLIC HOUSING AUTHORITIES AND TENANT MANAGEMENT CORPORATIONS

Jersey City Housing Authority (New Jersey)
  A. Harry Moore Tenant Management Corporation
  Curries Woods Tenant Management Corporation

Housing Authority of Louisville (Kentucky)
  Iroquois Homes Resident Management Corporation

New Haven Housing Authority (Connecticut)
  Que-View Tenant Management Corporation

Housing Authority of New Orleans (Louisiana)
  Calliope Tenant Management Corporation

Oklahoma City Housing Authority (Oklahoma)
  Sunrise Acres Tenant Management Corporation

Rochester Housing Authority (New York)
  Ashanti Tenant Management Corporation

BOARD OF DIRECTORS
MANPOWER DEMONSTRATION
RESEARCH CORPORATION

BASIC CONCLUSIONS ON THE NATIONAL TENANT MANAGEMENT DEMONSTRATION

NATURE OF THE DEMONSTRATION

The National Tenant Management Demonstration was designed in 1975 to test the potential benefits of having low-income public housing residents manage their own housing developments. The model for this demonstration evolved in St. Louis, Missouri, when, after several years of traumatic rent strikes, the tenants themselves were awarded management responsibility at several public housing developments.

Initial results in St. Louis seemed quite favorable. They included lower vacancy rates, improved rental collections, reduction of crime and vandalism, and improvement in the morale and self-confidence of the tenants. The Ford Foundation, which was an early supporter of the St. Louis experiment, and the U.S. Department of Housing and Urban Development (HUD) were interested in this approach to easing public housing problems. They recognized that a careful, limited test of tenant management was needed to assess its effectiveness under circumstances different from those in St. Louis.

Therefore, HUD and the Ford Foundation agreed to pursue a jointly sponsored national demonstration of tenant management in public housing. They believed that training, technical assistance, and improvement of the housing structures would be important ingredi-

1

ents if such a program were to succeed. HUD and the Ford Foundation therefore agreed to supply funding for technical assistance and training, physical improvements, and a careful evaluation of the program. In June 1975, the two funding partners asked the Manpower Demonstration Research Corporation (MDRC) to manage such a program. Its responsibilities were to design the program, determine its feasibility, help select the participating sites, conduct or arrange for training and technical assistance, monitor the sites, and evaluate the results.

The demonstration model devised by the planners of the National Tenant Management Demonstration involves a partnership between the local public housing authority (PHA) and the board of directors of a nonprofit tenant management corporation (TMC). Residents of each participating development elect a board of directors from among themselves. That board is trained in organizational skills and in the principles of real estate management. Major board responsibilities include formulating policy, determining the rules and regulations governing the development, and ensuring that residents can participate in policymaking and operations.

The routine daily management of each development is carried out by a staff hired from the resident population. The board chooses a resident manager at a point well into its own training process. That manager, with the aid of the board, then hires a staff. Staff training is the last step prior to signing a contract that transfers management control from the housing authority to the tenant management corporation.

Details of the working partnership between tenants and housing authority are specified in the management contract. The PHA delegates certain policy and management responsibilities to the TMC. Generally, the PHA still provides overall direction and sets broad performance criteria, while the TMC exercises direct control over day-to-day management. The housing authority retains ownership of the property and is ultimately responsible to HUD and the taxpayers for ensuring that the development is well maintained and that all laws and regulations are followed.

In selecting demonstration sites, three initial criteria were established: (1) housing authority commitment to the concept of tenant management, (2) organization and managerial potential of the tenants, and (3) existence of a cooperative relationship between housing authority and tenants. The support of city and state governments and of HUD's regional and area offices, geographic location, and the physical condition of the buildings were also considered. MDRC tried to include a broad variety of housing types, locations, populations, and predemonstration conditions. Following extensive field visits, discussions, and formal applications to HUD, a reasonable balance among these elements was achieved.

Seven public housing developments in six cities were selected as demonstration sites among 24 applicants. These sites were among 51 originally identified as potential sites by HUD regional offices. The seven developments selected were:

A. Harry Moore TMC
Jersey City, New Jersey

Curries Woods   NO
Jersey City, New Jersey

Iroquois Homes TM C
Louisville, Kentucky

Quinnipiac }
Riverview }   To become Que-View TMC   No
New Haven, Connecticut

Calliope   TMC
New Orleans, Louisiana

Sooner Haven }   No
387 scattered }   To become Sunrise Acres TMC
site units   }
Oklahoma City, Oklahoma

Olean Townhouses }   TMC
Capsule Dwellings }
Fairfield Village }   To become Ashanti TMC
Bronson Court   }
Edith Doran   }
Rochester, New York

These are predominantly family developments located in urban areas. Altogether, they contain 4,788 dwelling units housing 19,000 people. They have heavy concentrations of female-headed, welfare-dependent families, and the residents are predominantly black. The Urban Institute, a subcontractor for part of the research, found these demonstration sites similar to a representative sample of 168 other projects in 39 large housing authorities with respect to population, physical characteristics of the structures, and neighborhood environments. Since none of the demonstration projects has a predominantly elderly population, the sites have a younger average age of adults and a lower percentage of households receiving disability pensions and social security than the average public housing project.

Over the three years of the demonstration, the six public housing authorities received funds totaling $20.2 million from two HUD programs—$15 million from the Modernization Program (MOD) for physical improvements and $5.2 million from the Target Projects Program (TPP) for training, technical assistance, tenant salaries, and social services. In addition, MDRC made about $90,000 of its Ford Foundation grant available to the TMCs to cover incidental expenses.

NATURE OF THIS BOOK

This book represents the culmination of the national demonstration experience. It contains research findings on the results of the program and describes how tenant management was implemented; what changes, if any, occurred under tenant management; and how such changes came about. The research was conducted by MDRC with the assistance of the Urban Institute. It has four major components:

- Historic context: Examination of past and current tenant management efforts to allow comparison of those efforts and the national demonstration.

- Documentation: Description of the development of the program at the local level to identify possible explanations for results and to supply the information necessary for replication in other housing authorities.

- Impact: Assessment of the degree to which tenant management improved operating performance and increased resident satisfaction. It uses information from monthly and quarterly reports submitted by the sites on management performance indicators, as well as baseline and follow-up surveys conducted by the Urban Institute. The site reports and surveys are used to assess whether positive changes occurred under tenant management. The Urban

Institute also selected similar housing developments not under tenant management to assess whether any observed changes in the demonstration sites significantly differ from changes in similar developments during the same period.

- Cost analysis: Measurement of the cost of the demonstration, from the point of view of both one-time expenditures and regular line item costs in the site's operating budget. It compares costs under tenant management with operating costs before the demonstration in an effort to determine the added or decreased expenditures associated with tenant management. It also projects ongoing costs associated with tenant management.

MAJOR FINDINGS AND CONCLUSIONS

Tenant management was never regarded as an answer to all the problems of public housing. Many problems—long-term welfare dependency, high unemployment, and low education levels—are rooted in general social conditions extending far beyond the public housing projects themselves. The sponsors of this demonstration thought that if tenant management was administered with care and evaluated thoroughly, it might prove an effective form of property management under certain circumstances. Thus, the demonstration aimed at bettering the tenants' quality of life primarily by having them help improve property management. The major findings and conclusions of the National Tenant Management Demonstration—and recommendations for future action, where appropriate—are presented below.

1. In most of the public housing developments in the demonstration, tenant management worked just as well as previous management by housing authorities. This suggests that tenants can manage public housing projects effectively under certain conditions attainable in many projects. But it also indicates that, at least in the short run, tenant management does not usually produce results markedly superior to those stemming from conventional housing authority management.

Specifically, tenant management was not significantly better than housing authority management in terms of individual performance indicators such as average rent collections, vacancy rates, or speed of response to maintenance requests. However, resident satisfaction with overall management was higher in tenant-managed develop-

ments than it had been previously or than it was in other similar conventionally managed developments. Also, tenant management was
perceived as stricter than conventional management by the TMC
board and staff and by the tenant community.

None of the above findings depended upon poor past performance
by housing authority management; tenant managers were just as
effective as their predecessors, even where the latter had been performing well and where no traumatic events like the St. Louis rent
strikes had occurred. Nor did these findings depend upon the use of
MOD funds as a concomitant of tenant management. Therefore, we
believe tenant management could work effectively in a sizable fraction of existing public housing authorities, subject to the conditions
described further below.

2. Compared to traditional public housing management, tenant
management produced such additional benefits as (a) increased employment of residents, (b) a sense of personal development among
participants in the tenant management organization, and (c) a greater
overall satisfaction with the project management among residents,
but also incurred significant additional costs. While these benefits are
quite important, it is difficult—perhaps impossible—to quantify their
importance.

On-site tenant employment increased over the course of the demonstration and exceeded HUD's desired—but infrequently attained—
target of hiring 25 percent of project workers from among residents.
Many jobs were created, particularly in the TMC core management,
social services, and aide categories. However, it appeared that without continued supplemental funding from HUD, most of these added
jobs could not be sustained beyond the demonstration.

Increased personnel accounted for most of the additional costs
at the sites, adding from 13 to 62 percent to what continued traditional management would have cost. This wide range of added costs
resulted from variations in levels of both tenant employment and
numbers of units involved at each site. It indicated the range of additional costs likely to be required by tenant management. However,
many of the residents employed in tenant management positions
would otherwise have been on welfare or receiving other public
assistance. Among a sample of workers interviewed, 70 percent had
previously been receiving some type of public assistance that they no
longer required. Therefore, not all the additional personnel costs that
housing agencies would have to pay to sustain tenant management

represent net additional costs to society. Assessing the true magnitude of such net social costs, however, was beyond the scope of this demonstration.

3. Creating effective tenant management takes widely varying amounts of time in different developments and requires certain preconditions. The most important of these is a strongly positive and cooperative attitude on the part of the public housing authority and the ability of executive directors to communicate their commitment to this new idea to the PHA staff and to mobilize housing authority resources in implementing it. In addition, adequate time should be available to train residents in general organizational skills, as well as in the specific tasks of managing public housing. Many residents elected as board members had limited or no previous experience functioning in such a setting; they had to learn basic board skills before they could deal with tenant management issues effectively. However, neither extremely adverse prior conditions nor traumatic events like those preceding tenant management in St. Louis are necessary for successful tenant management.

4. Technical assistance is essential to the development of effective tenant management throughout its planning and implementation and well into the period after contract signing. The effectiveness of technical assistance depends upon support and acceptance from both the PHA and the TMC. However, identification and recruitment of adequate technical assistance personnel are difficult and time consuming because of the many skills required for this role. Board training took twice as long as had been anticipated by program planners, and provision of technical assistance to each board was needed throughout the course of the demonstration. Although this need diminished in intensity, the boards required ongoing help to consolidate and further develop their decisionmaking and planning abilities and to resolve internal conflicts. Moreover, the presence of non–PHA technical assistance appeared necessary for the TMC to develop as a truly independent entity. However, use of both PHA and non–PHA faculty in the training of board and staff seemed successful.

Therefore, any attempt to institute tenant management in a large number of public housing projects would probably be most effective if a single organization were responsible for arranging and overseeing the complex process of training and technical assistance.

5. Because the tenant management organizations formed during this demonstration were not in operation very long, it is difficult to

draw firm conclusions about their possible longer range impacts upon either management performance or resident satisfaction. Therefore, we strongly recommend that HUD support continued tenant management in these projects for several more years and carefully monitor and evaluate their performance through existing HUD channels. Such monitoring and evaluation should cover benefits and costs of the employment and community development impacts of tenant management. Future analysis of tenant management should focus not only on housing, but also on these broader nonhousing effects that are likely to produce significant social benefits and costs not dealt with in this demonstration.

6. The prerequisites of successful tenant management exist in varying degrees in public housing projects across the United States. Sufficient numbers of qualified residents were available to fill tenant management corporation board and staff positions in all but one of the projects in the demonstration. Although initial turnover among top level TMC staff was high, performance was generally adequate, and the continuity and strength of the TMC were not impaired. We believe that resident capabilities for adequate tenant management exist in nearly all other public housing projects as well.

There are greater variations in the attitudes of public housing authorities and their executive directors toward tenant management. When this demonstration began, very few expressed much interest in trying tenant management, even though major financial incentives to do so were offered. Their interest may rise once the results of the demonstration become known and they realize that tenant management does not unduly disrupt housing authority operations. However, maintaining the necessary continuity of housing authority support for tenant management is often difficult because of relatively rapid turnover among executive directors. Consequently, we believe that tenant management has mixed probabilities of success in the nation's public housing projects.

7. It would be unwise to mandate tenant management of public housing—either requiring it everywhere or prohibiting it everywhere. Rather, individual housing authorities should be able to pursue it if they so desire and if they meet certain preconditions. HUD should act as a sympathetic respondent to interest expressed locally in tenant management if it has enough resources to help local housing authorities finance the additional costs involved. However, in view of the limited benefits of tenant management, the additional costs it

requires, the administrative difficulties of establishing effective tenant management in any large number of public housing projects, and the stringent limits upon resources now available to HUD, we do not regard widespread implementation of tenant management as a high priority objective. Therefore, while we recommend that HUD continue the existing demonstration as noted above, we would not now expand tenant management further.

In conclusion, the demonstration has established that tenant management of public housing is feasible. It has also identified the conditions for success and most of the costs and mechanics of implementation. However, whether tenant management is worthwhile for a particular situation depends upon the importance attached to values that the demonstration was not designed to assess. These values include the satisfaction that low-income people derive from participation in the management of their housing affairs and the willingness of government to share public housing management prerogatives. Whether achieving these values is worth the added costs involved is preeminently a political decision.

1 THE ORIGINS OF THE DEMONSTRATION

Tenant management is one response to the profound problems that afflict public housing in the United States. These problems include the deteriorating physical condition of much of this housing and the financially pressed state of many public housing authorities. To a large extent, public housing has become home for a somewhat permanent class of economically depressed people often victimized by crime, drug abuse, and vandalism. For many public housing authorities, these multiple difficulties have resulted over the years in seemingly insurmountable management problems. For the residents, whose existence may be shaped by circumstances beyond their control, these problems have created a growing demand for greater participation. In response to these needs, the federal government has launched several initiatives that increasingly mandate tenant involvement. Tenant management seeks to deal with the problems of public housing within the context of that federal response.

The National Tenant Management Demonstration was designed to test the effectiveness of entrusting the residents of public housing with large areas of management responsibility. Authority was vested in an elected tenant board and in the staff it selected from among the tenant population. The basic model for the national demonstration originated with a tenant management experience in St. Louis, Missouri. While this was not the only existing model, its preliminary success indicated that it merited testing on a broader scale. Before the specific aspects of the demonstration itself are detailed, an examination of the historical setting of public housing will provide the context for the demonstration.

THE HISTORICAL SETTING: HIGHLIGHTS AND ISSUES

Public housing is the oldest and largest program of direct government housing assistance for the poor.[1] In the mid–1970s, it comprised about 2 percent of the housing stock in the United States and sheltered over 3 million people. Approximately 2,800 public housing agencies (PHAs) or local housing agencies (LHAs) were responsible for about 1.2 million units in approximately 10,000 projects, ranging in size from 10- or 20-unit complexes to huge developments with 1,500 units or more. The size of the PHAs, as measured by the number of units under management, also varied widely: about half managed 100 units or fewer, while about 13 percent (including all the housing authorities selected for participation in the demonstration) managed 500 units or more.

Public housing is an expensive program. Revenues come almost exclusively from rents and from the federal government, which subsidizes operating expenses and covers local debt service associated with initial construction costs. Washington guarantees over $12 billion in tax-exempt PHA securities. For the 1978 fiscal year, the federal government spent nearly $1.8 billion on public housing—over $1.1 billion for debt service and $0.7 billion in operating subsidies.

The U.S. Housing Act of 1937 (also known as the Wagner–Steagall Act) served as the cornerstone for all subsequent public housing legislation. The major purpose of the original act was to provide employment for construction workers idled by the Great Depression. Its secondary purpose was to house middle-class families dislocated by the Depression's economic ravages.[2] Although public housing was created originally for the temporarily poor, the chronically unem-

---

1. Chester W. Hartman, *Housing and Social Policy* (Englewood Cliffs, N.J.: Prentice-Hall, 1975), p. 113.

2. Alvin Rabushka and William G. Weissert, *Caseworkers or Police? How Tenants See Public Housing* (Stanford, Calif.: Hoover Institution Press, 1977), p. xvi.

ployed or impoverished have become its primary tenants. Yet not all of public housing has succeeded in meeting the challenge of serving the changing population.

The Supreme Court decided that the federal government could not build or own public housing, but it could finance state and local ownership by paying the original capital costs of construction. Accordingly, the Housing Act provided for financing with two components. The federal government was to cover debt service (amortization plus interest) through an Annual Contributions Contract, and tenant rents (linked to residents' incomes) were to support all administrative and operating costs. In addition, housing projects were exempt from paying local property taxes. Payment In Lieu Of Taxes (PILOT) by the housing authority guaranteed local services to the projects.

World War II transformed the economic, social, and political environment in which public housing had originated. During the war, industrial production was mobilized for military ends, and the postwar economic boom made irrelevant a program spawned during the Depression. Construction workers found ample jobs in private industry, and middle-class families acquired the means to move out of public housing. These families were increasingly replaced by tenants who were poor, welfare dependent, and black. The changing racial and socioeconomic composition of the tenant population became more apparent during the 1950s. The Korean War, the 1954 Supreme Court school integration decision, and several other factors shifted national priorities elsewhere, so that public housing became a dumping ground for poor inner-city residents displaced by urban renewal and highway construction.

By the 1960s and early 1970s, some large urban housing projects become characterized as "vertical slums." Physical appearance, sometimes the product of poor design, suffered from the aging process, deferral of repairs, and vandalism and resulted in developments unattractive to working-class families. It became necessary to fill vacant units with the unemployed and the welfare dependent, and especially in cases where these tenants became the majority, housing authorities found rent revenue inadequate to cover the increasing costs of operations. Under these pressures, those local housing authorities afflicted by these compound problems were forced to respond by increasing rents while services declined. In extreme cases, law-abiding tenants were frequently fearful for their safety and that of their children. Triple locks on apartment doors did little to allay anxiety and much to preclude the development of a sense of community.

The 1960s saw some important activities on the federal level, both in terms of housing legislation and in terms of the growing importance of the American poor on the federal domestic policy agenda. In 1961, housing legislation was enacted to supply federal subsidies for units occupied by the elderly and to give PHAs more flexibility in determining income limits and setting rents. A provision of the 1965 Housing and Urban Development Act freed PHAs of their obligation to pay all operating expenses out of rents collected, and in 1968 the federal government was authorized to subsidize the rents of very poor families with four or more dependent children. The Brooke Amendments (1969, 1970, 1971) to the 1937 Housing Act provided operating subsidies to PHAs on a permanent basis and granted additional reserve funds for those housing authorities facing severe financial problems. However, the net effect of the amendments, which set rent ceilings at 25 percent of tenants' incomes, was to impose an even greater financial burden on PHAs.

In 1967, as part of a new emphasis on guaranteeing due process, HUD issued its first directive dealing with tenants' rights, which specifically ensured that the tenant be given the reasons for an eviction, but did not require that those reasons constitute a good cause for eviction. Subsequent rules liberalized the practice of denying admission to or evicting tenants with illegitimate children or police records and established a model lease and grievance procedure for tenants. Moreover, the 1968 legislation required PHAs to provide education and occupational counseling and to stimulate tenant participation. Another factor strengthening tenants' rights was the extension to public housing of the Supreme Court's 1969 action striking down the residency requirement for welfare benefits.

The Modernization Program (MOD), created in 1968 in recognition of the financial inability of the PHAs to undertake major repairs of older public housing projects, provided federal funds for financing physical improvements. The 1968 act was one of several that also aimed at improving management practices. The Turnkey II program permitted PHAs to contract with private real estate firms to manage public housing projects under PHA jurisdiction. The Housing Management Improvement Program (HMIP) provided $25 million to 13 PHAs during fiscal years 1972–1975 to create and test new approaches for handling management problems. In 1974, the Target

Projects Program (TPP) replaced HMIP. Directed at "troubled" housing projects, TPP funds were to be used for software projects such as special social services, tenant education, and employment programs. A total of $35 million a year was made available through TPP, and along with MOD, the program was an important source of funding for the recipient sites, including those participating in the tenant management demonstration.

The Housing Act of 1974 attempted to alleviate the financial burden of the PHAs by recommending that they adopt a range of rents approach. This involved the selection of public housing applicants ranging from those tenants able to pay ceiling rents to those dependent on welfare, in order to encourage a greater economic mix among public housing residents as well as to enhance rent revenues. In addition, procedures were adopted to improve the financial viability of PHAs by guaranteeing prompt payment of rent and prompt eviction for nonpayment. PHA management and tenants were charged to work together to assure adequate security and maintenance, and HUD was authorized to provide up to $500 million each year in subsidies for operating expenses. This amount was increased by $60 million in 1975 and further in subsequent acts.

A key feature of the MOD, Turnkey II, HMIP, and TPP programs in their efforts to improve management was their provision for tenant input in deciding on both the allocation of monies and the determination of management policies. This concern reflected an impetus to involve the poor in the political process that had its roots in the tenets and tactics of the civil rights movement and that was institutionalized through the federal Office of Economic Opportunity (OEO). OEO supported and offered funding for activities using a strategy of community action that focused on the income, housing, and educational problems of the poor. An important aspect of this strategy was the mobilization of opposition toward traditional providers of these services using various confrontation type protests. The community action strategy also included supplanting these providers or gaining power to ensure that their activities reflected the self-determination of the poor.

Two organizations aided by the OEO momentum during the 1960s that had special relevance for public housing tenants were the National Welfare Rights Organization (NWRO) (1966) and the National Tenants Organization (NTO) (1969). Using protest tactics similar to those in many OEO–initiated efforts, these organizations moved to attack the problems of the poor in their respective focal areas—with the poor themselves, not their representatives, on the front lines of the protests. Through the myriad of activities fostered by OEO, the civil rights movement, NTO, NWRO, and many other community action programs, the poor gained greater power and were increasingly recognized as a force to be dealt with in the management of their lives.

PREDEMONSTRATION EXPERIMENTS IN TENANT MANAGEMENT[3]

Tenant management was the logical outgrowth of a set of historical trends involved in the effort to reverse the physical, financial and social deterioration of public housing.[4] It was anticipated that management by tenants would result in improved living conditions for several reasons. First, tenants could establish their own priorities in improving their developments by deciding how MOD monies should be spent. Second, tenants would respond more promptly to their fellow residents' housing and social service needs and could exert pressure on their peers to stop vandalism and to help make public housing developments more attractive places in which to live. Higher income residents might therefore be attracted to public housing to offset the low rents of welfare recipients. Third, rent rolls might also be increased, because tenant managers would be better informed than housing authority employees about the activities of their fellow tenants and would be able to identify tenants whose rents did not accurately reflect their current employment status. Finally, employment among tenants could be boosted directly by hiring residents for tenant management staff positions and indirectly through community development activities.

The National Tenant Management Demonstration was modeled on a specific set of roles and institutional arrangements developed be-

3. For a more complete discussion of predemonstration experiments in tenant management, see William A. Diaz, *Tenant Management: An Historical and Analytical Overview* (New York: Manpower Demonstration Research Corporation, 1979).

4. HUD has recently indicated that they believe improved management to have been the only important concern in the conception of the demonstration. MDRC records show that although management was often the stated issue in written material, the underlying issue in many discussions was the potential of tenant management to foster greater independence and self-determination among the residents.

tween the St. Louis Housing Authority and several tenant management corporations in public housing projects in that city. That model represents only one of a number of predemonstration efforts at tenant management, broadly defined here as granting some responsibility to residents for day-to-day management decisions. It is useful to examine these other efforts briefly in order to understand the variety of forms that tenant management can assume.

All these efforts can be ranked according to degree of tenant involvement. The Tenant Manager Program in Washington, D.C., falls at the low end of the scale. Initiated at two developments in 1973, extended to three other developments in 1977 as a result of TPP funding, and continuing until the present, the program merely entails the installation of a tenant as project manager. There are no requirements that other tenants be involved in any way. The manager's duties include the usual array of day-to-day management tasks, and policymaking responsibility is shared with PHA area supervisors and central office staff. [One of the original managers undertook to provide social services and recreational activities that do not ordinarily fall within the purview of conventional management.]

At the opposite end of the spectrum lies the Bromley-Heath program in Boston. An outgrowth of OEO efforts to explore tenant management on a demonstration basis, a TMC was established at the development in 1971. After a limited pilot program in which the TMC was responsible for some of the buildings comprising the development, the Boston Housing Authority signed a five-year contract with the TMC to manage the entire project. The contractual arrangements devolved virtually all management functions onto the TMC, including accounting, legal, and purchasing responsibilities. The Bromley-Heath Tenant Management Corporation thus functions as a "mini" housing authority.

Between these two extremes was another effort in Washington, D.C., that involved a private housing management corporation and an elected tenant governing board. After two years, the tenants there voted not to continue the arrangement. An effort in Hawaii, similar in structure to the national demonstration, was terminated after less than two years when federal funding ran out.

The third and most significant tenant management experience, also falling in the middle of the spectrum, was that of St. Louis. In 1954, a development called Pruitt–Igoe was built with great hope and public expectations of success. Meant to represent ideal public housing, its design was so innovative that it won an architectural award. By the 1960s, however,

> Robbers, burglars, narcotics pushers, and street gangs roamed at will through the buildings. Anarchy prevailed. Windows were broken faster than they could be replaced.
>
> The steam pipes were not covered and children were seriously burned. People fell out of windows or walked into elevator shafts to their deaths. . . .
>
> Last winter, with windows out, pipes froze and broke on some of the top floors, sending streams of water through the buildings and forming glaciers on the stairs.[5]

During the years of Pruitt–Igoe's decline, other precipitous events were taking place in St. Louis. Tenant power clashed with a financially beleaguered housing authority unable to halt the physical and social deterioration of its projects. Tenant management in St. Louis evolved as part of the settlement to a series of long and bitter rent strikes by public housing residents. Under this agreement, provisions were made for the election by tenants authoritywide of a Tenant Affairs Board (TAB) that would be significantly involved in formulating housing authority policy.

In the three years following the strike settlement, the TAB, with the support of the PHA, developed tenant associations—whose members had often been active in the ad hoc groups that had emerged during the strike—in each project. Strong tenant associations soon emerged at two developments—Carr Square Village and Darst—and the first two tenant management corporations were established at these sites. Board members were selected from existing tenant organizations, and these boards went on to hire tenant staffs. The Ford Foundation provided moral and financial support and assumed the cost of training, salaries, and technical assistance.

In March 1973, the first two developments signed management contracts with the housing authority. A year later, two other tenant management corporations, also supported by the Ford Foundation, followed suit; and a fifth was added in 1975. Ford Foundation staff members were instrumental in directing the attention of HUD central office personnel to the development of tenant management in St. Louis. With strong foundation encouragement, St. Louis was successful in obtaining TPP funds for the tenant management corpora-

---

5. Hartman, p. 120.

tions. Somewhat after their inception, the developments also received substantial funds under HUD's MOD program.

In addition to the sites involved in the national demonstration, the St. Louis experience also spawned interest in other communities, most notably in Newark, New Jersey, where a major tenant management program modeled on the St. Louis example is currently under way. Tenant management as it operates in St. Louis and in the national demonstration involves the tenant management corporation and the housing authority in a contractual relationship under which responsibility for the performance of management tasks is shared. Unlike tenant management at Bromley-Heath, where tenants have almost total independence, the housing authority retains control over accounting and purchasing, continues to set general personnel and wage policies, and collects rents. And in contrast to the Washington Tenant Manager Program, where the housing authority retains control over all decisionmaking, members of tenants' boards are charged with hiring and firing staff and with establishing rules and regulations, while their counterparts on the staff are responsible for supervising routine maintenance jobs, leasing vacant apartments, conducting rent reviews, delivering social services, and so on.

Early evaluations indicated that the St. Louis tenant management program effected improvements in several areas of both hard and soft management performance and that it compared favorably with past and current modes of management within the St. Louis Housing Authority. Other experiments with tenant management have also resulted in positive evaluations. Collectively, these experiences suggest that tenant management can work, but that it is not feasible in every development.

One factor that constrains the implementation and survival of the program is lack of tenant interest. Residents are sometimes unwilling to take on the demanding task of managing their own developments: they may lack the time, they may feel that management is the responsibility of the housing authority, or they may be satisfied with conventional management. Early reports also suggest that tenant management is costlier than conventional management and heavily dependent on the existence of federal funding initiatives and alternative, private funding sources.

THE NEED TO TEST THE MODEL

Neither the St. Louis experience nor those of other predemonstration experiments provided systematic evidence on the preconditions and outcomes associated with tenant management. In particular, they supplied few clues about the cooperation between housing authority and tenants that would lead to the successful implementation of the concept.

In mapping out the direction of a wider test of the St. Louis model, the funding agencies agreed to stage comparable tenant management efforts in a small number of cities, and to carefully evaluate the results and assess the impact of varying local conditions. The research findings and the lessons they suggested were expected to provide a much firmer basis for addressing the feasibility and viability of tenant management. HUD agreed to provide substantial allocations for the demonstration in the form of MOD, TPP, and research monies; and the Ford Foundation agreed to provide supplementary funds. In June 1975, HUD and the Ford Foundation designated the Manpower Demonstration Research Corporation (MDRC) as program manager for the demonstration with responsibility to determine its feasibility, select participating sites, conduct training, provide technical assistance, monitor site operations, and evaluate the results.

While hopeful that the results of the demonstration would be positive, the funding agencies recognized that regardless of its relative success, tenant management would not be a panacea for the problems currently inherent in much of public housing. Whatever judgments one makes about the potential of this innovation, one should bear in mind the basic plight of public housing—a system that does not have the financial resources to meet the needs of a tenant population suffering from very severe and long-standing deprivation. Tenant management alone cannot overcome these barriers, but it could, if successful, begin to reduce them.

2 THE DEMONSTRATION IDEA
Content, Organization, and Planning

The National Tenant Management Demonstration was conceived to test, under varying local conditions, the effectiveness of the St. Louis model to improve the operating performance of public housing management, expand tenant employment, and increase tenants' satisfaction with their housing. Program evaluators were to examine the relationship between tenants and PHAs and the quality of leadership in both necessary for a successful program. In addition, the demonstration would assess the accomplishments of tenant management and determine whether the additional costs, training, and technical assistance involved were worth the effort required. A study of the demonstration's outcomes should provide an assessment—however tentative—of the feasibility, viability, and initial consequences of tenant management as an option for public housing in the United States.

TENANT MANAGEMENT MODEL AND PROCESS

The demonstration model closely paralleled the St. Louis effort. A partnership between the housing authority and the tenant management corporation (TMC) was basic to both programs. The demonstration model defined the nature of the TMC, the respective responsibilities of each partner, and the key events in which the TMC assumed operating responsibility. This model served as the prototype

21

for the participating sites, but was flexible enough to allow for much variation.

The central element of the model is the tenant management corporation, the organizational mechanism through which tenant management is implemented and sustained. It is a nonprofit corporation, governed by an elected board of directors, and its membership includes all legal project residents over the age of 17.

After the board is elected by the tenant membership, the TMC becomes the single authoritative tenant entity at the development. The responsibilities of the TMC board include policy formation, developing rules and regulations governing project residency, and ensuring that tenants at large have the opportunity to participate in policymaking and operations. In cooperation with the housing authority, the board develops a roster of TMC staff positions to be filled by project residents. It recruits and selects the TMC manager and may, depending on local arrangements, participate in the selection of the remaining staff. Board members are elected to regular terms of office that ranged, during the demonstration, from one to three years. They receive no salary, but are compensated for out-of-pocket expenses such as babysitting, transportation, and telephone calls. The board members, along with the subsequently hired staff, play the pivotal roles in the TMC.

A minimum typical staff includes a tenant manager, who replaces the PHA's on-site manager after the PHA–TMC contract is signed, and building or lane managers. Lane managers, representatives from low-rise developments, and building managers, representatives from high-rise developments, are unique to tenant management. These positions were designed to diminish the distance between tenants and management by having a staff member residing in—or responsible for—each geographical area of a development to serve as a direct, two-way communication link between the tenant manager and the residents. The duties of building and lane managers include explaining project policies, enforcing rules and regulations, and providing services directly to residents within their areas of responsibility. They also convey tenants' needs, problems, complaints, and the like to the tenant manager. The TMC staff may also include an assistant manager, a social services and/or recreation director or aides, and a security force. With the exception of the manager, who replaces a PHA employee, the TMC staff represents an addition to PHA personnel (such as maintenance workers and clerks) at the project, who remain PHA employees, although they are usually supervised by the

TMC. For PHA personnel, existing collective bargaining agreements and/or civil service regulations continue to be observed under tenant management.

The model calls for the PHA and the TMC to sign a management contract that delegates to the TMC certain policy and management responsibilities associated with the day-to-day operation of the project. These responsibilities fall into four broad categories—policy development, budget preparation and control, management operations, and tenant relations. Specific responsibilities include tenant screening and selection (after eligibility has been determined by the PHA), apartment leasing, establishment of rules and regulations for continued occupancy, development of grievance procedures, budget preparation and monitoring, administration of annual rent review, follow-up on rent delinquency, initiation of evictions, and provision of routine maintenance. In the performance of these functions, the TMC works within existing HUD rules and regulations and under the supervision of the PHA, which retains ownership of the property and is ultimately responsible to HUD and the taxpayers for it. While the TMC assumes responsibility for some functions, the PHA retains authority over such others as payroll accounting, purchasing, legal processing of evictions, and the provision of extraordinary maintenance. The PHA also monitors TMC performance. Table 2-1 delineates the prototypical division of labor between the PHA and the TMC.

In addition to defining certain essential elements of tenant management, the demonstration model includes a sequence of steps, some of which overlap, for the ideal TMC developmental process.

- Planning Phase: Fashioning by interested residents of tenant management goals and a general approach to achieve them; determination of preliminary distribution of management functions between the PHA and future TMC; outlining the scope and length of TMC training; assessing the amount and kind of training and technical assistance that will be needed.

- Election of Board of Directors: Designation of a slate of candidates by fair and open means, assuring representation of various geographical areas of the project; development of election criteria and election mechanics; monitoring of the elections and certification of their results by a duly authorized body such as the League of Women Voters or the American Arbitration Association.

Table 2–1.   Division of Responsibility Under Tenant Management
Demonstration Prototype.

Tasks	TMC	TMC and PHA	PHA
Tenant selection and screening		X	
Development of annual operating budget		X	
Allocation of operating funds among selected budget line items	X		
Preparation and disbursement of TMC payroll			X
Provision to TMC of incentives to encourage cost savings and discourage overexpenditures			X
Leasing vacant apartments	X		
Institution of eviction proceedings and documentation of relevant information	X		
Processing of evictions, including legal proceedings and physical removal when appropriate			X
Physical collection of rents			X
Follow up on rent delinquencies	X		
Conduct of annual rent reviews	X		
Processing work orders for maintenance service requests	X		
Inspection and preparation of vacant apartments	X		
Supervision of on-site maintenance personnel	X		
Hiring, firing, and supervision of management personnel	X		

Source: MDRC file material.

- Incorporation of the Tenant Management Corporation: Taking the legal steps necessary to make the board of directors a non-profit corporation under the laws of each individual state, thus ensuring that it can receive funds and carry out business.

- Board Training: A general orientation to tenant management and public housing using the Program Sequence Guide (discussed in Chapter 6) as a framework; familiarizing the board with the policies and practices of the PHA; development of corporate bylaws and rules and regulations for the resident community; presentation of real estate management principles and practices; establishment of procedures for the recruitment and hiring of TMC staff.

- Recruitment and Hiring of TMC Staff: Development of job descriptions and qualifications; notifying residents of job availability; checking candidates' references and status as tenants; interviews for candidates and selection of future TMC employees.

- On the Job Training of the TMC Staff: Assignment of newly hired staff to work alongside their PHA counterparts and, where no counterpart exists, under the supervision of the PHA manager or tenant manager trainee. (During this period, the TMC board is still in training and receives oral and written reports on the staff trainees' progress.)

- Classroom Training of the TMC Staff: Formal, intensive presentation of real estate management principles and techniques—for example, finance, maintenance, and other day-to-day management issues—provided by appropriate PHA staff and consultants.

- Negotiation and Signing of the Management Contract: Gradual delegation to the TMC of responsibilities that it will fully assume upon consummation of the contract; discussion of the terms of the management contract, specifying the responsibilities of the TMC and PHA; creation of a site level budget; formal signing of the contract by the PHA and TMC.

- Assumption of Management Responsibility by the TMC: Reassignment of the PHA manager; TMC staff's full assumption of day-to-day project operation under supervision of the TMC board; TMC board's full assumption of policymaking and community relations functions.

ORGANIZATION AND MANAGEMENT
OF THE DEMONSTRATION

The structural and financial organization of the demonstration was rather complicated and unconventional. A variety of human and financial resources was mobilized to test the model described above. Figure 2–1 depicts the organization of the demonstration.

Four major organizational groups were involved in the effort—the U.S. Department of Housing and Urban Development (central and field offices), the Ford Foundation, the Manpower Demonstration Research Corporation, and the local participants (PHAs and the tenants living at the respective developments). Within HUD, two units were involved—the Office of Policy Development and Research, which monitored MDRC and provided funds for MDRC's administration and evaluation of the demonstration; and the Office of Housing, which provided MOD and TPP funding to the sites through its network of field offices. HUD and the Ford Foundation's Office of National Affairs, as sponsors of the program, provided the requisite funds to implement the demonstration and supervised the conduct of work by the demonstration manager, MDRC. A Project Review Committee was established among the sponsors of the demonstration to review program performance, provide policy direction for the demonstration, and resolve critical issues arising during its tenure.

To a large extent, MDRC acted as an intermediary between the program's sponsors and its participants, although there was also direct contact between them. At each site, the participating PHA and tenant group were responsible for local implementation of the program, with the active assistance, guidance, and supervision of MDRC.

Funding for the demonstration was budgeted at $21.4 million. Tables 2–2 and 2–3 summarize the funding structure of the demonstration. Table 2–3 indicates the distribution of MOD and TPP funds among the participating sites.

The total of $1.2 million from the Ford Foundation and HUD's Office of Policy Development and Research (PD&R) went directly to MDRC—$600,000 from PD&R earmarked for evaluation and $600,000 from the Ford Foundation to support MDRC's role as managing agent. The $20.2 million from HUD's Office of Housing went to the sites through the HUD field offices. On MDRC's recommendation, the sites received quarterly TPP payments from the re-

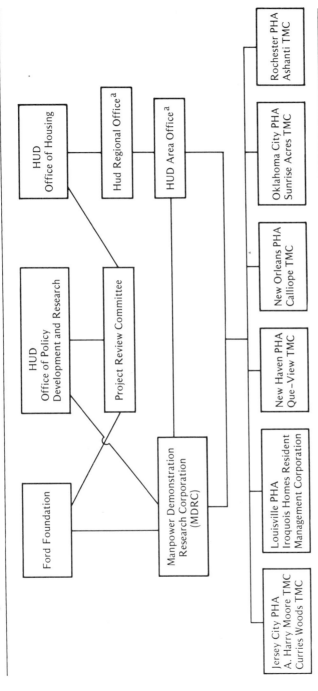

Figure 2–1.   Organization of the National Tenant Management Demonstration Program.

a. To simplify the presentation, HUD Regional and Area Offices have been represented by one box each. In reality, there were four Regional Offices, (I, II, III, and IV) and six Area Offices (Newark, Louisville, Hartford, New Orleans, Oklahoma City, and Buffalo) involved. However, the relationships were the same as indicated above with regard to each Regional Office and its respective Area Office(s) and each Area Office and its respective PHA.

Source: Derived from "Tenant Management Program: Program Design Organizational Relationships and Management/Work Plans," report prepared for the U.S. Department of Housing and Urban Development by the Manpower Demonstration Research Corporation, July 23, 1976 (mimeographed), Charts II and III.

Table 2–2. Funding Sources, Amounts, and Recipients: National Tenant Management Demonstration Program.

Source	Amount	Recipient
Ford Foundation	$ 600,000	MDRC
HUD, Office of Policy Development and Research	600,000	MDRC
HUD, Office of Housing Modernization program	15,000,000	Participating sites
Target Projects Program Monitoring and technical assistance	1,560,000	MDRC
Direct site expenditures	3,640,000	Participating sites
Total HUD	20,800,000	
Total	$21,400,000	

Source: MDRC file material.

Table 2–3. MOD and TPP Allocations to Participating Sites: National Tenant Management Demonstration Program.

Site	TPP Amount	MOD Amount	Total
Jersey City			
A. Harry Moore	$ 580,700	$ 997,000	$ 1,577,700
Curries Woods	581,000	1,015,000	1,596,000
Louisville	671,400	3,500,000	4,171,400
New Haven	442,100	1,650,000	2,092,100
New Orleans	2,010,500	6,524,000	8,534,500
Oklahoma City	514,300	1,007,000	1,521,300
Rochester	400,000	307,000	707,000
Total	$5,200,000	$15,000,000	$20,200,000

Note: The allocation of TPP and MOD funds was based upon the number of units at the sites and whether there had been TPP and MOD allocations in the recent past. In addition, for MOD amounts, the age and condition of the tenant management development were considered.

Source: U.S. Department of Housing and Urban Development, HUD News, No. 76–238, June 30, 1976.

spective HUD field offices. Out of the TPP portion ($5.2 million) of the latter allocation, MDRC received 30 percent ($1.56 million) from the participating sites to support its responsibilities for training, technical assistance, and monitoring. In addition, a portion of MDRC's grant from the Ford Foundation—an amount totaling almost $90,000—was made available to each TMC to cover incidental expenses other than those reimbursable under HUD funding.

MDRC'S ROLE: MANAGING THE DEMONSTRATION

In its role as demonstration manager, MDRC provided general oversight of the planning and implementation of the program. Once the parameters of the program design were sketched broadly, MDRC's role fell into three major functional categories—operations, research, and information. These were to be performed in a manner flexible enough to allow the individual sites to adjust their TMC organizational structures and models of operation to local circumstances. Sites were allowed to take other initiatives so long as they were in keeping with the general purpose, time schedule, and structure of the demonstration.

Program Operations

The category of program operations comprised training, technical assistance, and monitoring and reporting of ongoing activities at each site. These tasks were coordinated by the MDRC field representative assigned to each site, with the assistance of PHA staff, local technical assistants, and other consultants. From the inception of the demonstration, an important resource in program operations was the expertise in public housing brought to the program by McCormack, Baron and Associates, the consulting firm that had been instrumental in the implementation of tenant management in St. Louis. During the planning period, McCormack, Baron and Associates designed the Program Sequence Guide, which was the basic training and implementation plan for the demonstration sites. As the program got under way, they provided training and technical assistance at several of the sites and trained the locally recruited technical assistants in the fundamentals of tenant management, housing management, and budgeting skills.

MDRC field representatives were in weekly telephone contact with their respective sites and made at least one on-site visit per month. During the visits, they attended TMC meetings and training sessions and met with technical assistants and appropriate individuals from the TMC and the PHA to review progress and discuss problems. At these gatherings they also helped formulate plans. Field representatives and local technical assistants submitted monthly written reports and reviewed management performance data submitted monthly and quarterly by the demonstration sites.

Research

The research design[1] was organized into four major components— (1) historical context of the demonstration, (2) documentation of the demonstration, (3) impact of the demonstration, and (4) cost of the demonstration.

- The historical context component placed the demonstration in a comparative framework by examining other past and current tenant management efforts in public housing. It was hoped that an exploration of their forms, problems, successes, and failures would provide some preliminary insights into the viability of tenant management as an option for public housing.

- The documentation component focused on the evolution and development of the demonstration at the local level. Its descriptive and analytic account was guided by the following concerns—the effect of various local factors and characteristics on the development and success of tenant management, the problems and issues typical of the various phases of site operations, the organization of and progress in the areas of management responsibility, and the relationships among the various participants in the TMC and between the TMC and other important groups such as the PHA.

- The purpose of the impact component was to assess the extent to which tenant management achieved the major goals of the demon-

1. See Appendix A for a more detailed description of the research methodology.

stration and realized other anticipated and unanticipated consequences such as physical improvements, and PHA-wide changes in
policies, procedures, and community development.

• The cost component focused on the incremental cost of establishing and operating a tenant management corporation. The analysis
also considered the additional cost of operating an ongoing tenant
management corporation. On the benefit side, increases in revenue were discussed insofar as they affected increased costs.

Although this report is an institutional document weaving together
perspectives of MDRC's administrative, operations, and research
staff, the authors relied heavily on findings from the research effort.
Many data sources were utilized in the demonstration research. They
included archival materials, questionnaires, interviews, the Tenant
Management Information System (described below), field reports prepared by MDRC operations staff, and fiscal information and progress
reports routinely submitted to the demonstration sponsors. In addition, the impact component partially relied on a large-scale survey
conducted by the Urban Institute.[2]

The Urban Institute was selected because of its experience with
public housing research and its extensive data base on a large number
of public housing projects. Its primary function in the evaluation of
the demonstration was to (1) select a group of non-tenant-manage-
ment projects from its data base with which to compare the tenant
management sites and (2) collect and analyze survey data from both
groups before and after the implementation of tenant management at
the demonstration sites. The institute's data base consisted of information on some 170 randomly selected projects in 40 large PHAs
across the country. These projects provided the pool from which to
select the comparison (control) group for the tenant management
sites. After excluding projects with a predominantly elderly population from the pool, the tenant management sites were matched with
a subset of these projects. An attempt was made to achieve a match
that reflected similarity on the amount of TPP–MOD funds as well as
on an array of variables that previous Urban Institute research had
identified as important in an evaluation of performance. Eighteen

2. A full report of the Urban Institute Survey is contained in Suzanne B. Loux and
Robert Sadacca, "Analysis of Changes at Tenant Management Demonstration Projects,"
Working Paper #1335 (Washington, D.C.: Urban Institute, 1980).

control sites were selected for comparison with the six demonstration sites remaining in the program for its entirety.

Baseline (before) surveys were conducted in Spring 1976, before the implementation of tenant management, and follow-up (after) surveys were administered in Summer 1979 at both the demonstration and the control sites. For each of the PHAs represented, these surveys included interviews with a sample of public housing tenants at the tenant management and the control projects, selected HUD field office personnel, PHA board of commissioners' chairperson, PHA executive directors and questionnaires administered to the central office staff. The interviews were conducted using prestructured questionnaires developed by the Urban Institute. In addition to the institute's standard format requesting facts, evaluations, amount of satisfaction and opinions, at MDRC's request, other questions were added eliciting more detailed information about tenant participation in management, management–tenant interaction, and in 1979 only, activities of the tenant management corporation and attitudes toward tenant management. In their analysis, the Urban Institute aggregated the tenant management projects into one group and the control projects into another for comparison purposes. This survey included baseline (1976) and follow-up (1979) interviews with a sample of public housing tenants, selected HUD field office personnel, PHA board of commissioners' chairpersons, PHA executive directors, and other PHA staff at the project and central office levels. These interviews were administered at both the demonstration sites and a comparable set of sites selected by the Urban Institute that were not participating in the demonstration.

Tenant Management Information System

The Tenant Management Information System provided support to both the operations and the research efforts of the demonstration. It supplied the information necessary for careful monitoring of the demonstration and provided data primarily for the impact and cost components of the evaluation design. The system consisted of Monthly Information Reports, Quarterly Information Reports, and a manual of instructions for their completion. These reports were prepared by the participating housing authorities and submitted to MDRC. The monthly reports provided data on items such as occupancy, maintenance performance, and rent collections, while the quarterly reports included information on expenditures and income, tenant employment, and various other aspects of management performance.

Planning Phase

With the major organizational components in place, the design and planning phase of the demonstration was launched in June 1975, one year prior to its intended official beginning. During this phase, site selection criteria were developed, potential participants were identified and briefed about the demonstration, the evaluation design was formulated, and field visits were conducted to PHAs and their respective tenant groups that had applied for participation in the program. Following negotiations and completion of formal proposals for HUD funding, the tentative selection of sites was made. Finally, in June 1976, HUD officially selected the program participants.

In choosing the sites for the demonstration, program planners weighed a number of factors in an effort to achieve a balance geographically, physically, and demographically. Of primary interest was choosing both high-rise and low-rise developments that were neither deteriorated beyond reasonable TMC efforts nor in such good condition as to discourage incentives for improvement. The commitment and capabilities of the local housing authority, the interest and managerial potential of the site tenant organization, the cooperation between those two groups, and the expected cooperation from city and state governments and from HUD regional and area offices were also considered.

HUD suggested 51 PHAs for preliminary consideration; 24 authorities were subsequently interested enough to submit applications for consideration as demonstration sites. After a sequence of events, the applicant field was narrowed to six. Two of these dropped out later during the planning phase—the Cambridge (Massachusetts) and the Dallas Housing Authorities. They were replaced by the New Haven and the Oklahoma City Housing Authorities. The final six participants were:

PHA	*Project*
Housing Authority of the City of Jersey City	A. Harry Moore C Curries Woods NC
Housing Authority of Louisville	Iroquois Homes C
New Haven Housing Authority	Quinnipiac } Riverview } To become one TMC
Housing Authority of New Orleans	Calliope
Oklahoma City Housing Authority	Sooner Haven } 387 scattered } To become site units } one TMC
Rochester Housing Authority	Olean Townhouses } Capsule Dwellings } To become Fairfield Village } one TMC Bronson Court } Edith Doran }

Three of the six participating housing authorities, New Haven, Oklahoma City, and Rochester, decided to merge previously separate housing projects into one TMC. Jersey City was the only city with two separate sites, both high-rise projects. These two sites were chosen because, in addition to the working relationship already established between the PHA and tenant groups at both sites, the 1,376 units in the two projects combined represented one-third of the public housing for families in Jersey City and thus presented an opportunity to study the impact of tenant management on a large proportion of a housing authority's population.

Once projects were tentatively scheduled, MDRC held extensive discussions with representatives from the sites, and the preparation of proposals to HUD for TPP and MOD funding, as well as community organization activities geared to the election of TMC boards, began. The process of incorporation also commenced during this time, and additional activities included the identification of PHA tenant management liaisons and other PHA staff to be involved with the demonstration. Along with MDRC, the principals at each site formulated plans for locating and for training qualified technical assistant candidates. At only two sites were technical assistants chosen prior to the start of the demonstration.

On June 30, 1976, HUD and the Ford Foundation jointly issued a press release announcing the commencement of the demonstration, and on July 8, 1976, HUD advised the participating sites of their selection, officially marking the beginning of the National Tenant Management Demonstration.

3 STATUS OF TENANT MANAGEMENT AT THE DEMONSTRATION SITES

In order to provide a basis for the cross-site perspective used throughout most of the report, this chapter will briefly describe each of the participating sites and its progress toward tenant management. Rates of progress between the sites varied widely, and as these profiles show, rapid attainment of the various tenant management benchmarks did not always ensure permanent success. Of the seven sites, four most closely approximated the demonstration model and were considered to be the most viable by the demonstration's end, in June 1978.

A. HARRY MOORE TMC

In selecting the A. Harry Moore development in Jersey City for participation in the National Tenant Management Demonstration, program planners weighed several factors. For example, the development had relatively few households with working adults. An overwhelming portion of its population consisted of female-headed, welfare-dependent families. The development itself, a 25-year-old high-rise complex of 664 units, was in serious disrepair. Entry hall doorways were missing, the condition of the grounds was deplorable, and vandalism was widespread. In addition to the conditions specific to A. Harry Moore, there were potential union problems in Jersey City, where union job displacement was feared.

However, in spite of a history of high tenant turnover and a reputation as a poorly maintained, troubled site, the development had in its favor an active and vocal sitewide tenant organization and very strong building organizations. With the encouragement of the acting director of the Jersey City Housing Authority (JCHA), these organizations were already moving toward increased tenant responsibility. A. Harry Moore had received a MOD grant of $3 million in 1975, and work had already begun on the repair of incinerators, tiles, and roofing. In addition, tenants were beginning site beautification measures under a TPP grant.

The active interest in the demonstration displayed by the acting director and several crucial members of the board of commissioners allayed many initial reservations. However, there was no guarantee that the acting director would be appointed director or that the impact of MOD and TPP grants offered by the demonstration would not be overshadowed by the previous grants. Planners were reassured when attendance at the introductory public meetings held to explain tenant management was both sizable and impressive in terms of the questions asked by the residents. Interest in participation was clearly expressed.

As the site moved toward election of the board of directors, critical issues were dealt with effectively. The prior tenant organization had been seven separate groups, each able to work with the other, but lacking the authority to speak for the whole development. The board of directors would have that authority and would consist of one representative from each building. A preliminary work program outline for A. Harry Moore was drawn up, and meetings were held to formulate proposals for MOD and TPP budgets.

Turnout at the initial board election was good, and the seven-member board was elected, with the only male member as its chairperson. Interestingly, none of these board members had been a representative to the old tenant council, but all had been active participants in the preliminary tenant management meetings.

Board training began in July 1976. One year later, staff training began and lasted until September 1978, when the contract with the Jersey City Housing Authority was signed. McCormack, Baron and Associates and representatives from the housing authority conducted the training, and there was steady progress through the Program Sequence Guide.

Several problems did arise during the comparatively uneventful training of the board. Early in the process, complaints were made by an unaffiliated local maintenance union that tenant management constituted an unnegotiated change in working conditions and therefore violated fair labor practices. This resulted in the unions being promised that no employees would be laid off, demoted, or have their salary lowered because of tenant management; in addition, housing officials consented to the unionization of TMC employees, should they choose to organize.

The issue of nepotism arose during staff hiring, when a close relative of a board member applied for a staff job. To avoid tainting the TMC with charges of nepotism, the board amended its bylaws and excluded relatives from eligibility for full-time positions or any job funded by its operating budget. Summer youth jobs funded by CETA or part-time positions would be open to family members. The board also mandated that relatives already employed on the site must transfer to another development. The board's action on this issue was a clear example of its overall ability to function decisively and effectively as a cohesive body.

The board recruited and hired 22 staff members. The manager they chose had, in fact, been an original board member who resigned from the board specifically to apply for the position. Four of the seven building managers had been active in the former site committee, so the staff was fairly experienced as well as supportive of the tenant management concept. However, throughout the demonstration, issues concerning staff proved to be somewhat complex and troublesome.

The relationship between the board and the staff was strained from the start, and the difficulties were compounded at one point by a turnover in the position of manager. Staff came to view itself as doing the "dirty work" of the TMC—collecting delinquent rents, inspecting apartments, and locking out nonpaying tenants who were being evicted—while the board received the credit for community management. Staff morale was negatively affected by its feeling of being caught between the board and the resident population.

TMC employees were blamed for problems that were the responsibility of the board or for things that were beyond their control. For instance, the new manager was pressured by the TMC board to improve the site maintenance situation, one of the original goals of the demonstration. However, maintenance crew members—JCHA employees—were frequently absent, did not complete tenant service requests in a timely fashion, and generally allowed the site grounds to appear unkept. These problems affected the staff's image in the community, although they were, in fact, the result of the board's failure to follow up on its complaint to the housing authority. The manager held weekly meetings with the site crew to assign work schedules and follow up on service requests, but these efforts did not appear to improve the situation in a lasting way. The difficulty in dealing effectively with this maintenance problem led to mutual recriminations among the board, staff, and housing authority. Staff was also frustrated in its attempts to accelerate action on MOD projects that it felt would benefit the community. However, sloppy workmanship discovered by TMC staff caused delays in completion of much of this work.

Community tensions reached a climax when a dissident tenant group presented a list of complaints to the board. Board members agreed to consider the grievances and met with this group. The board's attentiveness to the tenant complaints helped mend community dissent and strengthen tenant management; and although it took nearly two years to resolve this problem, the housing authority, TMC board, and TMC staff were finally able to reorganize the maintenance department and impose a reasonable level of control.

At the end of the demonstration, in June 1978, the TMC was effectively and routinely managing the A. Harry Moore development. It received ongoing technical support from McCormack, Baron and Associates and the housing authority in facing the usual problems of managing large, multifamily urban housing complexes. The clear and consistent leadership of the board's chairperson was a key factor in A. Harry Moore's progress, as was the supportive attitude of the housing authority. The housing authority decentralized certain aspects of management, such as budgeting, to the site level at all other PHA–managed housing developments and was sufficiently encouraged by this experience to initiate tenant management in a third project and to plan to do so at a fourth.

CURRIES WOODS TMC

At the beginning of the demonstration, Curries Woods' well-organized, active tenant body led program planners to believe that the site residents were capable of taking on management responsibilities. The site—consisting of seven high-rise buildings built in 1959 and containing 712 apartments—had a strong tenant association, the United Community Council; a housing authority committed to tenant participation; and previous MOD funding. Yet Curries Woods was the only site in the demonstration that did not achieve the major threshold of tenant management, the signing of a management contract.

Contrary to initial beliefs, strong community support and the allegiance of tenant association participants did not automatically transfer to the tenant management corporation. In fact, the United Community Council wanted to co-exist with the TMC rather than disband, as required by the demonstration. This initial challenge to the TMC by the tenant association lay dormant for a period, but was later voiced by alternative resident associations such as the Concerned Tenants Committee and the 71 Merritt Street Tenants Association.

Initial community reaction to the TMC was favorable; attendance at tenant management introductory meetings was high, and many residents sought positions on the TMC board. Initially, the 14-member board began training with the A. Harry Moore board. Curries Woods board members were active in training sessions and seemed better organized than the A. Harry Moore group. But weak leadership did not inspire sustained enthusiasm, and by late summer, the lack of a quorum postponed many meetings and thus crippled the board. In later months, dissatisfied residents vocally criticized the TMC. This criticism, coupled with internal board struggles and poor attendance, left the board virtually paralyzed.

Tensions between the TMC and the community occurred largely because articulate, aggressive residents who had been involved in the earlier tenant association chose to challenge the TMC participants, whom they perceived as inarticulate and compromising, rather than to seek TMC board and staff positions. Community unrest was manifested not only in alternative tenant organizations but also in public forums where local politicians criticized the tenant management program. The weak TMC board was unable to defend itself against these criticisms or to manage the TMC. Finally, in the spring of 1977, under pressure from the housing authority, residents, and MDRC, the board members agreed to resign, but they felt forced from office and refused to advise the interim tenant committee.

The site's technical assistant helped to prepare for the September 1977 board election and to ease the transition to a new board. Some members had served on the earlier board, while others had been members of the interim committee. As with the previous board, attendance at training sessions soon dropped, with only nine of the 13 board members consistently attending the meetings. This board, however, showed more stability than its predecessor, and by January 1978, after three months of an accelerated but relatively smooth training process, it was ready to begin screening prospective tenants and soliciting staff resumes.

The TMC staff was hired by May 1978, and training progressed without considerable delay. Staff training was conducted primarily by the PHA, with some assistance from McCormack, Baron and Associates. During this period, staff members promoted tenant management throughout the community by holding building meetings, discussing residents' problems, and establishing a rapport with the housing authority. Resident cooperation with staff members varied among buildings; at several buildings meetings were well attended, and tenants participated in clean-up efforts.

The relationship between the board and staff was less cooperative. The board's continued efforts at site management undermined the staff's assumption of these responsibilities and evoked questions within the community as to who actually managed the site. Many residents were confused by what seemed to be tripartite management—the TMC staff, the TMC board, and the PHA site manager— and questioned the authority of the TMC, especially the TMC board. The housing authority augmented this confusion by bypassing the board, in whom they had little confidence, and dealing directly with the staff. Rather than working as partners, these groups often related to each other as adversaries. This breach was crucial in the Curries Woods board's failure to coalesce as an effective management body. Housing officials saw the board as incompetent and unwilling to work with the housing authority. The board responded with claims that the housing authority had undermined the first TMC board and was hoping to undermine the entire tenant management program by heightening community polarization.

The difficulties at Curries Woods were, no doubt, exacerbated by the fact that the PHA liaison was the sole technical advisor to the TMC during much of the first board period. Initially, when no qualified technical assistant could be found, all parties agreed that the liaison, who previously had worked successfully with the tenants, could carry out those functions effectively. However, as normal conflicts arose between the TMC and the PHA, the tenants came to feel that because the PHA liaison was a housing authority employee, he could not be trusted. Thus, during the early, formative period of the TMC, the board did not have a local advisor they trusted; and later, when independent technical assistants were hired, they lacked the expertise needed to guide the board into efficient management.

Because community dissatisfaction usually focused on the individuals who managed the TMC rather than on the program itself, by the demonstration's end, most residents neither actively denounced nor condoned the tenant management corporation. While the chaotic relationships made it impossible for the TMC to achieve a reasonable level of productivity, tenant management did bring some improvements to Curries Woods. The TMC board successfully organized a site security program composed of off duty city police officers and managed to involve local politicians in tenants' concerns. Demonstration monies also helped make improvements in Curries Woods' physically deteriorated buildings.

Although the Jersey City Housing Authority and Curries Woods TMC did not sign a management contract, they did agree to a six-month period of redirection during which JCHA would supervise the staff while the board would act in an advisory capacity. Should the board stabilize during this period, the tenants' organization and the housing authority could eventually enter into a contractual agreement. However, the board's history of attendance problems and high turnover, coupled with community quarrels, makes tenant management's future at Curries Woods questionable.

IROQUOIS HOMES RESIDENT MANAGEMENT CORPORATION

Iroquois Homes is made up of 72 low-rise buildings built in 1952 and containing 854 units; it is located in a predominately white, lower-middle-class community in Louisville. The site itself is currently more than 50 percent white. Prior to site selection, Louisville was in the midst of a racial upheaval as a result of a court-ordered school busing policy, but Iroquois, located in an antibusing neighborhood, survived the racial discord. Evidence of racial cooperation was manifested with the election of a black president and a white vice-president to the Iroquois Resident Council.

This element of racial integration was one of several factors weighed in choosing Iroquois as a demonstration site. In addition, Iroquois had a history of active resident participation. The resident council that functioned as advisor to the housing authority prior to the demonstration supported the concept of tenant management, which it perceived as a means to increase resident control and independence. The Housing Authority of Louisville (HAL), joined by Louisville's mayor and the citywide tenant organization, also fully supported the idea. In fact, HAL's executive director had been in the forefront of an earlier experiment in tenant management and was strongly committed to its value. These factors overshadowed any reservations program planners had in selecting Iroquois as a demonstration site, such as the absence of rent ceilings in HAL developments and the poor financial status of the housing authority.

Six of the nine members elected to the new Resident Management Corporation (RMC) were former members of the resident council. Although members of the new board lacked many of the skills necessary for effective organization, membership was stable, and board training, disrupted at times by a dissident group, was facilitated by HAL and MDRC field representatives and consultants. The board established a budget committee to review the RMC's budget and to outline its finances. New bylaws were distributed to the community for review and comment, a process that the board followed for any RMC action. The first board chairperson, an experienced resident council president, served from the inception of the RMC through May 1978.

The board survived a period of uncertainty within the housing authority that followed the resignation of the executive director in April 1977. After six months of operation under an acting director, HAL hired a permanent director who was enthusiastic about the tenant management concept.

Recruiting of staff members produced a generally low response. However, by October 1977, all staff positions were filled. Staff training lasted six months, and although both the board and the housing authority were apprehensive about giving the staff management responsibilities, the RMC staff has performed efficiently, and on July 13, 1978, the Resident Management Corporation signed a management contract with the Housing Authority of Louisville. Contract terms included the RMC's responsibility for budget and provisions concerning the repair of vacant and unrentable units, maintenance, and supervision of on-site HAL employees. An amendment was added in April 1979 to reconfirm the RMC's supervising role of HAL employees working at Iroquois. A postdemonstration contract is currently being negotiated that gives the RMC even greater budgeting responsibilities.

A real partnership between the RMC and HAL has emerged slowly. Although HAL upper level officials were cooperative, communications often broke down within the middle levels of the bureaucracy. HAL's initial reluctance to relinquish management responsibilities to the RMC was prompted by employees' fear of losing jobs to the RMC staff. The RMC, on the other hand, perceived HAL as being "too busy." Efforts to assuage these tensions resulted in the establishment of monthly meetings between HAL and the RMC as well as an orientation program for HAL employees designed to enhance the relationship between the two groups.

Community support for tenant management has also been occasionally troublesome. Most residents at Iroquois remained uninvolved in the RMC, and especially at the beginning of the demonstration, acceptance of the RMC board and staff was colored by suspicion and misunderstanding, engendered by local dissidents. Some members of the community felt that tenant management merely duplicated the role of the housing authority; others felt that tenant management was inappropriate for their community and should be reserved for more troubled developments. There were rumors that tenant management advocates wanted to replace whites with blacks in public housing communities, and this heightened racial tensions as the local media publicized these and other allegations. Negotiations with the housing authority and confrontations with dissatisfied residents, however, aided the RMC in developing leadership ability, expertise, and the impetus to emerge as a strong, cohesive group. Community relations efforts were undertaken to involve the resident population in tenant management and to clarify the role of the program within the community.

At the close of the demonstration, in June 1978, both the RMC and HAL were satisfied that the responsibilities delineated in their contract had been met. Many improvements in HAL's operation stemmed from the demonstration, and the housing authority felt that tenant-managed facilities decreased both vacancies and rent arrears. The RMC also appeared better able to complete maintenance work than central management. Corrections in record keeping increased the efficiency of HAL's modernization, accounting, and management departments. Other improvements included more accurate site budgeting and work logging. The impact of the program is evident in HAL's decision to implement tenant management in another public housing project through the assistance of Public Housing Urban Initiatives funds.

The Iroquois board is currently developing a marketing strategy to encourage higher income residents to move to Iroquois and has recently received a Ralston–Purina grant to finance future youth employment. In addition, a Community Development Block Grant award will finance maintenance repairs at the site.

Iroquois Homes developed into one of the most successful tenant management corporations in the demonstration. Motivated board members worked hard, and as a unified group became effective community leaders.

QUE-VIEW TMC

No doubt some of the difficulties that plagued tenant management in New Haven, such as the large and growing housing authority deficit, could have been anticipated. But the overall drain on staff energies and morale produced by a housing authority tottering on the brink of bankruptcy was not foreseen. Likewise, the strong-willed and somewhat intimidating presence of the initial executive director of the New Haven Housing Authority (NHHA) was recognized as a potential problem, but the instability within the housing authority that occurred after his departure was not anticipated. These were the major factors that undercut the potential of tenant management in New Haven and impeded the development of a partnership between the Que-View board and the housing authority.

The Que-View TMC consisted of two housing communities in the Fairhaven section of New Haven. Quinnipiac Terrace, with 248 units, dwarfed its sister site, Riverview Terrace, which consisted of only 12 apartments. Both developments were low-rise facilities, but Quinnipiac, built in 1941, was 29 years older than Riverview.

Many tensions among the TMC, NHHA, and MDRC surfaced during the board's training. NHHA's executive director dominated the

TMC, and many board members felt reluctant to express disagreement. A strained relationship between NHHA and MDRC also characterized the early demonstration period for Que-View. The housing authority viewed MDRC as a consultant, to be employed only when needed, rather than as an active program participant. Disagreements culminated in late 1976, when housing officials insisted that training be executed according to their own manual rather than the demonstration's Program Sequence Guide. In addition, the training consultants, McCormack, Baron and Associates, were dismissed, and their responsibilities were taken over by the NHHA executive director and his staff. Although the NHHA training manual was adequate, the housing authority staff did not have the experience or sensitivity to tenant needs to properly convey its contents in a TMC training context.

Domination of the tenant management corporation extended into the contract-signing period when the housing authority insisted that Que-View be among the first demonstration sites to sign a management contract and hurried the TMC participants' training in order to meet an October 1977 signing date. MDRC initially opposed this course, maintaining that the TMC board was unstable and lacked adequate training to enter into contractual agreement. It also questioned the TMC's preparedness, since staff hiring and training had not been completed. But it eventually went along with arguments presented by the TMC board itself that they were ready and that further delays would exacerbate existing hostilities between the TMC and its community. This early contract signing allowed the housing authority to dictate the agreement's contents, since the inexperienced board lacked both the skills and the confidence to challenge the NHHA. It also inflated the board and staff's sense of their own capacities, leading them to believe that they were more prepared to manage their community than in fact they were.

Internal problems within the TMC also kept Que-View from having a strong tenant management corporation. The board lacked leadership and was hesitant to confront issues concerning lease requirements, grievances, rent payments, and TMC participation. Board members were also intimidated by the TMC staff manager, a former board chairperson, who was an aggressive and formidable supervisor. As board chairperson she had often dominated her colleagues, and this carried over into her staff role.

There were internal staff problems as well, many originating in the staff hiring process when the Que-View TMC board hired two "manager trainees" before selecting a manager. As trainees, both residents had equal authority. After a short time, the board chose one trainee to be the assistant manager and the other trainee as the manager. In their new capacities, these staff members continued to compete with each other, causing resentment that handicapped their performance and divided their colleagues and the community.

Whether, in light of all these difficulties, a viable TMC could have eventually emerged is questionable. But in the end, the demonstration fell prey to the internal unrest and financial difficulties of the housing authority. In June 1978, after six months of extreme turmoil, the executive director resigned. His successor was not as supportive of the tenant management program and pursued a policy of "benign neglect." This further antagonized board members, who felt they were not receiving the necessary support from the housing authority. Throughout the demonstration period, NHHA's financial deficit increased, causing maintenance delays, a union strike, staff resignations, reduced tenant services, and drastic staff cuts. Although no TMC staff members were fired, the housing authority's hiring freeze prevented the filling of staff positions as they became vacant, including assistant manager, lane manager, and security officers. Maintenance delays affected the credibility of the TMC, because residents blamed the board and staff when needed repairs were not made.

Because the NHHA faced a large financial deficit, it was made clear that unless additional funds were available from HUD, the TMC would not be continued after the demonstration. However, even before learning whether funds would be allocated, the NHHA decided not to continue tenant management at Que-View. New Haven's experiment with tenant management has ended.

CALLIOPE DEVELOPMENT TMC

Although Calliope Development Tenant Management Corporation (CDTMC) initially showed little potential for effective leadership, the New Orleans TMC grew during the program to become a very stable management body. Early in the demonstration, internal strife virtually paralyzed the TMC board, but advantageous turnovers on the board, favorable working relations with the housing authority, and strong community support helped create conditions that allowed the tenants to develop into capable managers.

Calliope is located on 56 acres of land near downtown New Orleans and was the largest development in the National Tenant Management Demonstration. Its 95 low-rise buildings contain 1,550 units, the oldest ones erected in 1940. At the beginning of the demonstration, Calliope was in need of extensive refurbishment and modernization. Yet because of New Orleans' very tight market for low-income housing, there were virtually no vacancies at Calliope, and its rent collection rate was consistently over 90 percent.

For most of the 10 members on the TMC board, the demonstration was their first experience of participating in a decisionmaking process. Their lack of organizational experience became evident during training and was characterized by dissension among board members. To overcome this problem, MDRC training consultants and field representatives deviated from the training schedule to instruct the board in community organization, decisionmaking, and group relations. Although members regularly attended training, the board progressed slowly. In September 1976, a technical assistant who had worked previously in the city's social services division was hired. She worked with the TMC throughout the demonstration and was instrumental in pulling the board together and in helping them overcome many early difficulties.

The support of key Housing Authority of New Orleans (HANO) officials, especially its executive director, also helped the TMC board to increase its leadership capabilities. HANO was confident that tenant management could work, but questioned the capability of some board members to function in such a setting. Turnover within the board, however, removed troublesome members and thus helped pave the way for tenant management to progress at Calliope.

Housing authority support beyond the executive level was far from universal, however. Some HANO site employees, for example, were concerned that tenant management would leave them unemployed, but once HANO guaranteed their jobs, relationships improved considerably. A key factor in site progress was the hiring of the former site manager as Calliope's full-time technical assistant. He was able to bridge many gaps between the housing authority and the TMC and was well accepted by the residents. This trust was especially important because although they had completed formal training, board members still needed considerable assistance in dealing with the intricacies of managing such a large project.

Because of the need to strengthen leadership skills, the TMC board delayed hiring its staff until the fall of 1977. The large Calliope community provided a diverse tenant body from which capable leaders could be drawn. The board reviewed over 40 staff applications and, by November, hired 14 TMC employees. Many of these residents were qualified for management responsibilities by virtue of their educational histories or work experience.

Even with this relatively experienced pool to draw from, the board had difficulty matching the right person to the right job, and a good deal of shifting of positions took place. Perhaps the most significant was the board's reversing the positions of manager and assistant manager. The new manager, who started her TMC involvement as a clerk-typist, alleviated many conflicts within the staff and successfully led the TMC staff through the remainder of the demonstration. With the aid of the technical assistant and the promotion of the new manager, early tensions between board and staff (usually centered on staff complaints of board interference with staff prerogatives) were largely eliminated.

HANO and the TMC worked successfully as partners in site management. The residents of Calliope and HANO officials accepted the responsibilities delineated in the management contract, which was signed September 10, 1978. HANO's board of commissioners also supported tenant management, especially after the TMC's discovery of poor workmanship on the part of contractors hired by the HANO technical department. Such action, together with the revamping of the housing authority staff, led to improved modernization procedures at all New Orleans public housing sites. HANO later expanded tenant management to another site and asked Calliope TMC participants to help with the new program.

Unlike several demonstration communities, Calliope residents were generally very supportive of the TMC board and staff. The TMC board fostered this support by door-to-door canvassing, ticket sales to TMC-sponsored events, and staff application procedures that enabled residents to meet personally with board members. The TMC quarterly area meetings were consistently well attended. At these meetings, exchanges between TMC leaders and residents enabled tenants to participate actively in the tenant management corporation. Calliope proved to be a positive test of tenant management.

SUNRISE ACRES TMC

Oklahoma City was chosen to participate in the demonstration to ensure geographic representation, and of the PHAs in that area being considered for tenant management, the Oklahoma City Housing Authority's (OCHA) interest was the most sustained and seemed the most viable. While none of Sunrise Acres TMC's difficulties were unique to that site, their combination and intensity provide a good lesson in predicting when tenant management is likely to go awry. Program activities were characterized by a long period of disorganization with continuous turnover in trainers, field representatives, housing authority personnel, and board chairpersons.

The site's problems had been foreshadowed early in the demonstration: the OCHA's scattered site units were mixed with nearly identical private homes, and the housing authority could not readily identify its own property. There were also conflicts between the OCHA board of commissioners and its executive director, and the TMC evidenced a virtual void in leadership. This lack of leadership among the tenant representatives left the program without a real foundation, and the Sunrise Acres TMC was dropped from the National Tenant Management Demonstration after two years of participation.

Sunrise Acres incorporated several geographically and structurally distinct communities into one tenant management corporation. The most cohesive neighborhood was Sooner Haven, a conventional housing development of 150 units. Other developments included a four-block area of 170 unattached single family houses, 90 attached single family houses clustered in private neighborhoods, and 127 scattered single family units. As a result of this geographic dispersion, part of the site was isolated from the TMC. Since the housing authority did not know the precise location of the scattered site units, it is little wonder that many residents of the demonstration communities were unaware that they were part of the tenant management program. Some of those who did know, however, felt neglected because they had no real input into site management.

The lack of resident participation in TMC functions was obvious from the beginning. Only four residents initially filed for election to the TMC board. After an extended registration period this number increased to 16. Only 5 percent of the eligible voters cast ballots in the first board election. Board members' participation in the TMC decreased soon after their election, and because of the high absentee rate, nine additional members were appointed to the board in the fall of 1976 to ensure a quorum at meetings. This expansion required that board training begin anew since only one-third of the board had received prior training. Unfortunately, the new members followed the example of their predecessors and stopped attending TMC meetings.

Management problems within the housing authority compounded those of the TMC. Internal disputes among housing authority officials caused some employees to leave OCHA, including the executive director, who was forced to resign by the OCHA board of commissioners in 1977.

Although the executive director had not been personally active in Sunrise Acres' day-to-day activities, he had vocally supported the program. His successor, however, was even less supportive. From his initial encounters with the TMC, the new executive director insisted on maintaining control of the TMC's actions. He failed to delegate responsibilities to the board, and he demanded to interview candidates for the TMC staff and to approve any TMC expenditure of more than $10. In February 1978 he instructed his staff to write a management contract for OCHA and the TMC without involving the tenants. Although this contract was not signed until after the site had been dropped from the demonstration, the executive director's stance toward Sunrise Acres residents on this and other matters exemplified the housing authority's general attitude toward the demonstration.

The fluctuation of leadership at the housing authority was matched by the lack of leadership among the Sunrise Acres residents. Although training instructors worked continuously with the board, its members never acquired organizational or leadership skills, and the weakness of the board was evident throughout the community. Grounds deteriorated during the demonstration, modernization needs were not met, and communication between TMC officials and residents was minimal. Moreover, some board members refused to comply with apartment inspections, and their violation of rent rules further lowered tenant respect for the TMC.

Only the TMC staff members emerged as a really capable force as they moved successfully through the training curriculum. However, contrary to the basic demonstration model, most of Sunrise Acres' staff did not live in the development. Though the board canvassed the Sunrise Acres' community for staff applicants, qualified candidates did not emerge. The TMC therefore solicited and hired nonsite residents to fill most of the staff positions, including those of manager and assistant manager.

Hope for the Sunrise Acres TMC was further undermined by resentment and harassment of the TMC staff. Soon after the staff began functioning, the board began to voice petty complaints against staff members and to scrutinize their actions during working hours. These investigations, coupled with staff members' beliefs that the board was incompetent and that the staff performed the "dirty work," diminished the commitment of many TMC employees.

By the spring of 1978, it was clear that the narrow conception of tenant management held by the Sunrise Acres TMC board and OCHA officials blocked the growth of tenant management. Only a reconstitution of the board, coupled with intensive long-term training and a new commitment by the housing authority, could create a successful tenant management program at Sunrise Acres. None of these conditions appeared likely to materialize, especially in light of the limited time remaining for the demonstration. Thus, in mid–1978, Oklahoma City was dropped from the national demonstration.

ASHANTI TMC

In Rochester, New York, five separate public housing developments located within one square mile—Bronson Court, Capsule Dwellings, Edith–Doran Townhouses, Fairfield Villages, and Olean Townhouses—were combined to form one management unit called Ashanti, the newest and the smallest site of the demonstration. The oldest building in the five developments had been constructed in 1968, and together they contained only 211 units.

The demonstration value of a site such as Ashanti was that many middle-sized cities had relatively small developments that, by themselves, could not mount such a program, but that might be able to do so in cooperation with others. The Rochester Housing Authority's (RHA) area management structure provided the opportunity to test this alternative. There was one manager for the five developments, but each had its own tenant organization. With the merger of the five developments, the tenant associations continued to exist in the form of "block clubs" under the auspices of the tenant management corporation. Each of the five developments elected a representative to serve on the TMC board of directors.

The conversion of Ashanti from an area management unit to tenant management occurred without major difficulty. The smooth transition was due to the enthusiasm and support of the RHA and its board of commissioners and to the TMC board's leadership capabilities. The active participation of the RHA in board training and the very heavy infusion of technical assistance and training resources provided by a full-time tenant assistant and McCormack, Baron and Associates assisted in board growth and in the establishment of an excellent working rapport between the RHA and the TMC. In addition, the stability of the RHA's directorship supplied the necessary continuity for the implementation process.

Throughout board training, members demonstrated dedication and perseverance. Ashanti was the only site in the demonstration to complete the training phase for board members as scheduled. Attendance during training was excellent; almost every board member attended each session. While some members were somewhat timid initially, their active participation increased as they became more acquainted with management concepts and developed self-confidence. Two of the board members, the chairperson and the vice-chairperson, possessed leadership experience acquired from earlier tenant organization involvement. Together with the technical assistant and key RHA personnel, they were instrumental in the continued growth and resourcefulness of the board in managing tenant services and community concerns such as additional funding.

There was little board turnover at Ashanti; the initial chairperson remained in office through the crucial first two years of program operation. The positive attitude of board members coupled with the determination to make tenant management work resulted in early contract negotiations, and on June 10, 1977, less than one year after Ashanti residents elected their first board, the TMC and the RHA signed a management contract. Responsibilities delegated to the TMC included supervising on-site maintenance staff, security, monitoring budget issues, exercising authority over social services and tenant service requests, preparing vacant apartments, and scheduling interviews for prospective Ashanti residents.

Recruitment for management staff was initiated by board members who publicized job availabilities and descriptions for TMC management staff, clerical workers, and security personnel. Because the initial resident response was low, the board undertook additional recruitment efforts that included further district canvassing and the circulation of job notices. By early 1977, the TMC board had completed recruitment activities and hired management and support staff. The experience level of the new TMC staff varied; many had had prior work-related experience with community-oriented groups, and the housing manager had been a president of one of the tenant associations.

Staff training was conducted by a combination of RHA staff including the executive director, the technical assistant, training consultants, and MDRC staff. The TMC social service and recreation coordinator received special training from an RHA recreation center employee. Like the board, staff members completed their training according to schedule.

The TMC was not without its share of internal problems. Allegations were made by some residents that the TMC was being manipulated for the benefit of a few board members, and in one instance, charges of discrimination were lodged with the N.Y. State Equal Opportunity Commission. Others charged that the TMC failed to keep the community informed or relayed inaccurate information concerning tenant issues. Staff grievances and turnover also proved troublesome. Despite these problems, the Ashanti TMC maintained stability, efficiency, and effectiveness.

While the additional funding for increased social services, recreational programs, and tenant employment opportunities made residents receptive to tenant management, their participation in TMC meetings was not great. Prior to the start of the demonstration, Ashanti was in good physical condition, and tenant services were adequately delivered. Therefore, because the development was not beset by major problems, the residents saw very little need to participate in TMC meetings. Those needs or concerns that they deemed important could be expressed at the project level through their respective block club representatives.

The Rochester Housing Authority plans to continue tenant management at Ashanti, with postdemonstration plans varying little from the program model. Currently the TMC board is seeking additional funding from both private and public sectors. To date, the Rochester Community Chest and the United Way have awarded funds to the TMC in the amount of $7,000 to meet TMC personnel expenses.

4 THE TENANT PARTICIPANTS

This chapter examines the two groups of tenants chiefly responsible for making tenant management work—the board of directors and the staff of the tenant management corporations. Beyond essentially descriptive concerns, the chapter assesses those features that have contributed to the success of the tenant management corporations and identifies those elements that have caused problems in interpersonal relationships and job performance. The conclusions, positive and negative, that can be drawn from the experiences of board and staff members at the seven demonstration sites provide preliminary insight into the viability of tenant management there and at other sites where tenant management may be tried.

THE TENANT MANAGEMENT BOARD OF DIRECTORS

As the summaries in Chapter 3 indicate, the seven tenant management boards, working from a similar game plan, followed widely divergent paths. This section examines the extent to which these differences can be explained by factors in the early period of program implementation, before management contracts were signed.

Recruitment of Board Members

Strong leadership within the community of public housing residents is critical to implementation of the tenant management concept. It is an axiom of community organization that natural leaders are present in any assembly of individuals: sometimes they are officers and members of established groups; sometimes their leadership potential is latent and must be cultivated. Given the luxury of time, a plan might have been devised that deployed organizers to conduct intensive field work at potential sites to identify existing leaders and other talented individuals within the community. Because of the exigencies of the demonstration, however—the need to get tenant management off the ground in relatively short order—sites having an existing tenant association were selected for participation, although the tenant association at Calliope in New Orleans had been organized only a few months before the demonstration began. The demonstration model assumed that these tenant associations enjoyed community support and that leaders of tenant associations would run for, and be elected to, positions on the tenant management board of directors and thus build on existing community strengths.

The TMCs were organized by PHA and MDRC staff and, where they were used, by the technical assistants. The first board elections took place during the spring and summer of 1976. Voter response seemed quite high when compared to other special elections (such as for a school board) and even when compared to the turnout for municipal elections. There was an average participation rate of about 25 percent, the lowest being Oklahoma City's Sunrise Acres (5 percent) and the highest A. Harry Moore in Jersey City (40 percent).

The early experience of Rochester's Ashanti Tenant Management Corporation provides a "best case" example of the demonstration model in operation. Most of the members of Ashanti's first board of directors had been officers of the tenant associations at the five small developments that united to form the tenant management corporation. Propelled by the drive and ability of several strong members who were supported by their constituencies, the board proceeded quickly through training, and Ashanti was the first site in the demonstration to sign a management contract with the housing authority. In spite of this smooth beginning, however, Ashanti eventually experienced many of the same problems that faced other sites.

The transition from resident council to Resident Management Corporation at Iroquois Homes in Louisville was also fairly smooth. Two leaders of the earlier council were elected chairperson and vice-chairperson of the new board, and one other member of the council was elected to serve on the board. A later election brought three additional former council members to the RMC board.

At A. Harry Moore, the situation was a little different. The Jersey City Housing Authority had for several years promoted the development of both sitewide and building tenant groups to act as tenant advocates, but the tenant management board did not succeed in tapping the leadership of the sitewide committee. Although the resident population generally supported the A. Harry Moore TMC, throughout the demonstration ad hoc dissident groups continued to charge that the tenant management corporation focused on the management and performance goals of the housing authority rather than the needs of the community.

At these three sites, the electoral process produced boards that demonstrated capable, responsible leadership within a matter of months after the program was established. In New Orleans, however, leadership potential had to be identified and carefully nurtured by MDRC field representatives and technical assistants, together with the supportive leadership of the housing authority. After a year of absenteeism and dissension among board members, a single dominant leader with a loyal following emerged who, once elected to the position of board chairperson, has wielded power virtually single-handedly but effectively ever since.

While the electoral model could work reasonably well, it was not without its difficulties. Several recurring problems resulted in insufficient numbers of candidates running for board elections:

- Strong members of existing tenant organizations were not always eager to transfer their loyalties or involvement to a new organization;
- Some active members hoped to secure staff jobs;
- Board elections based on geographical representation pitted community leaders against one another; and
- Tenant association members did not necessarily want to join management's side.

Other problems were specific to individual sites. At Que-View in New Haven, while several members of the tenant association were elected to the board, the association itself had had little credibility within the community and was said to be no more than an ineffective voice for complaints to the housing authority. In spite of this, the initial weakness of the board might have been overcome had the housing authority made a concerted effort to build the board's organizational independence and strength.

Oklahoma City's program suffered from a lack of housing authority support. In addition, Sunrise Acres was geographically dispersed, and logistical difficulties were compounded by board members' widely varying interests and priorities. The first tenant board was reconstituted in the hope that absenteeism would decrease and membership would stabilize. But the new board, although able to overcome some of these problems and to progress through training and staff hiring, could not perform effectively without cooperation and support from the housing authority.

At Curries Woods in Jersey City, although some newly elected board members had previous experience in the sitewide organization, they represented factional interests rather than the community consensus. The model's stipulation that only the tenant management corporation be recognized as the official tenant entity—capable of receiving funds or making policy decisions—led to opposition by other tenant factions that ultimately helped cause the downfall of the original board.

The Curries Woods experience led some observers to suggest that the problem of securing leadership for the tenant management corporation could be solved by retaining the existing tenant association and adding management to its scope of responsibilities. However, there is no reason to assume that a tenant association, which acts primarily as an advocacy group, would want to expend its energies on complex and extensive managerial duties.

Characteristics of Board Members

Board members at the six sites still in operation at the end of the demonstration shared the problems of public housing residents in particular and of poor people in general: many board members lived in households without an employed adult, and many received public assistance.[1] The average board member left high school in the middle of the eleventh grade. Nine-tenths of all board members were women, and most were divorced or separated heads of households containing, on average, two or three children. Except in Louisville, virtually all board members were black. Three-quarters of board members were between the ages of 35 and 59, and 15 percent were 65 or over.

These characteristics reflected both the nature of the wider population living in the developments and the special demands that board membership placed on participants. Although many board members found it hard to estimate the time they spent each week on board matters, most said between 6 and 20 hours. A few described it as a 24-hour-a-day, seven-days-a-week job that often entailed responding to telephone calls, inquiries, and complaints from residents at any time, day or night.

These requirements account for the fact that the boards generally attracted neither people who worked full-time nor many young mothers of preschool age children. Time was also the major reason cited for the decision of some board members to resign or not seek reelection. Many resignations occurred early in the demonstration, when newly elected board members found that their positions entailed a far greater expenditure of time and energy than they had foreseen. When turnover occurred later in the demonstration, it was often because board members had the opportunity to return to work, take new jobs, or go back to school.

Another trait shared by board members at the different sites was long-time residency in their developments. Often they could recall a time when buildings and grounds were well maintained and when the developments had housed a "better class of tenants." They had been eyewitnesses to the deterioration that had taken place since. Consid-

---

1. Demographic data on board members were compiled from questionnaires completed by members of the boards and staffs at the six demonstration sites in the spring of 1979. Because of turnover among board members, they do not describe with complete accuracy the composition of the boards at the beginning of the demonstration or over its course (these data are unavailable), although at each of the sites there were several respondents who had been on the board since its inception. In addition, because some board members were unavailable to complete the questionnaire (they were out of town or otherwise away from the developments or did not attend board meetings regularly), the data do not describe the full complement of board members at the developments. These problems notwithstanding, the data do give a picture of the human resources available to the tenant management corporation boards of directors.

ering themselves stable, permanent residents of public housing, these tenants looked to tenant management as a way of making their communities once again clean, safe, pleasant places to live, without the stigma attached to a home in "the projects." And they wanted to be personally involved in that process.

Most board members were, by nature, doers and joiners. Most had been active in a variety of organizations, including tenant associations, church groups, school organizations, and social clubs, before they became involved with tenant management. They were not likely, however, to have been officers in these organizations, and they generally lacked experience in how decisionmaking organizations operate. Until this problem was addressed, many boards made little progress through the formal training curriculum.

Board Development

Building board strength was a major responsibility of the local technical assistants, who were eventually hired by MDRC for all sites except A. Harry Moore, where the PHA liaison served in this capacity. The role of technical assistants, along with the training in management procedures that board and staff members received, is discussed in Chapter 6.

If the major effort of the precontract period involved preparing the boards to act as boards—to work together to make responsible decisions—the period after contract signing tested how well the lessons presented during training were learned. This section describes the boards, their leadership, their stability, and the way in which they handled the major tasks required of them. Table 4-1 summarizes the salient findings.

Styles of Leadership. Four different kinds of leadership characterized the tenant management boards in the spring of 1979. At Curries Woods in Jersey City and at Que-View in New Haven, leadership could be described as weak; at Ashanti in Rochester and at Iroquois in Louisville, it was strong and diffused among many board members; and at Calliope in New Orleans it was strong and concentrated in a single individual, the board chairperson. Jersey City's A. Harry Moore's board fell between the latter two types. Although through much of its history it had been dominated, if not controlled, by the chairperson, a politically sophisticated clergyman, other board members eventually began to express their views more freely.

Throughout the course of the demonstration, strong leadership that won the respect and cooperation of fellow board members, the housing authority, and to some degree, the wider resident community has been associated with the presence of at least one assertive, decisive individual who was able both to control the behavior of fellow board members and to confront the housing authority when necessary. No such leader existed on the Que-View (New Haven) and Curries Woods (Jersey City) boards, in part, perhaps, because board members lacked confidence in their own abilities, in part because (at least at Que-View) there was an emphasis on achieving consensus among board members that made them unwilling to "rock the boat."

After a year of bitter squabbling at New Orleans' Calliope, capable leadership emerged in a feisty older woman who was elected chairperson and who has ruled the board with something close to an iron hand ever since. So complete was her authority that little other leadership has developed; when she was absent from board meetings, members seemed reluctant to make decisions. How a board would fare should such a chairperson resign is an open question.

The board in Louisville and the one in Rochester have each included at least two forceful personalities throughout the demonstration. Diffuse leadership can, of course, breed factionalism, and this was not entirely absent from these boards. It is a sign of the strength of both boards that they were able to overcome internal divisions and enlist several assertive personalities in a common cause.

During the early phase of program development, assertiveness was the trait that board members most prized in their leaders. As tenant management evolved, additional qualities became highly regarded; the ideal chairperson, as depicted in recent interviews, combined firmness with a willingness to listen to different points of view. The demands placed on the board as a whole also shifted over time. Once the staff was adequately performing day-to-day management functions and amicable relations had been established with the housing authority, it was no longer necessary for the board to be closely involved in all aspects of corporation affairs, and it could concentrate on its main business of making policy decisions.

Continuity in Board Membership. Stability in board membership had both advantages and drawbacks. On the plus side, a stable board

Table 4–1.   Characteristics of Tenant Management Corporation
Boards, June 1979.

Demonstration Site	Size and Structure	Attendance
Jersey City: A. Harry Moore Tenant Management Corporation	7 members—1 for each building.	Attendance of most members has been regular. There is one current vacancy.
Jersey City: Curries Woods Tenant Management Corporation	14–7–14 members—Because of attendance and other problems, the board has varied in size, with one or two representatives from each building.	Attendance has been spotty throughout; frequently a quorum has not been present.
Louisville: Iroquois Homes Resident Management Corporation	9 members—Geographically based, plus at large representation.	There is a solid core of members who attend regularly and a peripheral group whose attendance is irregular. There are two current vacancies.
New Haven: Que-View Tenant Management Corporation	6 members—Geographically based representation.	Attendance is regular. There is one vacancy.

Table 4-1. continued

Leadership Style	Extent of Turnover	Special Features Of Board Functioning
Strong, largely centered in chairperson, with increasing participation from other members.	Chairperson—There has been one chairperson throughout. Other members—Since the original election, there have been three changes in representation. There has been little disruption due to turnover.	The board functions well in identifying and resolving problems but has had a somewhat troubled relationship with staff. Relations with the housing authority are good.
Weak.	Chairperson—There have been three chairpersons; the most recent one was elected in 10/77. Other members—The original board was dissolved, and a new board was reconstituted in 9/77.	The board has been ridden with dissension and absenteeism throughout and has never won the support of the housing authority, the staff, or the community.
Strong and diffused among several members.	Chairperson—Two individuals have rotated as chairpersons. Other members—Although there was a moderate amount of turnover, little disruption resulted from the changes.	The board has several strong leaders and a well-developed subcommittee structure. Planning efforts include an annual plan against which progress is checked.
Weak.	Chairperson—There have been four chairpersons during the demonstration. These changes in leadership have had a disruptive effect on the TMC. Other members—All have been on the board since its inception.	The board has had difficulty in making decisions and tends to defer to the housing manager and the housing authority.

(Table 4-1. continued overleaf)

Table 4–1. continued

Demonstration Site	Size and Structure	Attendance
New Orleans: Calliope Development Tenant Management Corporation	9 members—Geographically based representation.	Attendance at the beginning of the demonstration was irregular; with a change of personnel it has improved.
Rochester: Ashanti Tenant Management Corporation	5 members—1 for each of the 5 developments comprising Ashanti.	Attendance has been regular, with the exception of one member, throughout the demonstration.

Note: Oklahoma City is not included because it did not complete the demonstration.
Source: MDRC files.

meant that most members were familiar with the goals and techniques of tenant management and that energies did not have to be diverted to training new members. In some cases it also meant that the resident population was satisfied with its chosen board's performance. On the other hand, board continuity that resulted from members running unopposed for reelection could suggest that the tenant management corporation had not been able to spark a high level of interest or participation on the part of the resident community. And as indicated in the preceding section, the continuous chairpersonship of a single figure could signal the weakness of the other board members. The board at A. Harry Moore in Jersey City was

Table 4—1. continued

Leadership Style	Extent of Turnover	Special Features Of Board Functioning
Strong and concentrated in the chairperson.	Chairperson—The initial chairperson was removed early in the demonstration; since then one person has presided continuously. Other members—Five of the original members remain on the board. Several board members who were disruptive resigned at various points.	Although the board has made immense strides since the beginning, when it was plagued with divisiveness, it still relies heavily on the chairperson for leadership, and absenteeism sometimes hampers decisionmaking.
Strong and diffused among several members.	Chairperson—There have been two chairpersons; both are current board members. Other members—Three of the five original members resigned and were replaced. There has been little disruption due to turnover.	Throughout, the board has been marked by strong leaders with political savvy in dealing with the housing authority.

under the leadership of one chairperson throughout the demonstration; at Calliope, one person had been chairperson since early 1977; and at Curries Woods, the same individual had been chairperson since the fall of that year. The remaining sites have all experienced turnover in the position of chairperson.

At Que-View in New Haven, four people have occupied the position of board chairperson. Of these, one resigned to apply for a staff position; one resigned before moving out of the development; and most recently, one left in favor of a younger woman who, it was hoped, could provide stronger leadership. While the majority of the Que-View board members had served since the inception of the demonstration, Que-View was a site where turnover at the top had a detrimental effect on the functioning of the rest of the board. Two of the resignations deprived the board of individuals who had demonstrated perhaps the greatest leadership capacity.

Turnover in the position of board chairperson may sometimes be seen as a demonstration of board strength rather than weakness, for it showed that boards were willing to coalesce behind more than one leader. After one person had served as RMC board chairperson for nearly two years, several members of the Louisville board apparently concluded that someone else deserved a chance. Although there is a general consensus that the new chairperson was not as dynamic a leader as her predecessor, the board continued to function smoothly under her stewardship. After a year, however, the former chairperson was reinstated.

At Ashanti, turnover occurred for another reason. When the first chairperson's wife was promoted to the top management position on the staff, he resigned his office and was succeeded by another vocal board member. The transition was particularly difficult because the former chairperson was reelected as a board member and had difficulty relinquishing his position of authority. Ashanti's technical assistant played a crucial role in smoothing ruffled feelings and ensuring his continued cooperation.

Beyond turnover at the top, the boards also experienced change among other members. Sometimes this was the consequence of regularly scheduled elections; more often, it was caused by resignations. As mentioned above, some board members did not anticipate the large commitment of time and energy, and others had to give up that commitment when they started new jobs or went back to school. Still others moved out of the developments. Finally, it appears that some members resigned because they felt that the board was ineffectual and preferred to voice their opposition from the outside rather than to participate from the inside. This was particularly the case at Curries Woods, where the board was constantly plagued by turnover. As a rule, however, former board members were not active in spearheading opposition to the tenant management corporations.

Board elections were seldom hotly contested affairs. On several occasions, residents seeking a place on the board or board members seeking reelection ran unopposed, sometimes, it would seem, because potential opponents were reluctant to risk defeat. Where TMC boards had a stable contingent of members from the beginning of the demonstration, turnover—whatever its cause—and the resulting need to assimilate new members did not create serious problems. Veteran board members were able to instruct new members in the goals and operations of tenant management, sometimes through efforts to provide systematic training for newcomers, sometimes simply through on the job experience. But where a basic cadre of board leaders was not retained, the turnover endemic to the demonstration seriously undermined the board's progress.

Continuity in membership has been a marked asset to the boards during the demonstration, but this continuity presented risks as well as strengths. There was little effort among the TMCs to nurture increased interest in board membership. Without a continuing influx of potential new leadership, there would be no new members prepared to take the places of longer term board members as they resigned or retired. Board members seemed only mildly concerned with this problem: although board seats were vacant at all sites except Ashanti in Rochester, the boards' efforts to fill these vacancies were lackadaisical. If failure on the part of community residents to come forward and fill vacant seats betokens lack of interest in the tenant management corporation or inability to take on the responsibilities of board membership, then the viability of the board, over the long term if not the short one, becomes an open question.

Patterns and Problems in Board Functioning. The following discussion is not intended as an evaluation of the overall effectiveness of the tenant boards. Such an evaluation involves a number of considerations, among them the way in which tenant management has affected management performance and the degree of support the tenant management corporation has garnered in the community. Both of these topics are treated in a subsequent chapter. Here, the aim is to describe the patterns that have arisen among the tenant boards and to assess their implications for the viability of the program.

Over the demonstration, the scope of board activities and the time demands placed on board members shifted. At the beginning of the demonstration, training sessions often took up several evenings a week, while at the end, board meetings occurred only weekly or biweekly. Nonetheless, most board members said they spent at least six hours a week on tenant-management-related matters. Once the tenant management staff took over day-to-day management, the board had other responsibilities—supervising staff performance, soliciting the views of residents, making policy decisions and communicating them to the community, securing additional funds from outside parties, and planning for the future.

Documentation interviews indicate that board confidence grew with experience. For many board members, conquering shyness was a difficult, although liberating, process. Speaking up was especially hard because it raised the specter of divisiveness. Particularly at the outset of the demonstration, lack of confidence often led board members to avoid or procrastinate on issues where there was disagreement. With time, however, came greater self-assurance and enhanced decisionmaking ability.

At every site, the boards had problems with staff members whose performance was poor. This is a normal management problem, but in tenant management, much of the board's reluctance to terminate unsatisfactory employees was grounded in sympathy for their fellow tenants and the knowledge that staff members needed the job and its income. Therefore, they usually looked for alternatives to firing, such as demotion and probation. While demotion often cured the problem, probation was a less effective remedy, and staff members were sometimes placed on probation several times before more decisive action was taken.

While the boards were not successful in dealing expeditiously with poor staff performance, they did not hesitate to monitor and criticize staff members, occasionally in ways that strained relations between the two groups. Board members sometimes trespassed on the housing manager's territory by complaining directly to staff members about behavior and job performance. In the Urban Institute survey, tenant management project managers did not indicate that board interference with staff functioning was viewed by staff as a major problem, although problems did seem to exist.[2]

Why the boards had problems observing the proper procedure in their dealings with the tenant management staffs is a question for which there is no simple answer. For one thing, board members themselves received training in management procedures, often working alongside housing authority personnel to become acquainted with the tasks that needed to be done, and they wanted to make sure that

2. Suzanne B. Loux and Robert Sadacca, "Analysis of Changes at Tenant Management Demonstration Projects," Working Paper #1335 (Washington, D.C.: Urban Institute, 1980). Tenant management project managers reported that board members making decisions that the staff should make was somewhat less than a medium-sized problem and "disagreed some" with the statement that board members tried to do the manager's job.

these tasks were properly performed. Then too, after the board members had completed training, many found themselves with free time and, not knowing quite what to do with themselves, intruded into areas where they were not welcome. Finally, unpaid board members had made a major commitment to tenant management—a commitment that some of them suspected the salaried members of the staff did not share. Some of the boards' requests might have appeared unreasonable to staff—for example, having to give up a weekend in order to conduct a clean-up campaign or having to patrol their buildings in the evenings without receiving extra compensation. These were the kinds of activities in which board members participated without receiving any compensation at all.

Two things made board and staff members more comfortable in their respective roles—the passage of time and the intervention of the technical assistants. The technical assistants helped TMC personnel define the limits of their separate spheres of activity and also aided the boards when problems developed with the housing authorities concerning matters on which the board had not received training. Indeed, at several sites, board members named the technical assistant as the first person they would turn to should such an issue arise.

A common criticism leveled at the boards, particularly by housing authority officials, was that the boards practiced "crisis management," handling problems as they occurred (and sometimes failing to deal with them until they truly became crises) rather than carrying on long-term planning. Iroquois in Louisville was the only board that engaged in advance planning for ends rather than means. Each year, the Iroquois board established a set of goals, and once a month it checked its own progress in achieving them. A serious shortcoming among many boards concerned community development and, most importantly, an effort to acquire additional funding for it. Although several boards considered soliciting funds from private and public agencies for the postdemonstration period, Louisville and Rochester were the only sites to have undertaken such an effort.

All this suggests that even in the best of cases, there was a continuing need for technical assistance to help the boards consolidate and further develop their decisionmaking and planning abilities and to conciliate internal conflicts. While the level of assistance can almost certainly be reduced in the postdemonstration period, it was probably unrealistic to expect that in three years most boards could have advanced to the point where they no longer needed the expertise and advice that sympathetic outsiders could provide.

THE TENANT MANAGEMENT STAFF

One of the major responsibilities of the tenant management board of directors during the precontract period was to oversee the recruitment and hiring of a staff to whom the daily business of management is entrusted. This section examines the characteristics, organization, and performance of staff at the six demonstration sites (excluding Oklahoma City).

Recruitment, Selection, and Characteristics of Staff Members

Staff job descriptions were posted, and applications were solicited through an assortment of techniques, including fliers distributed door to door or stuffed in mailboxes, posters, personal visits by board members, and at Calliope in New Orleans, a job fair. Although in some instances repeated recruiting efforts had to be made, the boards were eventually able to secure a sufficient number of qualified applicants from within the developments. At several sites, these candidates included former board members who resigned to seek salaried staff positions. According to interviews, the factors that spurred residents to apply for jobs with the tenant management corporation were different from those that induced others to join the boards. While staff applicants may have appreciated the opportunity to serve their communities, they were attracted chiefly by the conditions of work—the prospect of getting out of the house yet remaining close to home and family and of interacting with others rather than being confined to a desk or a factory post.

The importance of following open hiring procedures in order to deflect charges of favoritism was thoroughly impressed on board members. A related issue was whether immediate relatives of board members could be hired for staff positions. An antinepotism position was enunciated for the demonstration as a whole, but it was not rigidly enforced in the face of varying local conditions. What was insisted upon, however, was that each board arrive at a final decision only after a careful discussion of the issue. Thus, in Jersey City, the A. Harry Moore board decided that because the tenant population was large and diverse enough to provide an adequate supply of qualified applicants, relatives of board members would be ineligible for full-time tenant management corporation positions. The Louisville and Rochester boards, on the other hand, determined that as long as all eligible candidates for staff positions were carefully screened, the best candidates, regardless of relationship to board members, would be hired.

At most sites, job applicants were interviewed and their references were checked by board members, and they were then rated on a numerical scale according to a number of criteria that included appearance, work experience, education, past involvement in the community, rent payment record, and responses to the board members' questions. These scoring sheets figured prominently in each board's final hiring decisions.

Tenant management staff members, coming as they did from the same housing development, tended to share certain demographic characteristics with board members. They were predominantly black, female, and head of households.

Staff Organization, Past and Present

Table 4–2 shows the staff line-up at each of the sites as of June 1979 and summarizes the changes in staff organization as well as in personnel that have taken place during the demonstration.

Staff Size and Composition. Table 4–2 indicates that there was considerable variation among the sites in the size of the staff and the duties they performed apart from the number of dwelling units in the development. Staff size fluctuated over the course of the demonstration. In some instances, staff positions were added, and in other cases, positions were deleted as board members came to feel that the same quantity of work could be done equally well by fewer people.

Sometimes these events occurred at the same site: in Rochester, for instance, security aides and laundry room attendants were hired several months after the initial managerial staff had been installed, while the number of lane managers was cut back. At another site, factors entering into the board's decision to reduce staff included the inability of the first manager to organize work efficiently, the unsatisfactory performance of two of the four original lane managers, and the board's budget priorities. At a third site, the board, in dismiss-

Table 4–2.   Characteristics of Tenant Management Staff, June 1979.

Demonstration Site	TMC Staff Titles[a]	Turnover in Personnel	Special Features or Changes in Staff Responsibilities
Jersey City: A. Harry Moore Tenant Management Corporation (664 Units)	Housing Manager; Building Managers; Secretary; Security Officers; Mailroom Clerk.	The first Housing Manager resigned. A Building Manager was promoted to the position. One Building Manager position turned over because of death, and another due to poor health. In 5/79 the Social Service Coordinator resigned. Recreation Aides and Tutors were hired but then suspended because they had no supervisor and the school year was over. All these positions remained vacant until the demonstration's end.	Work is organized geographically, with each Building Manager responsible for performing a number of management functions in her building.
Jersey City: Curries Woods Tenant Management Corporation (712 Units)	Manager; Building Managers; Social Service Coordinator; Security Aides; Senior Citizens' Helper; Desk Clerk; Typist Clerk.	There has been turnover in every job title except that of Manager. The first Social Service Coordinator and a Building Manager were terminated.	Work is organized geographically, with each Building Manager responsible for a particular building.

Louisville: Iroquois Homes Resident Management Corporation (854 Units)	Manager; Assistant Managers[b]; Management Aides; Security Officers.	The first Manager was demoted to Assistant Manager, and a former board member became Manager. Originally, four Assistant Managers were hired. One resigned because of illness, and one was terminated. Security turnovers resulted from transfers and resignations.	At first the work was organized on a geographical basis, with Assistant Managers serving different areas of the development. After a general staff reorganization, tasks were divided along functional lines, with two Assistant Managers continuing to perform managerial duties and the other assuming social service functions.
New Haven: Que-View Tenant Management Corporation (260 Units)	Housing Manager; Lane Managers; Secretary.	The Assistant Manager resigned in mid-1978, after conflicts with the Manager. The resignations of the Secretary and one Lane Manager soon followed. By the end of the demonstration two more Lane Managers had resigned. Except for the Secretary, all of the above positions remained vacant until the end of the demonstration because of the New Haven Housing Authority's hiring freeze.	The duties of the Lane Managers are restricted to inspecting grounds, disseminating information to tenants, and assisting in the recreational programs because the board has been unwilling to allow anyone except the Housing Manager and the Assistant Manager to have access to residents' files.

Table 4–2. continued

Demonstration Site	TMC Staff Titles[a]	Turnover in Personnel	Special Features or Changes in Staff Responsibilities

New Orleans: Calliope Development Tenant Management Corporation
 	
(1,550 Units)
	Housing Manager; Housing Assistant Manager; Management Aides[c]; Account Clerk; Typist Clerks; Social Service Aides.	The only resignations were one Typist Clerk and one Management Aide during mid-1978. But a series of position exchanges followed these resignations: the Assistant Manager became a Management Aide; a Typist Clerk became Assistant Manager. The Assistant Manager and Housing Manager then switched positions.
		    In 6/79 the Social Service Coordinator was terminated and her position eliminated.
			After the position of Social Service Coordinator was eliminated, the Social Service Aides were supervised by the Housing Manager.
			    Work is organized geographically, with each Management Aide performing management functions in a particular area.

| Rochester: Ashanti Tenant Management Corporation (211 Units) | Housing Manager; Assistant Manager; Lane Managers; Clerk; Security Aides; Laundry Attendants. | In 7/78, the first Housing Manager was terminated. A Lane Manager was promoted to the top position. The Social Service Coordinator was terminated, and the position remains vacant. There have also been turnovers in the Lane Manager, Security, and Clerk positions. | Originally, the TMC hired five Lane Managers, each of whom was responsible for one of the five small developments at Ashanti. One Lane Manager was promoted to Housing Manager and another one to Clerk; the same duties are now divided among three Lane Managers, whose work includes some social service functions as well as management ones (e.g., Lane Managers assist residents with welfare problems). |

a. Positions listed here include only those jobs filled at the end of the demonstration. Vacant and eliminated positions are designated in the second column, Turnover in Personnel.

b. At Iroquois the Assistant Managers performed the Lane Manager responsibilities; Management Aides were office assistants.

c. At Calliope the Lane Manager duties were carried out by the Management Aides.

Note: Oklahoma City is not included because it did not complete the demonstration.

Source: MDRC files.

ing the social services coordinator, decided that the position was expendable. Three tenant management staff positions deserving special mention are the housing manager and social services coordinator positions, because they experienced a high degree of turnover; and the lane manager position, because it represents an innovation introduced by the demonstration to bring management closer to the residents and also experienced turnover.

The Housing Manager.   Changes of personnel were most frequent at the top; at four of the six sites, the first housing manager had to be replaced. Much of this turnover was probably inevitable, inasmuch as most applicants were inexperienced, and any prior work experience they had had seldom provided the board with clues about how they would fare in their new jobs. At one site, the housing manager was terminated after a housing authority evaluation found the manager to be ineffective in supervising staff and organizing work. Another resident manager had worked as a teacher's aide; in the new position, however, the manager proved ineffective in organizing work tasks and was unsympathetic toward residents. With the wisdom of hindsight, a board member at another site acknowledged that the board made a wrong choice in hiring its first housing manager because it was so taken with a candidate's pleasant, outgoing personality that it did not consider whether that candidate possessed the requisite firmness to deal with subordinates and recalcitrant tenants. A fourth housing manager was fired after being arrested for a minor offense (the case was later dismissed).[3]

An example of turnover that could have been avoided occurred at one site where the housing authority allowed two people to train for the top management position. Although the "loser" was appointed assistant manager, the rivalry that had developed during training continued after the trainees assumed management responsibilities. It sparked into a full-scale conflict that ended only when the assistant manager resigned.

The problem of finding new people to fill top management slots was mitigated by the fact that at all four sites where the housing manager was replaced, the vacancies were filled from within the tenant management corporation. At two sites, lane managers were promoted; at another site the housing manager and assistant housing

3. There were other infrequent instances of malfeasance followed by termination of the guilty party that did not pose special problems for the tenant management corporation but that represented instances of unpredictable turnover.

manager switched places; and at a third site, a board member resigned to become housing manager, while the housing manager was demoted to assistant housing manager. Thus, it appears that the early period after staff assumed management responsibility was one in which both inappropriate choices were weeded out and potential supervisory staff were identified and brought to the fore.

The Social Services Coordinator. The tenure of social services coordinator was as perilous as that of housing managers. At all but one of the sites where a social services coordinator was hired, the first person appointed was subsequently terminated. The high rate of turnover resulted not only from the incumbents' poor performance, including one instance of malfeasance, but also from the boards' failure to define responsibilities clearly.

Tenant management board training covered the provision of social services to site residents almost as an afterthought; the Program Sequence Guide discussed "soft management" only after an extended treatment of management principles, maintenance, marketing and leasing, security, and other "hard management" topics. When the social services coordinators assumed their new jobs, they often found the mandates they were given broad and vague—to help residents with personal problems, to refer them to other agencies where appropriate, to establish recreation programs, and so on.

While other members of the tenant management staff usually received extensive training for the responsibilities they would assume, the social services coordinators did not. Although they went through the same general management training as the rest of the staff, at only one site did they receive training especially geared to their future roles. In most cases, what the coordinators did was left to their own ingenuity and enterprise. As a rule, they solicited the cooperation and sometimes the advice of staff in local community agencies.

At one site these problems were compounded by the fact that a social services unit staffed by housing authority personnel continued to operate on the site. Despite repeated efforts (abetted by the technical assistants) to integrate and coordinate the functions of the housing authority unit with those of the new tenant management social services staff, an effective solution was blocked by continuing mutual jealousies. Attempts to delineate spheres of activity while respecting preexisting boundaries sometimes produced absurd results. Social services aides, for instance, were given responsibility for counseling residents about poor housekeeping practices, while housing authority staff continued to provide advice on family budgeting; the tenant management staff was charged with planning special holiday events, while the housing authority unit, as in the past, distributed Christmas toys.

In general, the coordinators appeared to have discharged their referral function adequately. Their performance was less satisfactory in the area of program development and follow-through. For instance, it took one social services coordinator over a year to get a recreation program going, and then it consisted largely of ceramics classes, sewing classes, and educational films, which drew only a limited audience.

Before attributing the problems of social services delivery to a lack of initiative and perseverance on the part of the people hired to fill the position, it should be noted that social services coordinators at several of the sites lacked support from the tenant management board. They complained that their proposals for new programs had not been given a hearing and that requests for space and materials were turned down.

The two sites where this role was performed satisfactorily share certain features that may account for the success more than the characteristics of the people in the position. Both sites were fairly isolated from the center of the city, and they had relatively large numbers of the elderly, a group both needy and appreciative of assistance.

The checkered experiences of the social services coordinators at the different sites, raise the question whether the position is feasible or desirable at all developments under tenant management. Some observers feel that the position is unnecessary at small scattered site developments or at sites where the housing authority has already established a social services staff. On the other hand, the social services coordinators performed valuable services for tenants at all the sites, including the two sites that eliminated this position. Public housing residents, by virtue of their low incomes, often face a host of problems whose solution requires negotiating a maze of social agencies and government bureaucracies; the social services coordinator could help residents cut through this tangle. And residents' children, too, could gain from organized recreation and tutoring programs that give them an alternative to "hanging out." Before deciding that the position of social services coordinator is expendable, it would probably make sense to attempt to strengthen the position by clearly identifying its purpose and ensuring that the person who holds it receives adequate training and resources.

The Lane Manager. At every site, the tenant management staff was larger than the on-site housing authority staff had been—an increase primarily accounted for by the lane managers. Lane managers—sometimes known as building or assistant managers or management aides—were usually the management representatives for a specific geographical area of the development. This staff position was critical to tenant management as embodied in the demonstration model, for it was the vehicle through which residents had most immediate access to, and interaction with, management. Through their close contact with the residents, lane managers also served as management's "eyes and ears" within the community. They were in a position to warn management of potential sources of unrest as well as to uncover illegal activities among tenants, such as unreported income.

According to the model, the lane manager was responsible for managerial duties and community organization in the section of the development where he or she lived. The lane manager referred residents' requests for maintenance to the central office and followed up to make sure they were attended to, determined building cleanliness and maintenance needs, inspected apartments to check on housekeeping practices and unreported maintenance problems, contacted rent-delinquent tenants, circulated fliers and informational literature, held building meetings, and generally served as the person to whom tenants first turned when they had a housing-related problem. In addition, as a neighbor, the lane manager was often privy to residents' personal problems and could bring these to the attention of the social services coordinator.

All sites initially hired several lane managers. The original organizational plan remained intact at both Jersey City sites and in New Orleans. In Rochester and Louisville, the tenant management boards decided to cut back on the number of lane managers, and in New Haven the staff was reduced through attrition and a hiring freeze.

Just as the number of lane managers differed from site to site and over time, so did their responsibilities. These appeared to be most varied in Rochester, where lane managers performed some of the functions elsewhere delegated to the social services coordinator, such as transporting elderly residents to the social security office and interviewing prospective tenants. In Louisville, the geographical organization of the assignment was abandoned completely in favor of a functional division of work, with one lane manager (or assistant manager) continuing to perform management tasks and another taking over the responsibilities of social services coordinator.

The lane managers's duties were most curtailed in New Haven, due to the board's reluctance to allow anyone except the housing manager and the assistant manager access to personal information about tenants, an attitude that seemed particularly ill advised because of the burden it placed on the housing manager. Given the small size of the development (260 units) and the restriction on the duties that lane managers performed, it was doubtful whether, if the hiring freeze were lifted, additional lane managers would have had much of a job to do, even though their positions were slated as part time.

The major risk in using lane managers was overstaffing—having too many people on staff without enough to do. However, in cases where the duties were clearly defined, the position did serve its intended purpose as a bridge between residents and management.

Staff Performance.   Ultimately, an evaluation of the tenant management staff, as of the board, must look at various management indicators—for example, the amount of rent arrearage, the vacancy rate, the per unit rent, and the like, which are examined in Chapter 7. Even without this, however, the general consensus among MDRC field representatives, housing authority personnel, and other observers was that after initial shakeups in personnel, the managerial staffs performed at least adequately, and sometimes better than conventional management. This finding was further confirmed by the Urban Institute survey in which housing authority personnel generally rated TMC staff management as equal to or slightly better than previous management.[4] The only site to receive an official housing authority staff evaluation was Ashanti in Rochester. The evaluation cited some positive gains, but also pointed out staff inefficiencies. The board found the evaluation to be excessively negative and protested. In Jersey City, the executive director of the housing authority considered the resident manager at A. Harry Moore to be one of his best project managers.

4. Suzanne B. Loux and Robert Sadacca, "Analysis of Changes at Tenant Management Demonstration Projects," Working Paper #1335 (Washington, D.C.: Urban Institute, 1980). PHA central office staff rated TMC management of the projects as 1.11 in comparison with prior PHA management where 0 = worst, 1 = same, and 2 = better.

Staff performed adequately even where tenant management board performance was problematic. Although the Curries Woods board in Jersey City had never displayed cohesiveness and decisionmaking ability, the staff carried out its duties competently. In New Haven, evaluation of Que-View's staff's performance was clouded by several considerations. These included the authoritywide hiring freeze that left staff size below the level necessary to take care of management functions in a timely manner, the board's decision to restrict the responsibilities of the lane manager, and a long strike of housing authority maintenance personnel. Nonetheless, it was widely acknowledged that the housing manager worked hard and had done a reasonable job with few resources.

Where problems arose with respect to staff performance, they generally centered on the twin issues of supervision and delegation. Some managers felt uncomfortable giving orders to, and some staff members resisted taking orders from, their fellow tenants. Possibly as a way of avoiding confrontation (and also of ensuring that the job would get done), top level managers sometimes took on tasks that should more properly have been delegated to lane managers. Technical assistants worked with the housing managers to sort out those duties that they should have attended to themselves from those that should have been handled by other staff. Learning to delegate responsibility consumed a great deal of time during training. This was due in part to the fact that as the demonstration progressed and duties changed, levels of responsibility also changed, and the human chemistry of the personalities involved required continuous accommodation.

The Burdens and Benefits of Board and Staff Participation

Involvement with tenant management has brought definite rewards to board and staff members of the corporations. For staff members, of course, the rewards were in large part financial, but both board and staff members cited an array of nonmaterial benefits that have come to them through participation in the demonstration. Involvement has also exacted sacrifices—of time, of other commitments, of friendships. In this section, board and staff members speak of the gains and losses they have experienced and of how they see their dual role as tenants and as managers.

Burdens of Participation. "I think I've kind of lost out on my children growing up . . . it seems like all of a sudden all of them were grown," is the way one board member at Iroquois expressed a theme that frequently recurs in the documentation interviews. The time commitment that tenant management demands—spending long evenings in training sessions and meetings and being constantly available to deal with irate or distressed residents—means that the families of board and staff members have to adjust their lives accordingly. This is not necessarily viewed as all bad. Some interview respondents feel that their children have gained in maturity from the independence that has been thrust upon them, but most voice regret that they have not been able to spend more time with their families. This problem, hardly unique to the demonstration, is one shared by many working women. In this instance, however, it is compounded by the fact that many of the board and staff members had previously perceived themselves only as homemakers with no other skills and by the widespread feelings that even when they are home, they "are on the job."

Board and staff members have sometimes become so dedicated to tenant management that relatives and friends accuse them of having lost all interest in anything else. Recreational activities and social life often are neglected. The former board chairperson at one site and his wife, the current housing manager, recount parallel versions of the same story. In his words: "Homewise, my wife, before she became part of [the program] used to tell me, 'I'm tired of hearing about that damn tenant management. That's all you talk about, you spend all your time there. You're never with the kids or me. We don't go out, we don't do this.' Then she became part of it, and now I tell her I'm tired of hearing. . . ."

Although being on the tenant management staff has brought financial gains to participants, these benefits have not been unalloyed. Rising incomes have brought rent increases for many staff members, and the requirement that all board and staff members behave in an exemplary manner has meant that rents must be paid on the first of the month. And some staff members speak of their initial qualms about leaving the security of welfare for the vicissitudes of an unfamiliar and impermanent job.

Board and staff members have also had to sacrifice amicable relations with some of their neighbors. Some residents of public housing resent the fact that their peers have access to files containing personal information about them. Hostility is also engendered when tenant management personnel, by virtue of their dual position as tenants and managers, find out and act on knowledge that other residents are behaving in ways that violate the rules—for instance, by failing to report increases in income, residing with individuals who are not on the lease, or keeping pets. And finally, some residents are annoyed that other tenants have any authority whatsoever over their conduct. As one lane manager expressed it: "If you have friends, this job honestly does make enemies out of them sooner or later. Because they feel, 'What right has she got? She lives out here just like me, she don't have no more than I do. What right does she have to come here and tell me what I got to do? She better get over there and clean her own yard or house or whatever.' "

Efforts to enforce the regulations have met with responses ranging from acquiescence to verbal slurs to threats of physical harm. Board and staff members have had garbage thrown on their lawns; one board chairperson had his windshield broken three times. Although a relatively small number of tenants at any site has been involved in such incidents, board and staff members have come to expect a certain degree of tenant hostility as part of the job.

Role Perceptions. Interview responses indicate that when staff members at the various developments encounter the antagonism of residents, they tend to respond in a similar vein. One lane manager put it this way:

> There were times when the tenants got uptight when I would go to them . . . for instance, inspecting their homes. I would tell them, "Look, I'm not the manager, I'm only here doing my job, I'm only carrying out orders. . . ."
>
> And a housing manager says: "I know I've a job to do and I just have to do it. And then I explain to them, You know, this is my job. Just because you're a friend of mine or a neighbor, I can't do you any different than I would anybody else."

The question then arises, How do tenant managers view the jobs they do and the orders they carry out? That is, How do they perceive their dual roles as tenants and as managers? A subsequent chapter examines this issue in relation to the tenant management corporations' interactions with the local housing authorities. Here the question is addressed with respect to the relations between tenant management personnel and other tenants.

In their dealings with fellow tenants, board and staff members side with management, but a management that they see as both stricter and more beneficent than housing authority management. At every site the board and staff who were interviewed maintained that they enforced the rules more rigorously than the housing authority. Those provisions that went unenforced (for instance, stipulations as to how tenants could decorate their apartments) had usually been ignored by the housing authority. Several respondents commented that in contrast to the twice yearly inspection conducted by tenant management staff, under housing authority management their apartments had not been inspected for years.

The training curriculum emphasizes the importance of rent collection to the entire management enterprise, and tenant managers assert that they are quicker than their housing authority counterparts in taking action on rent delinquencies and instituting eviction proceedings for nonpayment. At least one housing manager seems to believe that what is good for the tenant management corporation is also good for tenants, as a means of enforcing self-discipline and planning.

> It's taken me a long time to kind of straighten out the bad habits of some tenants. They're inclined to come in and give you half here and half there. I just put my foot down and said "No more of this." Really, it's helping the residents. This business of "I've got to give you my rent weekly because I cannot save it for a month," this is crazy. You've got to learn to do this. We've just put our foot down and said, "No, we can't accept that." I think we're really helping the residents. The rent collection has really gone up. We don't have too many problems now.

But if board and staff members are aware that they ask more of tenants, they are also convinced that they do more for them and are more responsive to their needs. They contrast their own around the clock availability to assist tenants who have lost keys or who need emergency repairs with the attitudes of housing authority personnel, who disappear from the site at 4:30 P.M. sharp. They pride themselves on the speed with which they respond to tenants' requests for services. And they see themselves as being in touch with tenants' problems and providing a sympathetic audience for their complaints, in large part because, as one housing manager put it, "you've had the same problems, the same miseries, the same frustrations that they are going through."

The Benefits of Participation.   The last comment notwithstanding, being a sympathetic listener and having the requisite patience to respond to tenants who are angry or upset are not traits that tenant managers automatically possess by dint of their shared status as residents of public housing. Rather, these are skills that must be learned and practiced in training sessions and on the job.

Many board and staff members surveyed in the spring of 1979 felt great satisfaction that they had acquired these abilities; when asked to name the best part of their experience with tenant management, a sizable number of them answered, "learning to work with people." Greater patience and understanding were just two of a panoply of positive personality changes they saw as produced by their involvement with tenant management. Several people said they had conquered shyness and overcome self-doubt and feelings of inferiority.

Pride in mastering the tenant management curriculum is reflected in this exchange between an interviewer and a board member whose formal education had ended after the fifth grade:

> The information I got, I didn't know I would be capable of absorbing all of this very important information that it takes to run and manage public housing, but I did. I did, I absorbed an awful lot. I have a lot of knowledge in my head. . . .
> So your feelings about yourself have changed?
> Changed considerably. (Laughing) I'm not as dumb as I thought I was.

And the development of self-worth and importance is also reflected in a lane manager's musings:

> I didn't have any confidence in myself. Ms. X [the assistant manager], if it weren't for her, I wouldn't be here, because she took me into her office and she gave me a good talking to. She told me that I didn't have any confidence in myself, because I felt that this job was more than my education called for. . . . Then I found out that I wasn't the only one low in education, and then it didn't bother me too much. . . . I stopped downing myself, and said that I was going to do the best I could. . . . I was afraid to ask them different things about coming to help me. . . . I didn't want to sound so dumb. But I stopped that. If I'm going to learn, I will have to ask. So I started asking, and didn't care what they said. The more I worked, I felt more like a business lady who carried a briefcase. Oh! I felt good. Coming to work nice and clean; carrying my briefcase made me feel real important. I still feel important about my work. I'd get up and tell my husband, "Well, I guess I'll go to the office."

These positive feelings have been enhanced by the fact of participation in a national demonstration, which occasionally afforded board and staff members the opportunity to travel to different places (for some, to take their first plane rides) and to meet their counterparts at other sites.

Staff members, of course, have derived financial benefits from their involvement with tenant management. Along with many board members, they expect their tenant management experience will stand them in good stead when it comes to finding other jobs in either real estate management or human services occupations.

Beyond these essentially personal rewards, board and staff members believe that they are engaged in an important mission, and they take pride in what they have been able to accomplish for their developments. The completion of physical improvements, the provision of transportation for the handicapped, the employment of a security force, even a quick response to a tenant's service request—all of these things heighten their sense not only of personal efficacy but also of altruism and public spirit. They are especially aware that they have been able to accomplish these things in the face of skepticism on the part of some housing authority personnel who doubted that tenants could do the job as well as experienced managers, if at all.

In short, what those involved with tenant management have tasted is power—power to change their own lives and power to change the communities in which they live. And having tasted it, they are reluctant to relinquish it. Asked what they would do should the tenant management corporation be dissolved at the conclusion of the demonstration, a few said that they would do nothing, that their energies had been burned out on this single activity that had become so central to their lives. But most said that they would remain active in the community, fighting to ensure that its needs were met. "They [the housing authority] would never just say, 'Well, it's all over. Be quiet.' Oh no. It'd never happen."

5 THE HOUSING AUTHORITY– TENANT MANAGEMENT CORPORATION RELATIONSHIP

The development of an open, cooperative relationship between the tenant management corporation and the housing authority is perhaps the single most critical factor for the successful implementation of tenant management. A partnership between the two relies on the acceptance of several key premises and principles. On one side, the tenant management corporation must realize that in taking on managerial responsibilities, it can no longer adopt an adversary stance vis-à-vis the housing authority and that it must work within the broad framework of housing authority operations. On the other side, the housing authority's executive director must make a philosophical commitment to the concept of tenant management (or at least to the value of testing that concept) and must impart that commitment to other housing authority staff. The housing authority must also be willing to make changes in its practices and procedures to accommodate tenant management. And both parties must be prepared to negotiate and then live with a reasonable division of responsibilities and of power.

In St. Louis, tenant management arose after a period of mutual mistrust and confrontation between tenants and the housing authority. Four years elapsed between the initial tenant strike and the implementation of tenant management at the first two housing authority developments, during which time a new relationship of mutual respect necessary for tenant management evolved between the tenants and the PHA.

As the demonstration neared its conclusion, a viable partnership between housing authority and tenant management corporation could be discerned at four of the original seven demonstration sites. At A. Harry Moore in Jersey City, Iroquois Homes in Louisville, Calliope Development in New Orleans, and Ashanti in Rochester, occasional problems and troublesome issues had been resolved, and a successful partnership had evolved. However, the other three sites were experiencing serious difficulties. At Curries Woods in Jersey City and Que-View in New Haven, relations between the tenant management corporation and the PHA—in both cases troubled from the outset—had deteriorated to a critical state. The Jersey City Housing Authority refused to sign a management contract with the Curries Woods board, while the Que-View Tenant Management Corporation—one of the first in the demonstration to sign a management contract—did not know whether its contract would be extended beyond the three-year demonstration period. (That state of ambiguity was resolved a few months later when the New Haven Housing Authority's Board of Commissioners voted to terminate the Que-View contract.) At the third troubled site, Oklahoma City, the situation became so aggravated that the site was dropped from the demonstration.

Where a partnership did exist, its achievement was not always easy. Frequent and open communication was required to conquer mistrust and to maintain amicable relations while unfamiliar policies and procedures were put in place; disagreements, at times intense, occasionally divided the parties. Furthermore, it would be misleading to view the tenant management corporation–housing authority relationship, even where it appears to be solid, as a partnership of peers. The housing authority starts off with the upper hand in the relationship because of its managerial experience, its role in board and staff training, and its control of materials and skilled labor. To be able to work effectively with the housing authority, the tenant management board needs a degree of assertiveness, unity, and self-assurance that is not always found among board members.

This chapter traces the patterns of cooperation and conflict between the tenant management corporations and the housing authorities as they have evolved over the course of the demonstration. It analyzes sources of strain in the relationship and examines how these strains have—or have not—been resolved. It assesses the advantages and drawbacks of participation in the demonstration from the housing authorities' standpoint and discusses their plans for the continuation or replication of tenant management.

PREDEMONSTRATION RELATIONSHIPS

An examination of the predemonstration relationships that existed between tenants and housing authorities in the demonstration cities provides some idea of the effort required to form a partnership. Although no such partnership existed prior to the demonstration, in some cases a foundation for a cooperative relationship had been laid. In five of the demonstration cities, a tenant member sat on the housing authority's board of commissioners, and in several of them, a citywide tenant organization interacted with the housing authority on specific matters. In addition, at most of the developments selected as demonstration sites, tenant associations were already in place, although they varied greatly in effectiveness. These tenant associations had generally received some measure of housing authority support, sometimes through community organization specialists deployed to assist in their establishment, sometimes through nominal allotments for operating expenses. The responsibilities of the tenant associations were restricted, however. At some sites, the tenant associations were the means by which residents provided input into modernization decisions, but at others, their responsibility was limited to such tasks as arranging outings for the children of the development or distributing food to needy families. Tenants were not involved in management duties at any site.

The relationships that existed between tenants and housing authorities ranged from indifference—with the parties interacting over routine matters such as rent collection or maintenance requests—to occasional tension, when tenants would mobilize to protest specific housing authority actions. Perhaps the best relationship had developed in Jersey City. There, a stable pattern of tenant participation in housing authority affairs had been established prior to the demonstration, and tenants were involved, through their sitewide and building organizations, in such decisions as the use of MOD and TPP funds. It is significant to note that neither Oklahoma City, whose public housing had received bad publicity in the local press, nor New Haven, whose housing authority was embroiled in conflict with the citywide Tenants' Representative Council, were originally slated for participation in the demonstration; both were substituted when other sites in the Northeast and Southwest dropped out of the program.

The experience of the tenant management demonstration suggests that the difficulties that marked the relationships between the New Haven and the Oklahoma City housing authority and their tenants foretold the problems that would appear once the demonstration was under way. Moreover, the fact that Curries Woods in Jersey City was unable to implement tenant management fully indicates that even a reasonably cooperative relationship between housing authority and public housing residents is no guarantee of program success and underscores the extent to which tenant management corporations in Oklahoma City and New Haven were at a distinct disadvantage from the beginning.

ATTITUDES OF HOUSING AUTHORITY PERSONNEL

The institution of tenant management inevitably imposes new demands on housing authority personnel at all levels and places them in a new relationship with public housing residents. The responses of housing authority administrators and staff, their perceptions of the newly emergent organization, and their reactions to the new roles in which they have been cast are critical determinants of the outcome of tenant management. While one person obviously cannot be credited with the success of the program or blamed for its failure, the executive director has been the central figure in shaping the attitudes and actions of lower echelon personnel. In the following section, the posture of the executive directors toward tenant management at the outset of the demonstration is discussed; how they ultimately came to evaluate the program is considered later in this chapter.

The Executive Director

The executive director's commitment to the concept of tenant management was recognized as important and was a factor considered in site selection.[1] As a result, executive directors at several of the sites had already demonstrated a high degree of interest in tenant management or other forms of tenant participation in public housing management.

Most executive directors were attracted to the demonstration, at least in part, because they subscribed to its basic premise—that greater control by tenants over their housing environment would lead to improvements in its general condition. An exception to this generalization was the original executive director of the New Haven Housing Authority, who, although reluctant to participate in the demonstration, was ultimately lured by the prospect of funding for his financially pressed housing authority. Skeptical about what he viewed as the program's "hidden" premise—that tenants could manage better than housing professionals—he believed that the wholesale infusion of funds, rather than any inherent value in tenant management, would be responsible for positive outcomes that might result from the demonstration.

Once the demonstration was under way, the interaction of the executive directors with the tenant management corporations was marked by two distinct styles of leadership. In Rochester, New Haven, and to some degree, Louisville, the executive directors devoted a good deal of personal time to the implementation of the program; in the other cities, the executive directors maintained a more distant stance. Although the personal attention of the executive director was associated with the relatively rapid signing of a management contract, an independent, effective tenant management corporation did not necessarily result. In retrospect, it is difficult to conclude that either of these styles of interaction per se was critical to the development of a successful relationship between tenant management corporation and housing authority. What seems to have been more important was the executive director's ability to impress

---

1. Suzanne B. Loux and Robert Sadacca, "Analysis of Changes at Tenant Management Demonstration Projects," Working Paper #1335 (Washington, D.C.: Urban Institute, 1980). The executive directors uniformly agreed that in order for a tenant management program to succeed, the executive directors must give it high priority.

on housing authority staff his commitment to the concept of tenant management and to ensure their full cooperation with the tenant management board and staff.

The executive director of the Rochester Housing Authority estimated that at the beginning of the program he spent as much as 15 hours a week on tenant-management-related affairs, including evening meetings at the tenant management corporation office. Moreover, he insisted that housing authority personnel refrain from taking any action on matters affecting Ashanti without first discussing the situation with the tenant management board, thereby allowing the board to develop as an independent entity. Where differences of opinion between the housing authority and the board emerged, they were resolved in an atmosphere of open discussion and mutual respect. Due both to this cooperative relationship and to the unusually extensive organization experience of the members of Ashanti's board of directors, the board proceeded quickly through training, and Ashanti was the first tenant management corporation to sign a management contract with the housing authority.

As an aside, it may be noted that while the executive director's early attention to and support of the program accelerated the tenant management corporation's progress, his personal involvement, though not his support, diminished considerably after the signing of the management contract. He then delegated the tenant-management-related functions he had previously performed to the housing authority's deputy director.

By contrast, the personal involvement of the executive directors in Louisville and New Haven was probably counterproductive to the establishment of a successful relationship between the housing authority and the tenant management corporation, although for different reasons and with different ultimate outcomes. The consistently troubled relationship between the New Haven Housing Authority and the Que-View Tenant Management Corporation will be discussed throughout this chapter. Here it is enough to point out that the New Haven Housing Authority's executive director, having pressed for the removal of outside trainers, devoted much of his own time to the program, visiting the site as often as twice a week to deliver lectures from the housing authority's training manual. The executive director's forceful personality deterred board members from asking questions and expressing doubts, and his presence on the scene thus inhibited the development of a competent board capable of negotiating with the housing authority from a position of strength. The housing authority became the main arbiter of what tenant management—a concept it had never wholly supported—was and was not and of what it could and could not do. Despite the board's weakness, the executive director pushed to have a management contract signed early on, and Que-View was the second site in the demonstration to enter into such a contract.

In the case of Louisville, the support accorded the program by the executive director of the Housing Authority of Louisville at the beginning of the demonstration apparently was threatening to housing authority staff, who viewed his accessibility to members of the tenant management board as his allowing tenants to go over their heads. Already alienated from the director for a variety of reasons, staff may have transferred this animosity to the program he was seen as favoring. He was eventually replaced by a new director who had both more respect from staff and a positive attitude toward tenant management. The Iroquois board, however, was strong enough to overcome the obstacles hostile staff members erected, and after an initial period of mutual distrust, the Housing Authority of Louisville and the Iroquois Homes Resident Management Corporation developed a satisfactory, if sometimes strained, working relationship.

The second group of housing authority executive directors maintained a more routine, less personalized relationship with the tenant management program. After instituting the procedures necessary to get the program off the ground, they adopted a "hands-off" policy with respect to day-to-day program operations. For example, attendance at board training sessions was a responsibility usually assigned to the person designated as housing authority liaison to the program. This attitude seemed to be the expression of an explicit philosophy to prevent tenant management from becoming a "pet project" receiving extraordinary attention at the expense of other equally important efforts.

Just as the direct personal involvement of the executive director did not necessarily signal commitment to the concept of a strong, independent tenant management corporation nor ensure the support of other housing authority staff, so too, this second style of operation produced mixed results. In the best instances, exemplified by A. Harry Moore in Jersey City and Calliope in New Orleans, generally harmonious and cooperative relationships developed, although some areas of interaction (e.g., maintenance and modernization) continue to present difficulties.

The most complex case is typified by Oklahoma City. The original executive director, while philosophically interested in tenant management, was embroiled in difficulties with the board of commissioners, and as a result, housing authority staff never really became involved in the program. His replacement perpetuated this lack of involvement and never exhibited any interest in, or understanding of, the program. The result was that—for different reasons—neither executive director participated regularly in board training sessions, made any effort to win over those members of the board of commissioners who were opposed to tenant management, or impressed on staff the necessity of sharing responsibilities with the tenant management corporation. Without either querying or informing the tenant management corporation, the housing authority carried out plans to use TPP funds allocated for the demonstration to hire security guards, thus denying the board any say in a matter of critical concern to the development. Similarly, the housing authority received only nominal input from the tenant management corporation about the use of MOD funds. In effect, the Oklahoma City Housing Authority conducted its business as much as possible as if the Sunrise Acres Tenant Management Corporation did not exist.

Ensuring that housing authority personnel understand the aims of the demonstration and follow through in their support and cooperation is a particularly important responsibility of the executive director, given the high turnover in that position. The executive director in many cases was not in office to see the program through to completion. There was turnover in the position of the executive director in four of the six cities where the demonstration was mounted (only the heads of the Jersey City and Rochester Housing Authorities remained at the end). In all of these cases, the departure of the first executive director and the ensuing period of instability within the housing authority impeded the tenant management corporation's development.

While Oklahoma City's first executive director never expressed more than lukewarm enthusiasm for the demonstration, the program fared worse under his successor, who committed no housing authority resources to it. The new executive director of the Housing Authority of Louisville was sympathetic to tenant management, but could give the program only limited attention when he assumed his new responsibilities. In New Orleans, the extremely supportive initial executive director was replaced first by an acting director who, knowing his tenure was temporary, did little more than maintain the housing authority in a holding pattern. Because his eventual successor was not appointed until very near the end of the demonstration, his ultimate attitude toward the program was not known.

The departure and replacement of the executive director of the New Haven Housing Authority merely exacerbated the already ailing condition of the Que-View Tenant Management Corporation. Although his successor had been deputy director of the housing authority, he had not been involved in the original planning for the demonstration and was unfamiliar with the philosophy and practices of tenant management. In addition, most staff members who were knowledgeable about the program left soon after the initial executive director. The new executive director inherited a housing authority fraught with problems—among them, impending bankruptcy—and tenant management was, perhaps necessarily, low on his list of priorities. Finally, some Que-View board and staff members, especially the housing manager, found it hard to get along with the new deputy director authorized to deal with tenant management matters.

The Housing Authority Board of Commissioners

The attitude of the housing authority board of commissioners toward the tenant management corporation has largely been a function of the commissioners' relationship with the executive director. In Rochester, Jersey City, and New Orleans, board members have joined the executive director in endorsing the tenant management experiment, but generally have stepped back from direct involvement with the program.

In both Oklahoma City and Louisville, on the other hand, the board of commissioners lacked confidence in the competence of the first executive director and in both cases intervened in tenant management corporation affairs. Their involvement at worst threatened the autonomy of the tenant management corporation and at best slowed its progress. In Oklahoma City, for instance, the board of commissioners attempted to have a say in the selection of tenant staff members and went so far as to interview applicants for these positions. In Louisville, when the first executive director left, the Iroquois board took its case for tenant management directly to the commissioners in an effort to muster support for the program. This public relations effort eventually paid off.

Other Housing Authority Staff

Where the executive director has shown little interest in or support of tenant management, that attitude has quickly been translated to his or her staff. But the converse does not always hold; the executive director's support of the program has not always been sufficient to ensure the cooperation of other staff members. Sometimes that cooperation has been extended from the beginning: the former site manager at Ashanti still telephones the tenant management corporation housing manager periodically to offer his help with problems. But even in Rochester, which in many respects provides a model of positive housing authority–tenant management relationships, the knowledge that the executive director stood squarely behind the tenant management corporation did not prevent the housing authority's on-site maintenance personnel from resisting Ashanti's efforts to exercise control.

Resistance to the tenant management corporation by housing authority personnel stems from various sources. Some staff members harbor negative attitudes toward public housing residents, regarding them as the passive objects of administrative directives or as the active causes of the ills that have befallen public housing. Tenants, on the other hand, feel that housing authority staff have doubted their ability to master the technical aspects of maintenance, security, modernization, and the myriad other details associated with management. In addition, owing to the fact that most tenant management board and staff members are women, a measure of sexism has often compounded their skepticism. One executive director cited as a reason for hostility the resentment that arises when a "new kid on the block" gets special treatment, while the efforts of more experienced staff are taken for granted.

In addition, the program has inevitably meant changes in policies and procedures, and with change has come uncertainty and sometimes inconvenience. On-site personnel often were fearful that they would lose their jobs to tenants; and although regular housing authority staff have not been dismissed, they sometimes were transferred to assignments they considered less desirable. At times, tenant management has entailed changes that run counter to established, or newly established, ways of doing things. For instance, shortly before the demonstration began, Louisville had implemented a centralized maintenance system, but for purposes of the demonstration, Iroquois became the only development in the housing authority to have its own, on-site maintenance crew.

Tenant management has also placed additional demands on some staff members who have been expected not only to fulfill their customary responsibilities but also to assist in the training of tenant management personnel and to take on additional activities associated with the demonstration. A prime example involves the development of site-specific budgets. A central tenet of the program has been that the tenant management corporation control its own budget and that in order to do this, it must have accurate and up to date accounting of its revenues and expenditures.

None of the housing authorities had instituted site-specific budgeting prior to the inception of the demonstration, and the design and implementation of a new accounting system was a major task. Some accounting departments were able to convert to the new system relatively quickly; this was the case in Rochester and Jersey City, where the executive directors believed that project-based budgeting would benefit the housing authority as a whole, not merely the demonstration site. In New Orleans, site-specific budgeting was already in use for many aspects of HANO's projects, making the transition for the remaining items fairly smooth at Calliope. However, in Louisville site-specific budgets were implemented for the entire housing authority, and the changeover had not been completed before the demonstration ended. In New Haven the effort to develop a site-specific budget for Que-View ceased when the executive director and the head of the data-processing department left the housing authority. The failure of these housing authorities to proceed with dispatch in developing this important tenant management tool has been a source of continuing strain.

Relations between the tenant management corporation and the maintenance and modernization departments have also been less than amicable at many of the sites. On-site maintenance staff often resented taking orders from tenants, especially female tenants. Housing authority staff frequently considered the details of modernization too arcane for public housing residents to assimilate and excluded tenant management personnel from discussion of specifications and openings of competitive bids. Further, tenant management board and staff members charged modernization department employees with holding up progress even beyond the usual bureaucratic delays. They also accused modernization staff of being willing to settle for shoddy work, and at several sites, board members withheld payment to contractors until they had made repairs on work that had been done incorrectly. In Louisville, the Iroquois board appears to have disrupted an allegedly improper relationship between certain contractors and the modernization department.

The tenant management corporations followed several routes to gain the cooperation of housing authority staff. While differences between the tenant management corporation and the housing authority were usually settled through meetings with lower level housing authority staff, sometimes residents went over their heads to appeal directly to the executive director. Some change came naturally; as tenant management personnel acquired and demonstrated increased expertise, they won the respect of initially skeptical housing professionals. And time also alleviated fears that tenant management would be accompanied by large-scale layoffs and other disruptions. On the other hand, some change was enforced from above; at nearly every site it was necessary to transfer a site manager or maintenance supervisor whose hostility toward the tenant management corporation proved intractable.

The necessity of dealing with recalcitrant housing authority staff had varying effects on the different tenant management corporations. In Louisville, the uncooperative attitude of the modernization department spurred the board to gather its own forces. Its tenacity in insisting that it participate in decisionmaking and that it pay only for quality work resulted in both the eventual replacement of the housing authority's modernization coordinator and a greater degree of board strength and self-confidence. On the other hand, at Curries Woods, distrust of the housing authority liaison and feelings of impotence with respect to decisionmaking resulted in dissatisfaction actively expressed in the refusal of board members to proceed with training and more passively expressed in high absenteeism and turnover.

The relationship between the A. Harry Moore Tenant Management Corporation board and the Jersey City Housing Authority was a case unto itself. All parties described it as a close, cooperative partnership. But the tenant management corporation encountered at least as much resistance on the part of the on-site maintenance crew as did any site in the demonstration. Although the board's reaction to these difficulties was one of concern, it was unwilling to press the housing authority to correct the situation and appeared to accept its rationale that the problems were ones that afflicted the entire system — overly bureaucratic procedures and inadequate staff. While to some extent this explanation may be valid, the point is that the board, to preserve a smooth working relationship with the housing authority, opted against a more activist stance that might have produced more favorable and immediate results for the development. The reluctance of board members to stand up to the housing authority is probably rooted in part in their personalities, but it may also reflect the fact that the housing authority liaison (who acted as technical assistant) did not encourage the board to question housing authority practices and policies.

THE MANAGEMENT CONTRACT

Two interpretations can be assigned to the management contract that the tenant management corporation signs with the housing authority. The first considers the document a statement of the formal relationship between the two parties, one that determines the actual responsibilities granted to the tenant management corporation, how closely these responsibilities conform to the demonstration model, and the extent to which the contract protects the tenant management corporation and its employees in the event of a change in administration within the housing authority.

The second interpretation, advanced by the executive directors of the Rochester and Jersey City housing authorities, regards the contract as a document that is primarily symbolic. Its signing marks the transition from one stage to another in the development of the housing authority–tenant management corporation relationship. But according to this view, the signing of a contract cannot guarantee either that the relationship will be amicable and cooperative or that the provisions of the contract will be adhered to.

The experience of New Haven's TMC suggests that while both interpretations have some validity, the second is more discerning. In conformity with the demonstration model, the Que-View contract ceded the tenant management corporation responsibility for tenant selection; leasing of units; rent reviews; follow-ups on rent delinquencies; and the selection, supervision, and termination of tenant management corporation staff. However, contrary to the model, the contract provided Que-View with neither control of nor input into the budgetary process; instead, the housing authority allocated funds among budget line items. In denying the TMC budget control, the contract negated a central feature of the program.

The experience of Que-View in the postcontract period suggests that a sheet of paper cannot protect the tenant management corporation if the housing authority fails to live up to its obligations. Although the Que-View contract stipulated that the tenant management corporation had responsibility for supervising on-site maintenance personnel, the housing authority reassigned maintenance staff without consulting the TMC. The contract stated that the housing authority would provide the tenant management corporation with monthly reports on income and expenditures, but the housing authority seldom met this contractual obligation. A change of leadership in the New Haven Housing Authority meant that the contract provided even less of a buttress for the tenant management corporation because the new executive director and his deputy did not become familiar with its contents and, furthermore, showed little sympathy for the concept of tenant management in general.

Those who hold to the second interpretation of the management contract could well argue that the contractual arrangements between Que-View and the New Haven Housing Authority were less significant than the long history of mutual mistrust between the two parties, the reluctance of the housing authority to transfer power to Que-View tenants, and the tendency of the Que-View board to defer to housing authority decisions. Conflicts surrounding the sharing of authority resulted in charges and countercharges and often ended with the tenant management corporation's bitter but resigned acceptance of the housing authority's dictates. And indeed, the only practical recourse available to Que-View would have been to terminate the contract—that is, to write itself out of existence.

At sites where the relationship between tenant management corporation and housing authority had been less conflict ridden, the contracts that were negotiated adhered more closely to the St. Louis model. These contracts met with the general approval of housing authority administrators and tenant management boards, and complaints that one party or the other had not lived up to its responsibilities were few and muted. Except at Louisville, there was little sentiment in favor of large-scale contract revisions. The Housing Authority of Louisville staff and Iroquois board members agreed that the initial contract had been essentially correct in somewhat limiting the scope of responsibilities of the newly instituted tenant management corporation, but concurred that a revised contract should grant the resident management corporation a larger role in budgetary matters, confer on it the authority to institute on-site leasing procedures, and delineate more clearly its power to hire and fire staff. Clearly, the importance given to the technicalities of contract language made the Louisville contract far more than a mere symbolic document.

THE HOUSING AUTHORITIES VIEW
THE DEMONSTRATION

The executive directors participating in the demonstration were a diverse group. They were mixed in terms of age, race, and experience, and the only characteristic that might have distinguished the directors of the more successful programs from other housing authority directors as a whole was that they were generally newer to public housing management. Within the demonstration itself it is not possible to characterize either the qualities or the predispositions that separated those executive directors who were associated with successful TMCs from those who were not.

At the close of the demonstration, four of the five executive directors of participating housing authorities told MDRC researchers that even with the wisdom of hindsight, they would unequivocally opt to participate in the demonstration all over again. Their informal assessment of the value of participation convinced them that the gains outweighed the time demands and disruptions that tenant management entailed. They did not necessarily view tenant management as having improved managerial practices and performance; two of the executive directors interviewed favored the program at least as much because of their belief in giving residents a greater say over their own homes and lives as because of any concrete benefits they felt tenant management brought to the developments. These four executive directors intended to continue with tenant management after the demonstration has elapsed, and all were at least considering extending tenant management to other developments in their housing authorities.

The fifth respondent, the current executive director of the New Haven Housing Authority, saw few gains of any kind stemming from the program. Two months after the end of the demonstration, the Board of Commissioners of the New Haven Housing Authority voted to terminate the contract with the Que-View Tenant Management Corporation and to return the development to conventional management.

Time Demands and Disruptions

Executive directors met with TMC boards concerning such issues as budgeting, maintenance, modernization, and general TMC management responsibilities. As previously discussed, the extent of the executive director's participation in the program varied by site. Regardless of the personal time involved, most of the executive directors agreed that participation in the demonstration consumed a disproportionate amount of staff time and energy. The housing manager coordinator for the Rochester Housing Authority's family units, for example, traced his activities for a month and found that he spent twice as much time at Ashanti as at any of the other family developments under his supervision.

These time demands did not decrease over the course of the demonstration. The executive director of the Rochester Housing Authority asserted that while the tenant management corporation no longer imposed demands on his own time, these burdens had merely been shifted to other housing authority personnel. Although the liaison to the Calliope TMC in New Orleans felt that his role had become less time consuming, his counterparts in Jersey City and Louisville did not share that assessment.

For the most part, the executive directors viewed these extra time demands as necessary and perhaps inevitable. If tenant management was worth doing, said the executive director of the Housing Authority of Louisville, it was worth doing right. His counterpart in Jersey City believed that the additional demands imposed by A. Harry Moore and Curries Woods were attributable not to particular administrative problems associated with tenant management but to the fact that tenant managers were more in touch with residents' needs

and therefore more likely to bring problems to the housing authority's attention. The Rochester executive director maintained that the
housing authority had expected to devote additional time to Ashanti.
But he also expressed a desire to treat Ashanti like any other family
development and noted that in the postdemonstration period, the
housing authority would have to weigh the extra attention tenant
management required against the benefits it produced.

Except in New Haven, where the executive director viewed what
he considered the rash decisions of Que-View's board and staff as
impeding the smooth transaction of housing authority business, no
executive director saw the demonstration as unduly disruptive of
housing authority operations. Some saw those disruptions as positive—for example, the changes involved in the implementation of a
more responsive accounting system or the elimination of irregulari-
ties in the modernization department. Several executive directors
mentioned that the program had created jealousy on the part of
other developments, which envied the time and money expended on
the demonstration site. But the executive director of the Jersey City
Housing Authority interpreted this resentment in a positive light, as a
goad to other developments to become more organized.

Benefits of Participation

The executive directors who were interviewed expressed basic satisfaction with the management performance of the tenant management corporation at four of the six demonstration sites. The current
executive director in New Haven was one of the dissenters. Although
the housing authority liaison to Que-View believed that tenant management had resulted in a higher average rent and a reduced vacancy
rate (a gain vitiated when the housing authority, due to fiscal pressures, abolished its vacancy preparation crew), the executive director,
and especially his deputy, were highly critical of Que-View's board
and staff.

Ironically, given Ashanti's position in the vanguard of the demonstration (as the first tenant management corporation to sign a
contract with the housing authority), the Rochester Housing Authority has been less than enthralled with Ashanti's management performance. At the time that the interviews were conducted, Ashanti
was the only site in the demonstration to have undergone a formal

evaluation by the housing authority. The evaluation uncovered, among other things, an excessive amount of board involvement in day-to-day operations and a lack of clarity as to the responsibilities of the lane manager. Although under tenant management the amount of rent in arrears and the vacancy rate declined, Ashanti's performance in these respects was not as good as that of the housing authority's other family developments. Despite these negative indicators, the executive director's support for Ashanti was evidenced by his stated intention to extend tenant management at the site even if HUD funding should no longer be available. His commitment to tenant management appears to be grounded not in a belief that residents can effect turnarounds in managerial performance (in discussing why the Rochester Housing Authority had entered the demonstration, this factor was played down), but in a philosophical belief that tenants should have a greater say in governing their communities.

To some degree, these views were shared by the executive director of the Housing Authority of Louisville, who held that tenant management should be regarded as desirable in and of itself, regardless of any benefits in the way of improved management performance. These benefits, he felt, were minimal; in his view, the demonstration site had been adequately run before the advent of tenant management. Although he conceded that Iroquois' resident manager had done a good job, he believed that the extensive technical and financial assistance the development had received placed it in a "can't lose" situation, and he attributed Iroquois' drop in vacancies to renovations that would have been undertaken with or without tenant managers on the site. He appeared to regard tenant management as an innovation worth trying, but he also expressed interest in experimenting with other forms of management, such as contracting with a private management company.

The executive director of the Jersey City Housing Authority was no less committed than the others to the philosophy of tenant management; it was under his leadership that significant tenant participation in decisionmaking began. Unlike the other two executive directors, however, he was highly enthusiastic about the performance of tenant managers. He rated the performance of A. Harry Moore's housing manager as equal to or better than that of any other manager employed by the housing authority. He mentioned, too, the positive response of residents of the development and praised the board for dealing with general problems arising in the community, as well as with strictly housing-related matters. Although his opinion of the Curries Woods board was much less sanguine, he commented that the staff at the site had performed well, reducing the rate of rent arrearages and cutting the number of vacancies.

The positive assessment of the tenant management corporation's management performance was shared by the acting executive director of the Housing Authority of New Orleans. He asserted that maintenance at Calliope had improved and that rent delinquencies had dropped. He also cited cleaner grounds as evidence that Calliope residents had responded well to this management innovation.

The Urban Institute survey material reports that regular central office housing authority personnel believe tenant management is workable, but probably only at carefully selected projects.[2] They were generally impressed with the dedication of the tenants involved in the demonstration and with their level of cooperation with regular staff.[3]

If most executive directors did not feel that tenant management had interfered excessively with housing authority operations, neither did they tend to see the program as having improved those operations significantly. The benefits of participation were perhaps felt most profoundly in Rochester. There, the project-based budgeting developed for Ashanti was considered such a valuable management tool that it was extended throughout the housing authority. In addition, the executive director mentioned that in the process of training Ashanti's board and staff, the housing authority had updated its rental and occupancy policies and had attended to numerous "housekeeping procedures" that needed revision but had been left in abeyance.

Elsewhere, except for the development of site-specific budgets, most executive directors did not feel that changes that might logically be associated with tenant management were in fact produced

---

2. Suzanne B. Loux and Robert Sadacca, "Analysis of Changes at Tenant Management Demonstration Projects," Working Paper #1335 (Washington, D.C.: Urban Institute, 1980). On a scale where 3 = agree strongly, 2 = agree some, 1 = disagree some, and 0 = disagree, the central office staff scores averaged 2.16 when asked to indicate their level of agreement with the statement, "tenant management can probably only work at carefully selected projects."

3. Ibid. In their evaluation of the TMC boards, the central office rated them between "good" and "very good" on cooperation with PHA regular staff (2.05) and on interest in making tenant management a success (2.37) where 3 = very good, 2 = good, 1 = poor and 0 = very poor.

by it. However, in the Urban Institute interviews, the majority (67 percent) of executive directors reported that changes have taken place at other projects due to tenant management. The executive director at Louisville argued that his support of decentralized operations antedated his involvement with the demonstration, and his counterpart in Jersey City maintained that while improved systems for tracking occupancy and reporting vacancies were "part and parcel" of tenant management, these changes might have been introduced even without the impetus it provided. Few procedural or policy changes were cited by the executive directors in New Haven or New Orleans.

On the other hand, it might be argued that the executive directors have a vested interest in viewing their housing authorities as well-run and innovative. They did not mention, for example, that the tenant management corporations at several sites saved the housing authorities thousands of dollars by refusing to pay for shoddy modernization work. In addition, tenant management board and staff members have pointed up the performance, and sometimes secured the removal, of incompetent (and occasionally venal) housing authority personnel. And they have introduced innovative ways of doing things: Iroquois' self-help paint program, in which tenants were supplied with paint to refurbish their own apartments and volunteers were recruited to paint the residences of the elderly, is an example of a beneficial and cost-effective practice that was transferred to other Housing Authority of Louisville developments.

Finally, the tenant management demonstration has brought a new level of awareness of tenants' capabilities and interests to housing authority staff. Housing authority personnel have come to admire the commitment of tenant management corporation board members, who have spent long hours in training sessions and meetings with at best minimal remuneration, and to respect the efforts of staff members to combine tight management with responsiveness to residents' needs.

The Extension of Tenant Management

Perhaps the greatest effect of the demonstration on the housing authorities has been that it has widened the avenues for future tenant participation in policy and management decisions. Whether they were convinced by the ideology of tenant management or by its achievements, four of the five executive directors interviewed were contemplating or had actually initiated the extension of tenant management, not only at the demonstration sites but also at other developments.

Continuation of tenant management at Calliope and Iroquois was, however, conditional on the receipt of additional HUD funding. The executive directors in New Orleans and Louisville did not believe that the costs associated with tenant management's additional personnel could be borne by their housing authorities' operating budgets, and the former argued that it was unrealistic to expect that tenant management could ever generate enough revenue to become self-supporting. On the other hand, the housing authority had embarked on the demonstration with the intention of continuing tenant management at Ashanti, whether or not additional HUD funding was made available. In the absence of such funding, Ashanti would have to cut back its security staff and eliminate the social services coordinator's position, but the basic managerial structure would remain intact. And the Jersey City Housing Authority executive director told the interviewer that the housing authority gave the tenant management program high budget priority and would continue to support it at A. Harry Moore and at Curries Woods, if that site eventually achieved tenant management, whatever HUD's refunding decision.

None of the four executive directors saw reasons to change the tenant management model; all anticipated that after the demonstration ended, the tenant management boards would continue to make policy decisions, and the staff would continue to carry out day-to-day management tasks. The only change suggested for future tenant management efforts was that more time be allotted for both formal and on the job training of TMC staff. In addition, the executive directors generally recognized a need for continued technical assistance, although on a much reduced level (a few days a month).

The situation at Curries Woods prompted the only exception. There, the executive director intended to extend tenant management for a six-month period, during which time the Curries Woods staff would continue to work under the direction of the housing authority site manager rather than under the tenant management corporation's board of directors. He expressed the hope that during this interim period the board, freed of management oversight responsibilities, would jell into a capable policymaking body that could eventually enter into a management contract with the housing authority.

The willingness of the executive directors to test tenant management and to provide the necessary support does not necessarily mean that the program will be extended to other developments. In Jersey City and New Orleans, where the executive directors were most pleased with residents' management performance, efforts to institute tenant management at other housing authority projects were under way at the close of the demonstration, supported in part by HUD Urban Initiatives funds. The lure of federal funding, rather than a particular attachment to the tenant management model, seems to have spurred the Housing Authority of Louisville to pursue tenant management at another site. Although the executive director of the Rochester Housing Authority mentioned one family development as a possible candidate for tenant management, his attitude toward the program might best be characterized as wait and see. At the time he was interviewed, he was not sufficiently impressed with Ashanti's managerial competence to be convinced that the housing authority should devote itself to the repetition of a long and arduous process.

Both the executive directors who had made plans to extend tenant management to other sites and those who were considering expansion were certain about one thing: tenant management cannot work everywhere. All agreed that the program requires the presence of strong leaders in the resident community who enjoy wide respect and who are capable of being trained. The events at Curries Woods and Sunrise Acres reinforce this view, but the overall experience of the demonstration indicates that an interested, cooperative housing authority is perhaps more vital to effective tenant management.

6 TRAINING AND TECHNICAL ASSISTANCE

The design of the national demonstration called for the tenant management board and staff to receive extensive training in the details of public housing management. The design did not, however, anticipate the tenants' lack of background in dealing with crucial organizational issues. This lack of experience became apparent as the first boards of directors were elected. The original training model was modified accordingly almost from the outset, in recognition of the boards' need to address basic organizational activities—setting agendas and conducting meetings, dealing with internal dynamics, and planning and carrying out activities. Not until this was achieved could they accomplish the requisite tasks.

This chapter discusses both the original conception and the actual implementation of training and technical assistance at the demonstration sites. While a relatively uniform manner of providing such assistance was envisioned, there were in fact wide variations in the type and continuity of the assistance that was supplied as well as in the people or firms who provided it. In exploring these variations, the aim is to identify those factors related to training and technical assistance that fostered or inhibited program development.

MODIFICATION IN THE PROGRAM MODEL

At the outset of the demonstration, McCormack, Baron and Associates, a consulting firm with extensive experience in tenant management dating from the St. Louis program, was engaged both to design and to participate in implementing the training and technical assistance component of the demonstration. Specifically, they were charged with developing a curriculum and lesson plans (what was to be known as the Program Sequence Guide) for the training of technical assistants and of the tenant management boards and staffs. To the extent possible given the firm's small size, they were also to conduct training at the demonstration sites or to guide its delivery.

In addition, MDRC planned to hire a technical assistant for each demonstration site before beginning operations. The role of the technical assistant was envisioned as complex, challenging, and demanding of a range of talents. Because this person's job was to reinforce or actually lead the training sessions devised by McCormack, Baron and Associates, as well as to guide the board in making informed policy decisions, he or she had to be knowledgeable about public housing operations, including accounting and finance, property management, and social services. The technical assistant also had to be supportive and sympathetic to tenant management board and staff members, helping them resolve internal problems and restore flagging energies. In addition, the technical assistant would be responsible for facilitating the tenant management corporation's initial dealing with the wider community, so that experience in community organization and group dynamics was also required.

Because of anticipated disagreements between the housing authority and the tenant management corporation, the technical assistant needed to be a skilled negotiator, acting at times as tenant advocate, at other times as a disinterested third party. Finally, the nature of the demonstration required that the technical assistant be able to prepare written reports and be available for the duration of the program on a full-time or part-time basis.

During both the design phase and program implementation, fundamental alterations were made in the nature and the amount of technical and training assistance provided to the sites. These alterations resulted from a number of considerations and, in turn, were to have a major impact on the progress of the demonstration.

One deviation from the program design was the fact that by the beginning of the demonstration, technical assistants had been hired at only two of the seven sites. The most difficult problem was the recruitment of technical assistants with the desired knowledge and range of experience who were acceptable to the three groups most immediately involved—the housing authority, the tenant management corporation, and MDRC. As a result, from the outset there was considerable variation in the amount and nature of the technical assistance provided to the sites.

The cases of Rochester and New Orleans illustrate two different but successful ways of providing technical assistance. In Rochester, the hiring process went exceptionally smoothly. There MDRC was able to engage a former member of the housing authority's board of commissioners. In addition to his housing background and experience, he had previously been successful in assisting local community organizations, and these organizational skills were to prove important in helping the TMC deal with a wide variety of situations such as peer pressures, developing and maintaining open communication with housing authority personnel, general management concerns, and crisis intervention.

In New Orleans, referrals from local universities, private consulting firms, housing authority personnel, and the League of Women Voters produced three candidates who were serious possibilities to fill the technical assistant position. All had very broad community organizational skills but limited knowledge of housing authority operations. The person finally chosen was a trained social worker with experience in the area of group agencies. Considering the highly disorganized state of Calliope's tenant management board, it was decided that expertise in this area was more appropriate to Calliope's immediate needs than extensive knowledge of housing authority operations, and that later, a second, part-time technical assistant could be hired to help with the specific aspects of property management. This, in fact, did occur: the first technical assistant worked to help the board develop organizational strength and to create leadership ability; the former on-site housing authority manager was then hired as the second technical assistant. He brought to that position thorough familiarity with housing authority procedures and a demonstrated ability to work with both housing authority and tenant management staff.

Another major divergence from the program model was the decision not to give systematic training in public housing management to the technical assistants prior to the start of the demonstration. This decision was reached for two reasons—because the hiring of technical assistants had been delayed and because the extensive training program outlined by McCormack, Baron and Associates would require a minimum of several months and, within the demonstration's time constraints, would constitute an unjustifiable delay in program operations.

Although an attempt was made to compensate for this change by holding several short training sessions for technical assistants to clarify roles and share information and experiences, the technical assistants were basically placed in the position of learning the fundamentals of public housing management one step ahead of the tenant management board members whom they were responsible for assisting. When, as was frequently the case, they lacked the requisite technical knowledge to present training materials, their credibility with both the boards and the housing authorities was diminished, and the progress of the demonstration was slowed.

In the remainder of this chapter, technical assistance and training are discussed as separate program elements. Although training is defined here as a formalized, classroom effort—complemented by on the job experience—and technical assistance as a broader, less confined process, there is a great deal of overlap between the two.

TECHNICAL ASSISTANCE

As a result of the modifications in program design, noted above, the provision of technical assistance did not proceed in orderly and consistent fashion across the sites. Table 6–1 highlights these differences, and indicates that over the course of the demonstration, a complex set of arrangements for the provision of technical assistance evolved.

Those people who were responsible for providing technical assistance to the sites during the early period of the demonstration had certain common functions. Their initial responsibility was to arrange for the election of the tenant management corporation boards. Then came the task of coordinating with the housing authority the schedule, format, and faculty for the board's formal training. At the same time, the technical assistant helped the board begin to operate as a policymaking entity, assisting it in preparing its corporate bylaws, formulating rules and regulations for residents, and establishing a positive relationship with the resident community through such vehicles as sitewide meetings and newsletters. Another major activity of the technical assistant was to help the board and the housing authority forge an open, constructive relationship and to resolve such potentially nettlesome issues as the development of site-specific budgets and the monitoring of modernization work. Staff organization was the tenant management corporation boards' next area of concern, and they received a great deal of support and guidance in formulating job descriptions, hiring procedures, and personnel policies.

Staff hiring and training was the immediate precursor to the negotiation and signing of the management contract. By October 1978, contracts had been signed at all sites except Oklahoma City and Curries Woods in Jersey City. This had taken longer than anticipated. Once the basic relationship between tenant management corporation and housing authority had been established and board and staff were carrying out their respective functions, the technical assistant could, and generally did, step back from intense, day-to-day involvement with the affairs of the tenant management corporation and provide advice and mediate conflicts on an as needed basis.

Technical assistance efforts met with varying degrees of success. At Rochester, the tenant management board, aided by the knowledgeable technical assistant who served in that position throughout the demonstration, developed into a stable and competent management organization. Although the development of management skills was slower in Louisville and New Orleans, there too the technical assistants helped the boards build a sense of organizational competence and independence.

While technical assistants were undoubtedly essential to the success of the program at these sites, it is difficult to measure the extent of their contribution. Where technical assistance was effective, it worked in conjunction with other important factors—tenant management board members with prior organizational experience and/or natural leadership ability and housing authority executive directors who were committed to the concept of tenant management.

The several sites where technical assistance was unsuccessful confirm that its effectiveness depends on support and acceptance from both the housing authority and the tenant management corporation.

Table 6–1.   Technical Assistance and Training at the Tenant Management Sites.

Demonstration Site	Early Board and Staff Development	Staff Training and Contract Signing	Postcontract Operations
Jersey City: A. Harry Moore Tenant Management Corporation	A housing authority liaison functioned to a large degree as technical assistant and played this role throughout the demonstration. McCormack, Baron and Associates provided technical assistance as necessary. Good relations with the housing authority were established.	The PHA liaison continued in his capacity as technical assistant with ongoing support from McCormack, Baron and Associates.	
Jersey City: Curries Woods Tenant Management Corporation	The housing authority liaison initially functioned to a large degree as a technical assistant. McCormack, Baron and Associates provided technical assistance as necessary. These personnel were not successful in helping the board resolve problems of internal dissension and community nonsupport. A part-time technical assistant was hired in March 1977 to help reorganize the tenant management board and to win community support. This technical assistant resigned in March 1978. A full-	McCormack, Baron and Associates continued to serve as training consultants to the board and staff and often mediated issues between the JCHA and the TMC. The technical assistant worked with McCormack, Baron and Associates in these efforts and also helped resolve internal tensions within the TMC and with the community. But though the staff completed training with the assistance of these consultants, Curries Woods could not resolve enough of its problems to proceed to the point of initiating contract negotiations.	Not applicable

Louisville: Iroquois Homes Resident Management Corporation	time technical assistant was hired in January 1978 and remained with the site for the rest of the demonstration. He continued the community organization strategy. MDRC initially assigned a special consultant to organize the board. The tension, present because of the school busing issue, provided the opportunity for training in community and political organization. Two part-time technical assistants who were familiar with community development and the functioning of public agencies were hired in March 1977; they focused on strengthening the board's internal organization through committees and such concepts as management by objective.	The technical assistants focused on board decisionmaking and management organization and coordinated staff training with the PHA liaison. They also arranged for supplemental training, demonstrating that all resources necessary for staff training were available within the city.	Rather than introduce issues on which they felt the board should focus (as during the earlier phases), the technical assistants relied more on the tenant management corporation to identify issues and provided the support and guidance necessary to resolve them. They mediated among the board, staff, and wider community.
New Haven: Que-View Tenant Management Corporation	A local lawyer was retained as a technical assistant prior to program start-up and remained until May 1977. McCormack, Baron and Associates provided some technical assistance. The housing authority insisted that technical assistance be provided only in the presence of a housing authority representative.	The first technical assistant resigned, and the tenant management corporation relied on housing authority and MDRC operation staff for assistance.	In March 1978 two special consultants were hired to assist the board in decisionmaking and conflict resolution techniques.

(Table 6–1. continued overleaf)

Table 6–1. continued

Demonstration Site	Early Board and Staff Development	Staff Training and Contract Signing	Postcontract Operations
New Orleans: Calliope Development Tenant Management Corporation	MDRC assigned a special consultant to assist in early organizing activities. In September 1976 a part-time technical assistant, experienced in community organization, was hired and remained throughout the demonstration. In May 1977 a second part-time technical assistant was hired. This technical assistant, however, failed to gain the board's confidence and remained only until November 1977. McCormack, Baron and Associates visited the site several times but did not provide ongoing technical assistance. The consultant and technical assistant helped the board to deal with attacks from the tenant community and with its own lack of stability. Good relations with the housing authority were established.	A full-time technical assistant, the former housing authority project manager, was hired in February 1978. His managerial experience and familiarity with housing authority personnel and procedures were of benefit to the board and staff and facilitated cooperation between the tenant management corporation and the housing authority. The original part-time technical assistant continued to focus on board development, while the new technical assistant concentrated on staff training.	The technical assistants continued to help the board identify problems, reach well-considered decisions, establish a professional relationship with staff, and interact with the housing authority. Technical assistants remained involved in all program issues.

| Oklahoma City: Sunrise Acres Tenant Management Corporation | MDRC assigned a special consultant to assist in organizing board elections. McCormack, Baron and Associates visited the site to plan a specialized training program, but the plans were aborted because of high turnover. The first technical assistant, hired on a part-time basis in November 1976, was terminated in July 1977. In August 1977 a second part-time technical assistant was hired. She was joined in October 1977 by a full-time technical assistant; these technical assistants assisted in board training. Both of these consultants stayed with the program until the site was dropped from the demonstration. | After a slow start-up and a revision of the training manual, the technical assistants coordinated the training of the board. They worked with the PHA on assigning appropriate staff to conduct the various aspects of training. | Not applicable (site dropped from demonstration before a contract was consumated). |

(*Table 6–1. continued overleaf*)

Table 6–1. continued

Demonstration Site	Early Board and Staff Development	Staff Training and Contract Signing	Postcontract Operations
Rochester: Ashanti Tenant Management Corporation	A full-time technical assistant, who was knowledgeable about community development and who had previously sat on the Housing Authority Board of Commissioners was hired before program start-up and remained throughout the demonstration. McCormack, Baron and Associates also provided technical assistance. Good relations with the housing authority were established. The technical assistant helped the board with staff hiring.	The technical assistant aided the staff with classroom and on the job training. He helped draft the management contract and mediated between the tenant management board and the housing authority. McCormack, Baron and Associates conducted 10 weeks of formal staff training in conjunction with the PHA.	The technical assistant functioned as an advisor to the TMC. He acted as ombudsman, helping to avoid crises and to resolve ongoing problems among board, staff, PHA, and the wider tenant community. His position was full-time until December 1977 and part-time from then until the fall of 1978; thereafter, he visited the site monthly. McCormack, Baron and Associates continued to provide in-service training for board and staff throughout the demonstration.

Source: MDRC files.

In New Haven, for example, the executive director's intention to dominate the TMC board was manifested by his efforts to prevent meetings between the tenant management board or staff and the MDRC-hired technical assistant without the presence of a housing authority representative. In the generally indifferent atmosphere of the Oklahoma City Housing Authority, technical assistance to the Sunrise Acres Tenant Management Corporation was also ineffective.

In Jersey City, where a qualified technical assistant could not initially be found, the parties agreed that the housing authority liaison to the two Jersey City tenant management corporations, working in conjunction with McCormack, Baron and Associates, could perform technical assistance functions. Although this employee had been active in organizing tenants in various other efforts, he failed to win the confidence of the Curries Woods tenant management board. The two technical assistants subsequently hired to take over these duties were versed in community organization but lacked knowledge and experience with housing management and thus could not secure the housing authority's respect. As a result, progress at Curries Woods was severely hindered.

While every technical assistant at a given site need not have housing management expertise, the Curries Woods case suggests that at least one such person must be available to provide technical guidance when the board requires it. There are, however, drawbacks to using a housing authority employee for this purpose. Although the same housing authority liaison who had trouble at Curries Woods did establish a successful relationship with the A. Harry Moore board, it was thought that an independent technical assistant might have contributed more significantly to the board's development. If a technical assistant remains a housing authority employee, his or her loyalties could be questioned, and the board's sense of having an advocate in matters of conflict with the housing authority would be undermined. In New Orleans, when the on-site manager was hired as the second technical assistant, he took a leave of absence from the housing authority and devoted himself to the TMC board, thus reassuring the board of his support.

There are some similarities between the roles of technical assistant and PHA liaison, but there are also fundamental differences. The principal function of the liaison is to coordinate and expedite tenant management corporation business within the housing authority, while a major task of the technical assistant is to help the tenant management corporation clarify its options and choose among them. In presenting primarily the policies and points of view of the housing authority to the A. Harry Moore board, the liaison tended to curtail its choices to those acceptable to the housing authority. As a consequence, at community meetings some residents of the development expressed the opinion that the tenant management corporation was merely an extension of the housing authority with little power to effect change.

TRAINING

The training curriculum was designed to present, in 34 lessons over the course of nine months, the basic technical information that first the board and then, building on that, the staff needed to know in order to assume management responsibilities. The areas covered in the Program Sequence Guide include the legislative background of public housing, the philosophy of tenant management, and the organization of a tenant management corporation; principles of real estate management; the operation of a maintenance and custodial program; the use of MOD and TPP funds; marketing and leasing procedures; security considerations; and "soft management" and community organization.

The demanding job of organizing the delivery of training fell to the technical assistant and required close cooperation with the housing authority, particularly with the housing authority liaison. Once the tenant management corporation board had been elected, their formal classroom training began. The technical assistant scheduled classes and selected faculty members (including McCormack, Baron and Associates, MDRC operations staff, and housing authority personnel). The technical assistant also conducted review sessions with the board to ensure that the concepts had been learned.

Because staff training followed board training, and because a good deal of the material was identical, staff benefited from the experience acquired during board training. While similar to board training, staff training was conducted primarily by housing authority personnel and focused on the more technical aspects of housing management. Classroom sessions were often supplemented by on the job training. To implement this on the job staff training program, the technical assistant and the housing authority liaison worked together to find appropriate housing authority personnel to act as trainers. When no housing authority staff members performed duties analogous to those set forth in tenant management corporation job descriptions (as was the case with the lane manager and social services coordinator positions), the technical assistant helped the housing authority make ad hoc training provisions. The technical assistant also met with the staff during this training process to review progress and resolve problems.

As was the case with technical assistance, training efforts encountered various problems and met with varying degrees of success at the different sites. Except at Ashanti in Rochester, the implementation of formal board training was delayed because a technical assistant had not been designated and/or because the board required preliminary assistance in basic group dynamics. In Rochester, McCormack, Baron and Associates began formal board training immediately; the executive director arranged for housing authority staff to serve as instructors as needed; the technical assistant followed up each lesson with an informal review; and board training was successfully completed early in 1977. Staff training proceeded equally smoothly.

McCormack, Baron and Associates also initiated training in Jersey City, with the Jersey City Housing Authority liaison acting as technical assistant. The A. Harry Moore board, and subsequently the staff, made steady progress through the curriculum; but the Curries Woods board, beset by internal problems, discontinued formal training with McCormack, Baron and Associates and did not resume until almost two years later with a reconstituted board and a technical assistant hired by MDRC.

While the ongoing assistance of McCormack, Baron and Associates produced outstanding results, some TMCs were successfully trained through other resources. For instance, in both Louisville and New Orleans, the housing authority took the lead in presenting the board-training curriculum. The commitment of the executive directors to the tenant management concept provided the high level impetus for the successful completion of training in spite of the ambivalence of some of the middle level housing authority personnel who ran the training sessions.

Staff training in Louisville was conducted in a somewhat unique fashion. First, a retired housing authority site manager was hired to supervise the entire on the job training component. Second, classroom training conducted by housing authority staff was supplemented by training sessions led by a number of professionals from the Louisville area, including a local attorney, a real estate manager, a city government official, and a member of a local civic organization. While this arrangement required a good deal of work on the part of the technical assistants (as well as the judgment to know when a presentation by the housing authority could not be dispensed with), it exposed staff to a wide range of viewpoints, in addition to developing the required level of technical expertise.

An early indication of the problems that later developed in New Haven came when the executive director and the housing authority liaison insisted on taking over from McCormack, Baron and Associates and conducting board training using housing authority materials rather than the Program Sequence Guide. On occasion, the board expressed its dissatisfaction with this arrangement, but was unable to effect any change. The imposing manner of the executive director and the PHA liaison discouraged questioning, and the board was exposed only to the housing authority's concept of tenant management. Formal staff training at Que-View was also conducted without a technical assistant on hand to coordinate activities. However, the tenant manager sat in on housing authority site manager meetings and felt that this was an effective means of on the job training.

Board and staff training were most disorganized at Sunrise Acres in Oklahoma City. Because the technical assistants assigned to the site did not have the requisite technical background, most training presentations were conducted by Oklahoma City Housing Authority personnel, many of whom were unfamiliar with and unsupportive of the tenant management concept. MDRC operations staff attempted to fill the breach, but they too lacked technical expertise, and changes in staff assignments hindered continuity.

In response to an MDRC questionnaire administered to board and staff members at the six remaining sites in the spring of 1979, most stated that the training they had received had prepared them quite well for the management duties they had to assume; moreover, they were proud of having mastered so much information in a relatively short time. Although they generally found the Program Sequence Guide an excellent management curriculum, certain complaints about training did surface across the sites. Several board members felt, for example, that the Program Sequence Guide was too detailed in its technical coverage and was more appropriate for staff members concerned with day-to-day operations. However, where the Program

Sequence Guide was deficient (in matters of group process, for instance), technical assistants generally devised means of filling the gap.

The quality of instruction was also a source of some dissatisfaction to board and staff members either because technical assistants lacked expertise in housing management or because housing authority staff were unable to present material in an interesting manner or were ambivalent about the tenant management program. In addition, trainees often felt that on the job training was poorly coordinated. The housing authority staff member responsible for training the tenant management staff counterpart usually had a full-time job and saw this responsibility as an additional burden. When no housing authority counterpart for a tenant management position existed, the training that was delivered tended to be catch-as-catch-can.

McCormack, Baron and Associates received special praise for its ability to present clear, lively lessons. And when housing authority staff were motivated to participate wholeheartedly in training tenant management corporation members, better relations between the two parties frequently resulted.

7 ACHIEVEMENT OF DEMONSTRATION GOALS

The demonstration was designed to test the effectiveness of tenant management as a means of improving public housing management, expanding tenant employment, and increasing tenants' satisfaction with their housing. In addition, the infusion of large amounts of MOD funds to the participating developments was expected to produce significant physical improvements. Earlier chapters, such as those on the TMC board and staff and on the PHA, provided insights into these areas, but did not cover the specific program goals. This chapter examines program outcomes in terms of the purposes of the demonstration as outlined in its design.

REAL ESTATE MANAGEMENT

The quality of real estate management performance is important for assessing the viability of tenant management as an option for public housing communities in the United States. While some housing authority directors who participated in the demonstration indicated that the actual performance of the tenant management corporation may be less important than the benefits derived from community participation, the tenants must perform at least as well as conventional management to be considered effective. If rents cannot be collected in a timely fashion, vacancies kept low, and tenants' maintenance requests responded to promptly, the social, financial, and physical condition of the housing will deteriorate, and public housing's mandate to provide decent, safe, and sanitary housing will be negated. Moreover, one of the fundamental beliefs on which the tenant management concept is based is that public housing residents can manage effectively because of their more intimate knowledge of tenants' needs, desires, and behaviors as well as their own self-interest in achieving and maintaining improvements in management. This seems to have been the case in St. Louis, the model for the demonstration, where tenant management compared favorably with other modes of management within the St. Louis Housing Authority.[1]

The demonstration goal of improving operating performance over that of conventional housing authority management was perhaps an unrealistic one. The demonstration was designed to last just three years, and one of the primary lessons learned by program sponsors was that the training of both board and staff took considerably longer than anticipated. In fact, as mentioned earlier, only one site (Rochester) actually signed a management contract within the nine-month period originally allotted for training. Three of the sites that achieved tenant management did not complete training and sign contracts until something over two years after the start of the demonstration. (Iroquois in Louisville signed in July 1978, and both A. Harry Moore in Jersey City and Calliope in New Orleans signed in September 1978.) Thus, they actually managed the developments on their own for less than one year before the demonstration officially ended. Given the complexity involved in public housing management, it hardly seems possible that inexperienced residents could have been expected to do better than experienced housing personnel.

In assessing the management performance of the tenant management corporations, three dimensions—rent, occupancy, and maintenance—were evaluated. In terms of rent, concern is with the average monthly rent due per unit as well as with rent collection and delinquency. The discussion of occupancy includes attention to vacancies and the preparation of vacant units. The section on maintenance focuses on routine maintenance work completion.

Determining whether change occurred in any of these management performance areas during the demonstration is a fairly straightfor-

---

1. Richard D. Baron, *Tenant Management: A Rationale for a National Demonstration of Management Innovation* (St. Louis: McCormack and Associates, n.d.).

ward process. However, determining how much—if any—of that change to attribute to the effects of the demonstration is a more complex process. In this context, the demonstration includes far more than the concept of tenants managing a public housing development. The demonstration also included an enrichment of resources in the form of MOD and TPP funds, the provision of expertise in the form of technical assistance and specialized training, national attention and publicity, and other benefits not characteristic of ordinary operating conditions. Moreover, the program undoubtedly elevated the status of the individuals involved and prompted a commitment from them to make it work.

A major task in the analysis is sorting out whether the demonstration or other factors, singly or in concert, account for any of the changes identified. There are a number of factors outside the demonstration that could have contributed to any change that occurred. First, simply participating in an innovative experience in and of itself often produces change; the special attention received—the so called Hawthorne effect—motivates better performance. Second, it is also possible that change was due to the fact that PHAs participating in the demonstration were required to make certain management and other improvements at the sites prior to the transfer of management responsibility to the tenant management corporation. In some cases where they were not achieved before the management contract was signed, a commitment to do so was included in the contract. A third possibility is that whatever change occurred was due to PHA-wide forces and conditions affecting all PHA developments or to other local forces and conditions to which the tenant management site was subject. This was an especially compelling possibility in examining vacancy rates, since the local private housing market and the PHA-wide occupancy situation can have an important impact on a project regardless of tenant management. The fourth possible explanation views change in management performance at the demonstration sites as the result of a normal evolutionary or maturation process that would have occurred anyway without tenant management.

Although these various explanations are analytically distinct, they often combine to produce an observed effect. Moreover, it is not possible in the analysis that follows to show positively that the enriched resources of the demonstration or the actual effectiveness of tenants as managers were responsible for any one of the changes identified. Instead, the possible factors that could account for the change are examined. The strategy utilized is, first, to examine the trends in management performance at the six tenant management sites participating in the demonstration throughout its full term[2] to ascertain whether or not change occurred.[3] Second, if change occurred, performance in the period before and after the transfer of management responsibility is compared. In assessing whether the observed changes can be attributed to the demonstration or perhaps to tenant management, other candidate explanations are examined to a limited extent by looking at larger PHA–wide forces or conditions, the local housing market, and the performance of a group of control sites. The use of a control group of sites permitted a limited assessment of what would have occurred in the absence of tenant management. Statistically significant differences between these sites and those in the demonstration could be validly attributed to the program. The absence of such differences would imply that changes occurring at the demonstration sites were part of the normal evolutionary process common to public housing developments with or without tenant management.

Several data sources were utilized in the analysis—the Tenant Management Information System (TMIS), a survey conducted by the Urban Institute, and a housing market analysis of the tenant management cities. The TMIS, consisting of monthly and quarterly reports prepared by participating PHAs, was developed for the demonstration. It provided information regarding such areas of management performance as rents, rent collection rates, vacancy rates, and maintenance. The Urban Institute survey consisted of a 1976 predemonstration interview effort and a 1979 follow-up at the tenant management sites and at a comparable group of sites that were neither in the demonstration nor had tenant management. These sites served as a basis of comparison and are called control sites. Interviews were conducted with the PHA executive directors and other central office staff, with managers at the tenant management developments and at the projects serving as their controls, and with a sample of project employees and a random sample of tenants. The information collected dealt with evaluations of and satisfaction with project conditions and the tenant organization and with performance in terms of

2. Oklahoma City was not included.

3. A .10 level of significance is used throughout the discussion as the statistical criterion against which to determine whether change occurred and to denote a difference. A trend or a difference is statistically significant only if it is highly unlikely that it could have occurred by chance alone. Results are considered statistically significant if they can be assigned a probability of chance occurrence of no more than 10 cases in 100 ($p = .10$).

selected conventional management indicators.[4] The local housing market analysis for the tenant management sites included an examination of the major trends in housing supply and demand as they related to low-income families for the years 1976–1979, the period of the demonstration.

Rents

It is to the advantage of any management entity to maximize the dollar amount of rents collected. In keeping with this maxim, all tenant management corporations sought to increase rental income as an explicit demonstration goal. However, achievement of this goal posed a dilemma for tenant management corporations as managers of housing where limits based on income are placed on eligibility. With a legislative mandate limiting public housing eligibility to persons of low income, rents had to be maximized in ways other than allowing them to rise to whatever level the market would bear.

Two major strategies were available to the tenant management corporation in obtaining more rental income—maximizing the legitimate rent charged and the rate of collection. The latter strategy is relatively straightforward and needs no explanation. However, the operation of the former is more complex and involves two techniques. The first is the most potent tool available for the purpose of increasing rental income for current residents of public housing. It is the timely administration of rent reviews, which involves monitoring any changes[5] in residents' incomes in order to modify rents charged in accordance with those changes.

Rent reviews are conducted either upon lease expiration for each individual unit or at one specific time during the year for all units. At this time, the income and employment status of each adult occupant in each unit is verified. Rent reviews can have a positive effect upon project revenues if there have been certain changes in status among residents—for example, family members who have obtained employment during the year, members who have received increases

4. A more detailed description of the data sources and methodology used in the research is contained in Appendix A. A full report of the Urban Institute's demonstration survey effort is available from MDRC.

5. Most tenants' rent is based on a percentage of family income.

in social security or welfare benefits, and additional wage earners occupying the unit. Careful rent reviews can also increase average monthly rent due per unit when there has been extensive underreporting of income to PHA staff. TMC staff members' resident status puts them in a position of knowing who is living in a given unit and is working or has received increases in salary or benefit payments.

The second means of increasing rental income applies to new applicants for public housing and involves attracting eligible higher income tenants. The Housing and Community Development Act of 1974 encouraged the development of tenant selection criteria designed to ensure that projects include households with a broad range of incomes. During the demonstration, all tenant management corporations were concerned with tenant selection strategies that would increase the number of residents who were able to pay maximum rents.

One potential disincentive to employing any or all of these techniques for maximizing rental income would have to be overcome by a tenant management corporation—or a housing authority, for that matter—operating without the special status accorded the demonstration. According to the Performance Funding System, which determines the amount of annual federal subsidy a given PHA receives for operating expenses, a PHA's allocation is reduced in a subsequent year by the amount of income it receives in a given year. The dilemma arises between the need to maximize rents to cover operating costs on the one hand and the disincentives to do so given the resultant reduction in subsidy. In fact, rental income at the demonstration sites never increased enough to affect the PHA's subsidy allocations. But as a way of partially offsetting this potential dilemma, PHAs informally agreed not to alter the tenant management site's share of the total PHA subsidy during the demonstration. However, under nondemonstration conditions, this might not occur.

In this section, changes in average monthly rent due per unit are looked at to ascertain if any increases occurred in established rents. In addition, the extent to which the tenant management corporation was able to maximize the collection of established rents is examined by looking at three indicators—average monthly rent collected per unit, monthly rent collection rate, and the percentage of units owing more than one month's rent.

Average Monthly Rent Due.   Table 7-1 and Figure 7-1 show findings on average monthly rent due—that is, the current rent due
divided by the total number of units occupied at the beginning of the
month. Because rent is tied to residents' incomes, it can be expected
to increase with inflation, as residents' wages or welfare grants are
augmented by cost of living allowances. The data on average monthly
rent due shown here, as well as the data on average monthly rent collected in the following section, were therefore controlled for inflation,[6] so that these data are presented in 1976 constant dollars.

The data in Table 7-1 and Figure 7-1 suggest a mixed picture.
At three of the six sites (A. Harry Moore in Jersey City, New Haven,
and New Orleans), the amount of average monthly rent due rose
significantly over the course of the demonstration. These increases
ranged from 4 percent at A. Harry Moore to 20 percent in New
Haven when the first and the last quarters of the program are compared. Moreover, these three sites also show significant increases
in the postcontract period, when the tenant management corporation was managing the development, in comparison with the period
prior to management transfer. In Louisville, there was a 6.4 percent
drop in the average monthly rent due between the quarter ending
March 31, 1977 (the first quarter for which data from this site were
available), and the end of the demonstration. This decline is also evident when the precontract and postcontract periods are compared.
At Curries Woods in Jersey City average monthly rent due fluctuated
over the course of the demonstration and on the whole showed an
overall significant increase. No change in this indicator was apparent
at Rochester. Overall, then, average monthly rent due rose at three
sites, fell at two, and shows no change at one.

Other data, aggregated for the tenant management sites and separated for the control sites, suggest that there was a greater increase
in average monthly rent due at the tenant management sites than
at the control projects. Significantly more tenant management ten-

6. Adjustments for inflation were made using factors computed on a local basis by
HUD for determining the level of subsidy under the Performance Funding System. *Low-
Income Housing Program—PHA Owned Rental Housing, Performance Funding System*
(Washington, D.C.: U.S. Department of Housing and Urban Development, HUD 52723D,
annual), Appendix 13, Table 4. For a more complete discussion of the HUD factors, see
Chapter 8.

Table 7-1.   Performance Indicators in the Tenant Management Demonstration by Site and Calendar Quarter, Average Monthly Rent Due per Unit, (*1976 constant dollars*).[a]

	Monthly Average in Quarter Ending					
Site	*Dec. 1976*	*March 1977*	*June 1977*	*Sept. 1977*	*Dec. 1977*	*March 1978*
Jersey City A. Harry Moore	69.54[d]	67.30	66.74	66.85	67.04	67.98
Jersey City Curries Woods	67.53	66.67	67.20	66.71	67.77	66.53
Louisville Iroquois Home	N/A	42.30[d]	45.79	43.20	41.79	42.04
New Haven Que-View	67.58	66.49	70.37	71.61	71.15	72.80
New Orleans Calliope	38.22[d]	37.60	37.48	38.17	37.93	38.00
Rochester Ashanti	65.65	59.29	58.79	60.98	67.06	63.50

a. Average monthly rent due per unit is defined as the current rent due (rent roll adjusted for prorated rent of turnover units and allowance provided) divided by the total number of occupied units at the start of the month. These calculations have been adjusted for inflation to show rents in 1976 constant dollars.

b. Estimate of the probability that changes in average monthly rent due per unit over the course of the demonstration are attributable to chance. This estimate takes into account the differences in average monthly rent due from quarter to quarter for each of the eleven quarters of the demonstration.

c. Estimate of the probability that changes in average monthly rent due per unit between the precontract periods are attributable to chance. This estimate contrasts the average monthly rent due for the entire period subsequent to contract signing. The number of quarters in the pre- and postcontract periods vary by site.

d. Based on two months' data.

c. Significant at the .10 level or above.

N/AP—Not applicable.

N/A—Not available.

—Indicates the boundary line between the pre- and postcontract periods.

Source: Tabulation of data in the Tenant Management Information System.

Table 7-1. continued

June 1978	Sept. 1978	Dec. 1978	March 1979	June 1979	Demo. P Value[b]	Pre vs. Post P Value[c]
			Monthly Average in Quarter Ending			
69.20	69.95	68.18	72.09	72.53	0.001[e]	0.001[e]
64.81	63.29	60.89	65.41	67.23	0.001[e]	N/AP
44.56	42.39	39.17	38.91	39.58	0.000[e]	0.000[e]
72.89	73.82	74.51	75.85	80.78	0.000[e]	0.000[e]
38.53	40.19	40.70	40.75	41.82	0.000[e]	0.000[e]
59.45	56.59	64.71	62.58	63.33	0.309	0.619

ants reported that their rent had gone up in the last two years (1977–1979) than did tenants at the control sites.[7]

Explaining these changes is not as simple as documenting their occurrence. Between 1976 and 1979, tenants' educational level, average annual income, and working status were measured at the demonstration sites treated as a group and at the nondemonstration

7. Suzanne B. Loux and Robert Sadacca, "Analysis of Changes at Tenant Management Demonstration Projects," Working Paper #1335 (Washington, D.C.: Urban Institute, 1980). Eighty percent of the tenants interviewed had lived at the development at least two years. The gain score (1979 minus 1976) for the tenant management sites (.39) differed significantly from that for the control sites (.08) on "Resident's rent went up, down or stayed the same in the last two years" at the .10 level. In addition, significantly more tenants reported in 1979 than in 1976 that their rent had increased. The gain score was used as the measure to assess the amount of change that had occurred between 1976, when the baseline survey was conducted, and 1979, when the follow-up survey occurred. The score represents the difference between the 1976 value of a variable and the 1979 one. See Appendix A for further details.

PERFORMANCE INDICATORS IN THE TENANT MANAGEMENT DEMONSTRATION BY SITE AND CALENDAR QUARTER

Figure 7-1 · AVERAGE MONTHLY RENT DUE ($)

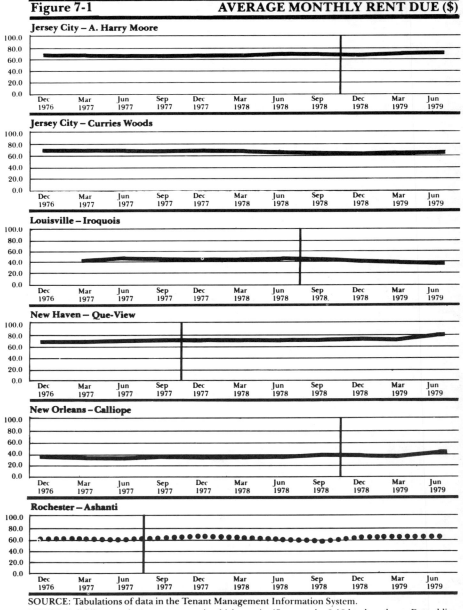

SOURCE: Tabulations of data in the Tenant Management Information System.

NOTES: Solid line graphs represent trends which are significant at the 0.10 level or above. Dotted line graphs represent trends which are not significant at the 0.10 level. Vertical line indicates the boundary between the pre- and post-contract periods.

Jersey City — Curries Woods had no signed agreement during this period.

counterparts, also aggregated. Increases occurred for both groups on all three measurements, but only at the tenant management sites was the improvement in working status significantly better. This improvement may have been the result both of the demonstration's efforts to attract higher income tenants and of the jobs created for residents by the demonstration itself. The significant increases in tenants' average annual income and education level and the fact that only 20 percent of the tenants interviewed were new tenants within the past two years combine to suggest that these newer tenants may have possibly been higher income tenants.

These findings suggest that increases in average monthly rent due per unit over the course of the demonstration may be attributable to two factors—the tenant management sites' success in implementing new tenant selection criteria and their ability to administer rent reviews in a timely manner. However, some tenant management sites appear to have been somewhat less forceful in administering rent reviews (for example, Jersey City). In Louisville, the one site where there was a decline in average monthly rent due, this was in all likelihood caused by concentration on the serious problem of preparing and filling vacant units.

Rent Collection and Delinquency

Rent collection and rent delinquency show a mixed picture during the course of the demonstration. There was neither overall improvement nor a worsening condition at the majority of the sites, indicating that the TMCs were able to do as well as conventional management in this area.

Average Rent Collected Per Unit. Quite separate from the rent due per unit is the amount of rent that was actually collected each month. The average monthly rent collected per unit is defined as the total rent collected from tenants in residence all or part of the month divided by the total number of dwelling units in the development. This figure therefore reflects not only the tenant management staff's ability to collect rents but also their success in filling vacant units.

Three sites (New Haven, New Orleans, and Rochester) showed significant increases in the average rent collected per unit per month, adjusted for inflation (see Table 7–2 and Figure 7–2). This significant increase ranged (between first and last quarters) from 8 percent

Table 7-2. Performance Indicators in the Tenant Management
Demonstration by Site and Calendar Quarter, Average Monthly
Rent Collected per Unit (*1976 constant dollars*).[a]

	Monthly Average in Quarter Ending					
Site	Dec. 1976	March 1977	June 1977	Sept. 1977	Dec. 1977	March 1978
Jersey City A. Harry Moore	59.78[d]	65.75	63.28	57.50	62.71	67.02
Jersey City Curries Woods	64.61	66.89	64.22	61.87	63.62	66.95
Louisville Iroquois Home	N/A	35.30[d]	38.56	38.10	35.54	34.35
New Haven Que-View	58.72	62.18	63.03	64.28	65.15	68.20
New Orleans Calliope	38.21	37.16	37.32	37.45	37.66	38.56
Rochester Ashanti	56.26	58.36	55.46	54.80	63.00	61.40

a. Average monthly rent collected per unit is defined as the total rent collected from tenants in occupancy all or part of the month divided by the number of dwelling units in the development. These calculations have been adjusted for inflation to show rents in 1976 constant dollars.

b. Estimate of the probability that changes in average monthly rent collected per unit over the course of the demonstration are attributable to chance. This estimate takes into account the differences in average monthly rent collected from quarter to quarter for each of the eleven quarters of the demonstration.

c. Estimate of the probability that changes in average monthly rent collected per unit between the precontract and postcontract periods are attributable to chance. This estimate contrasts the average monthly rent collected for the entire period subsequent to contract signing. The number of quarters in the pre- and postcontract periods vary by site.

d. Based on two months' data.

e. Significant at the .10 level or above.

N/AP—Not applicable.

N/A—Not available.

—Indicates the boundary line between the pre- and postcontract period.

Source: Tabulation of data in the Tenant Management Information System.

Table 7–2. continued

Monthly Average in Quarter Ending						
June 1978	Sept. 1978	Dec. 1978	March 1979	June 1979	Demo. P Value[b]	Pre vs. Post P Value[c]
67.37	64.90	65.22	70.93	71.05	0.295	0.032[e]
61.99	59.65	59.39	66.09	64.17	0.937	N/AP
32.68	35.10	32.83	37.01	36.78	0.387	0.784
68.35	70.34	70.37	72.15	72.79	0.006[e]	0.000[e]
38.31	39.94	39.29	41.65	41.20	0.004[e]	0.000[e]
54.95	53.29	57.38	65.04	61.06	0.075[e]	0.304

in New Orleans to 24 percent in New Haven. For New Orleans and New Haven, but not for Rochester, average rent collected during the postcontract period was significantly higher than for the precontract period. In Louisville and at Curries Woods, there were no significant changes in average rent collected per unit over the course of the demonstration.

Rent Collection Rate. Table 7–3 indicates that the sites did not substantially increase their performance in collecting due rents. Only three sites showed significant changes in the rent collection rate — that is, the ratio of total dollars collected to total amount due — over the course of the demonstration. Of these, at two (A. Harry Moore in Jersey City and Louisville) there was a significant increase indicating improvement. Only in Louisville was there a significant increase in the postcontract period (see Table 7–3 and Figure 7–3). The period

PERFORMANCE INDICATORS IN THE TENANT MANAGEMENT DEMONSTRATION BY SITE AND CALENDAR QUARTER

Figure 7-2 **AVERAGE MONTHLY RENT COLLECTED ($)**

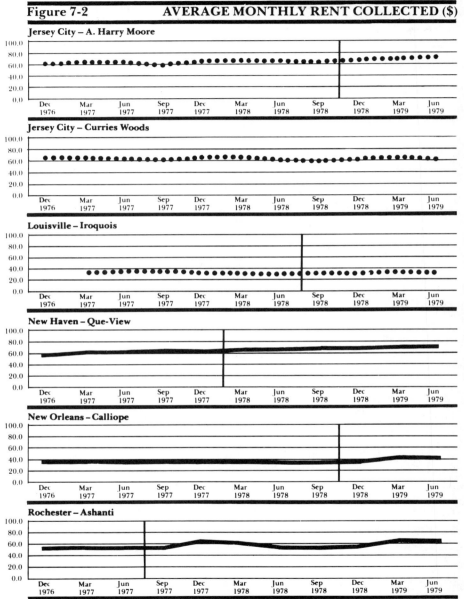

SOURCE: Tabulations of data in the Tenant Management Information System.

NOTES: Solid line graphs represent trends which are significant at the 0.10 level or above. Dotted line graphs represent trends which are not significant at the 0.10 level. Vertical line indicates the boundary between the pre- and post-contract periods.

PERFORMANCE INDICATORS IN THE TENANT MANAGEMENT DEMONSTRATION BY SITE AND CALENDAR QUARTER

Figure 7-3   **RENT COLLECTION RATE (%)**

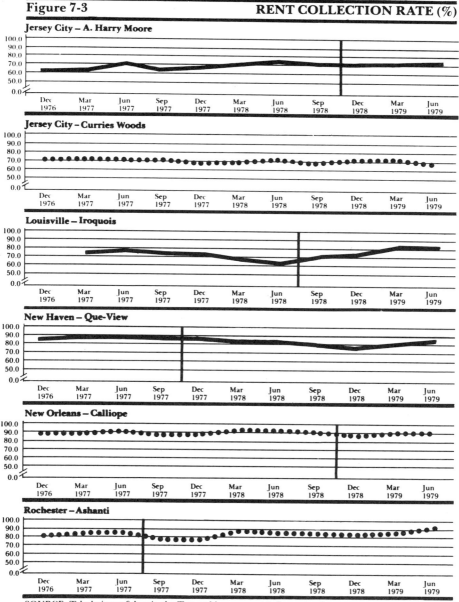

SOURCE: Tabulations of data in the Tenant Management Information System.

NOTES: Solid line graphs represent trends which are significant at the 0.10 level or above. Dotted line graphs represent trends which are not significant at the 0.10 level. Vertical line indicates the boundary between the pre- and post-contract periods.

Table 7-3. Performance Indicators in the Tenant Management Demonstration by Site and Calendar Quarter, Rent Collection Rate (*percent*).[a]

Site	Monthly Average in Quarter Ending					
	Dec. 1976	March 1977	June 1977	Sept. 1977	Dec. 1977	March 1978
Jersey City A. Harry Moore	62.5	63.2	71.7	64.0	67.0	71.0
Jersey City Curries Woods	71.4	70.3	70.7	70.9	68.2	68.0
Louisville Iroquois Home	N/A	75.9[d]	77.7	73.2	73.4	68.0
New Haven Que-View	86.1	89.4	89.7	88.8	88.6	81.6
New Orleans Calliope	89.1	90.1	91.1	88.1	89.7	92.1
Rochester Ashanti	80.0	84.7	87.3	77.2	78.6	87.5

a. Rent collection rate is defined as the proportion of total rent due (arrears and current month) collected in the month.

b. Estimate of the probability that changes in the rent collection rate over the course of the demonstration are attributable to chance. This estimate takes into account the differences in the rent collection rate from quarter to quarter for each of the eleven quarters of the demonstration.

c. Estimate of the probability that changes in the rent collection rate between the precontract and postcontract periods are attributable to chance. This estimate contrasts with rent collection rate for the entire period prior to contract signing with the rent collection rate for the entire period subsequent to contract signing. The number of quarters in the pre- and postcontract periods vary by site.

d. Based on two months' data.

e. Significant at the .10 level or above.

N/AP—Not applicable.

N/A—Not available.

—Indicates the boundary between the pre- and postcontract period.

Source: Tabulation of data in the Tenant Management Information System.

Table 7-3. continued

Monthly Average in Quarter Ending						
June 1978	*Sept. 1978*	*Dec. 1978*	*March 1979*	*June 1979*	*Demo. P Value*[b]	*Pre vs. Post P Value*[c]
75.7	71.0	70.8	70.2	74.1	0.10[e]	0.20
72.5	69.5	71.2	72.4	67.0	0.97	N/AP
61.1	71.0	74.4	82.6	83.6	0.003[e]	0.02[e]
82.2	79.5	76.2	81.6	85.0	0.000[e]	0.000[e]
92.0	91.0	88.8	91.8	90.9	0.28	0.91
87.9	84.9	83.9	87.5	93.7	0.15	0.69

prior to management transfer was characterized by a decline to a low of 61 percent, followed thereafter, during the postcontract period, by an increase to 84 percent at the end of the demonstration.

The rent collection rate in New Haven suffered during the demonstration, declining significantly. It reached a low of 76 percent in the quarter ending December 1978. In addition, there was also a significant decrease between the pre- and postcontract periods. This decrease in New Haven, together with no discernible change in three sites (Curries Woods in Jersey City, New Orleans, and Rochester), produce a generally poor showing during the demonstration in terms of impact on rent collection rates.

Percentage of Units Owing More than One Month's Rent. Only three sites showed significant improvement in this indicator (A. Harry Moore in Jersey City, Rochester, and Louisville; see Table 7-4 and

Table 7-4.   Performance Indicators in the Tenant Management Demonstration by Site and Calendar Quarter, Units Owing Over One Month's Rent (*percent*).[a]

Site	Dec. 1976	March 1977	June 1977	Sept. 1977	Dec. 1977	March 1978
	Monthly Average in Quarter Ending					
Jersey City A. Harry Moore	18.2	18.1	9.3	12.9	13.4	11.7
Jersey City Curries Woods	9.3	12.7	10.3	9.7	11.7	11.7
Louisville Iroquois Home	N/A	5.5	5.6	4.9	3.8	5.7
New Haven Que-View	1.6	1.6	1.9	2.1	1.5	2.7
New Orleans Calliope	2.3	3.6	2.7	3.4	2.3	1.7
Rochester Ashanti	11.9	5.6	3.7	11.3	7.6	2.0

a. Percent of units owing over one month's rent is defined as the proportion of occupied units at the end of the month for which tenant owes more than one month's rent.

b. Estimate of the probability that changes in the percentage of units owing over one month's rent over the course of the demonstration are attributable to chance. This estimate takes into account the differences in the percentage of units owing over one month's rent from quarter to quarter for each of the eleven quarters of the demonstration.

c. Estimate of the probability that changes in units owing over one month's rent between the precontract and postcontract periods are attributable to chance. This estimate contrasts the percentage of units owing over one month's rent for the entire period prior to contract signing with the percentage of units owing over one month's rent for the entire period subsequent to contract signing. The numbers of quarters in the pre- and postcontract periods vary by site.

d. Significant at the .10 level or above.

N/AP—Not applicable.

N/A—Not available.

—Indicates the boundary line between the pre- and postcontract period.

Source: Tabulation of data in the Tenant Management Information System.

Table 7–4. continued

| Monthly Average in Quarter Ending | | | | | | |
June 1978	Sept. 1978	Dec. 1978	March 1979	June 1979	Demo. P Value[b]	Pre vs. Post P Value[c]
7.7	10.0	10.8	11.1	10.5	0.000[d]	0.22
9.7	11.2	11.2	10.4	13.4	0.33	N/AP
5.1	6.4	6.1	4.2	3.9	0.01[d]	0.74
3.8	4.3	5.2	4.7	3.7	0.000[d]	0.000[d]
1.4	2.4	3.0	2.4	1.9	0.06[d]	0.89
2.0	1.8	3.0	10.0	0.5	0.01[d]	0.26

Figure 7–4. Despite an overall significant decrease at these sites, the percentage of units owing more than one month's rent fluctuated. At none of the three sites showing improvement did the transfer of management to the tenant management corporation seem to make a difference; a comparison of pre- and postcontract rates shows no significant difference.

In New Haven, the situation worsened, with the percentage of units owing more than one month's rent increasing significantly, not only over the course of the demonstration, but also during the postcontract period. New Orleans' experience demonstrates no clearly discernible linear trend indicating a pattern of increase or decrease. A high of 3.6 percent and a low of 1.4 percent characterized the precontract period in New Orleans, while the postcontract period saw a decrease from 3 to 1.9 percent over the last three quarters of the

PERFORMANCE INDICATORS IN THE TENANT MANAGEMENT DEMONSTRATION BY SITE AND CALENDAR QUARTER

Figure 7-4   UNITS OWING OVER ONE MONTH'S RENT (%)

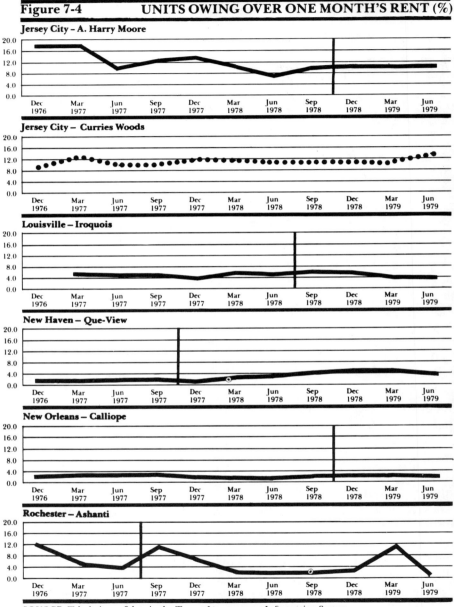

SOURCE: Tabulations of data in the Tenant Management Information System.

NOTES: Solid line graphs represent trends which are significant at the 0.10 level or above. Dotted line graphs represent trends which are not significant at the 0.10 level. Vertical line indicates the boundary between the pre- and post-contract periods.

demonstration. No significant change in the percentage of units owing more than one month's rent was evident at Curries Woods in Jersey City.

The Urban Institute survey indicates that there was no significantly greater improvement at the demonstration sites alone or in comparison to their nondemonstration counterparts in matters of rent collection and delinquency. It also corroborates the finding that the tenant management sites as a group experienced little change in rent collection and delinquency between 1976 and 1979.[8] This suggests that the tenant management sites were no better or worse off than their control counterparts.[9] These findings suggest that tenant management did not have a noticeable effect on this area.

Occupancy

The level of occupancy in any type of rental housing is inextricably linked to the ability to generate income. Consequently, the ability to reduce vacancies is an important measure of management performance; the lower the vacancy rate, the higher the overall project income. Given the importance of vacancies to project income, the tenant management sites sought to decrease their incidence over the course of the demonstration.

However, in any effort to fill vacant units, a management entity is subject to conditions prevailing in the local private housing market that affect the choices of the tenants whom management is trying to attract to its own vacant dwelling units. Consequently, it could be expected that the local housing market would have a significant impact on the ability of the tenant management corporations to reach their goals with respect to vacancy reduction and improvement in other management areas.

The availability of decent, affordable housing in the private market affects both the occupancy level of public housing and other per-

8. Suzanne B. Loux and Robert Sadacca, "Analysis of Changes at Tenant Management Demonstration Projects," Working Paper #1335 (Washington, D.C.: Urban Institute, 1980). The gain source (1979 minus 1976) for the tenant management sites for "percent rent delinquent units" was not statistically significant at the .10 level (14 percent in 1976 and 14.8 percent in 1979).

9. Ibid. The gain score (1979 minus 1976) for the tenant management sites (0.8) did not differ significantly from that for the control sites (1.2) on the "percent rate delinquent units."

formance measures such as rent collection rates and per unit rental income. When the local housing market is "tight,"[10] the acceptable alternatives to public housing are reduced. Under such circumstances, public housing residents are probably more responsive in meeting such obligations as prompt payment of rent because there is little chance of their finding comparable housing should they be evicted. A tight market could also aid public housing managers in attracting higher income tenants, if fewer private market alternatives were available or if the price differential between public and private housing was compelling.

In light of its importance in interpreting changes in management performance, especially in the area of vacancy, an examination of the local housing market at each of the demonstration sites was undertaken. This examination included an investigation of major trends in housing supply and demand as they relate to low-income families for the years 1976 to 1979, roughly the period of the demonstration. On the demand side of the equation, major population and economic trends were explored; on the supply side, the number of available dwelling units was tabulated, and net change over time was measured by factoring in demolition, abandonment, and new construction. To the extent possible, major changes in the quality of the available units were examined. Data representing demand for other subsidized housing—such as the availability of housing at other PHA developments—were also examined, as were data indicating the availability and supply of private, nonsubsidized housing generally affordable by low-income households.

Despite these efforts, the information uncovered in the housing market analysis was limited.[11] It should also be understood that data for housing market analyses are often inadequate with respect to

10. Traditionally, a 5 percent vacancy rate has served as the rule of thumb in measuring the adequacy of the available housing supply. A vacancy rate in excess of 5 percent has been viewed as sufficient to afford housing consumers reasonable choice within a given market. A vacancy rate of less than 5 percent has been generally accepted as an index of tight supply or an "owner's market."

11. Data sources for the analysis included the 1970 census; Housing Assistance Plans; PHA data on vacancy rates and applications for housing; and interviews with PHA personnel, city community development officials, and knowledgeable private market brokers. A Housing Assistance Plan is a mandatory component of an application for a Community Development Block Grant. It includes a description of a city or locale's existing housing inventory as well as estimates of current demand and need for housing. The limitations of the data used introduce several caveats that should be kept in mind. Overall vacancy rates are not particularly useful in describing the market for households of particular sizes or eco-

both availability and reliability. In the discussion that follows, vacancy rates during the demonstration are examined, followed by a consideration of the role of the local housing markets in any changes identified and the role of the tenant management corporation in the attribution of such changes.

Vacancy Rate. All sites experienced improvement in occupancy over the course of the demonstration as indicated by the significant decline in vacancy rates presented in Table 7–5 and Figure 7–5. However, a similar improvement also occurred among the control counterparts, indicating that tenant management did no better, but certainly no worse, than conventional PHA management. In three sites (A. Harry Moore in Jersey City, New Haven, and Rochester), there were significant differences between the pre- and postcontract periods, indicating greater success in reducing vacancies after the transfer of management to the tenant management corporation. Although the vacancy rate in New Haven dropped from 10 percent in the first quarter to less than 3 percent in the eighth, it began climbing again, reaching 8 percent by the end of the demonstration. However, this late reversal was not strong enough to negate the significant reduction (9 versus 5.1 percent) in vacancies between the pre- and postcontract periods. In Rochester, there were some fluctuations, but postcontract vacancy rates were significantly lower than precontract ones.

   Although the vacancy rates in Louisville and New Orleans decreased significantly over the course of the demonstration, the pattern of change differed from that for the other sites. The trend in Louisville included a four-quarter period (October 1977 and September 1978) during which the vacancy rate went as high as 17 percent before it began to decline to the 5.6 percent figure shown in the last quarter of the demonstration. In New Orleans, vacancies remained quite low throughout the demonstration; at no point did the rate reach 1 percent. What fluctuations there were seemed erratic and not associated with the development of the tenant management corporation.

---

nomic situations. Nor do they provide insight into aspects of housing quality — standard or substandard conditions, aesthetic factors, availability of transportation, neighborhood reputation for crime and safety — that significantly affect housing consumption. Still another factor that was virtually impossible to assess was the degree to which landlords discriminate against certain consumers, particularly minority families who are welfare dependent.

Table 7-5.   Performance Indicators in the Tenant Management
Demonstration by Site and Calendar Quarter, Vacancy Rate
(*percent*).[a]

	Monthly Average in Quarter Ending					
Site	*Dec. 1976*	*March 1977*	*June 1977*	*Sept. 1977*	*Dec. 1977*	*March 1978*
Jersey City A. Harry Moore	7.7	5.3	5.7	6.6	5.2	4.4
Jersey City Curries Woods	1.5	1.8	3.5	4.8	2.6	1.4
Louisville Iroquois Home	12.3	13.1	11.4	8.3	9.0	9.8
New Haven Que-View	10.2	8.6	9.1	8.1	5.7	4.4
New Orleans Calliope	0.2	0.3	0.5	0.7	0.3	0.1
Rochester Ashanti	6.7	7.2	4.4	2.6	4.4	3.7

a. Vacancy rate is defined as the proportion of total project dwelling units vacant at the end of the month.

b. Estimate of the probability that changes in vacancy rate over the course of the demonstration are attributable to chance. This estimate takes into account the differences in vacancy rate from quarter to quarter for each of the eleven quarters of the demonstration.

c. Estimate of the probability that changes in vacancy rate between the precontract and postcontract periods are attributable to chance. This estimate contrasts the vacancy rate for the entire period prior to contract signing with vacancy rate for the entire period subsequent to contract signing. The numbers of quarters in the pre- and postcontract periods vary by site.

d. Significant at the .10 level or above.

N/AP—Not applicable.

—Indicates the boundary line between the pre- and postcontract periods.

Source: Tabulation of data in the Tenant Management Information System.

Table 7-5. continued

| *Monthly Average in Quarter Ending* | | | | | | |
June 1978	*Sept. 1978*	*Dec. 1978*	*March 1979*	*June 1979*	*Demo. P Value[b]*	*Pre vs. Post P Value[c]*
2.0	2.0	2.6	2.6	2.5	0.000[d]	0.003[d]
1.0	1.0	1.0	1.3	1.1	0.000[d]	N/AP
13.4	17.1	11.9	5.9	5.6	0.000[d]	0.48
2.5	2.8	4.7	7.2	8.2	0.000[d]	0.000[d]
0.2	0.2	0.4	0.5	0.1	0.000[d]	0.88
3.2	4.9	4.4	2.5	1.4	0.000[d]	0.000[d]

The housing market analysis provides a framework for conclusions to be drawn for Louisville, New Haven, and New Orleans.[12] In both Louisville and New Haven, forces internal to the PHA seemed responsible for the changes in the vacancy rates rather than the more general housing market. In Louisville, despite a "soft" market for private rental housing (vacancy rates hovered near 7.5 percent throughout the demonstration), with affordable alternatives available for low-income individuals, demand for public housing remained high. The

12. There was insufficient data for the other three sites. In Rochester there was only limited data available on the demand for public housing and the vacancy rates for conventionally managed PHA projects. The PHA was unable to provide information on applications for housing prior to January 1977, and there were no data available for vacancies PHA-wide for 1976 and 1978. In Jersey City, there was no information on the private housing market for 1976, and only very limited data on vacancy rates in conventionally managed PHA projects and on total number of PHA applications for housing in 1976.

PERFORMANCE INDICATORS IN THE TENANT MANAGEMENT DEMONSTRATION BY SITE AND CALENDAR QUARTER

Figure 7-5   **VACANCY RATE (%)**

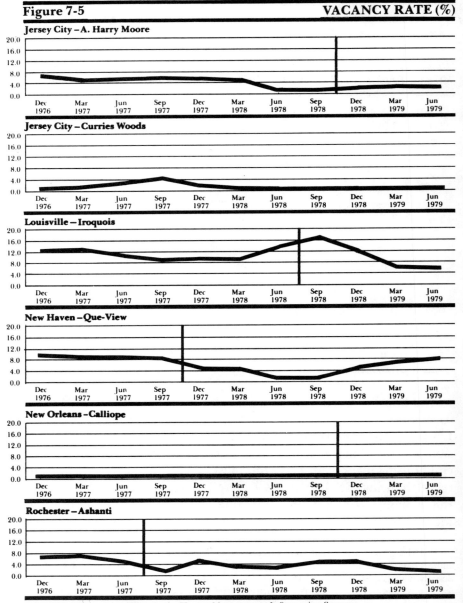

SOURCE: Tabulations of data in the Tenant Management Information System.

NOTES: Solid line graphs represent trends which are significant at the 0.10 level or above. Dotted line graphs represent trends which are not significant at the 0.10 level. Vertical line indicates the boundary between the pre- and post-contract periods.

fluctuations in the vacancy rates for the tenant management site cannot be differentiated from those that characterized other family developments as they responded to management control efforts of the PHA.

In New Haven, the market for private rental housing varied, but in a manner that was not useful in explaining changes in the vacancy rate at the tenant management site. That is, during those periods in which the private rental housing market tightened, the vacancy rate at the tenant management site rose. As the market became soft, vacancies at the tenant management site fell. Factors affecting the PHA as a whole do seem to have had an impact, since vacancy rates for all family developments exhibited a pattern similar to that of the tenant management site. These changes seem related to the worsening financial condition of the housing authority and its inability to commit resources to vacant unit preparation.

Only in New Orleans was the private rental housing market a possible factor in explaining the observed trends in vacancy at the tenant management site. There, the private rental market tightened in the last year of the demonstration, and the vacancy rate dropped as low as 1 percent. The increase in the demand for public housing and the decrease in the vacancy rate for the PHA as a whole resulted from this. There was no discernible difference in the vacancy rate pattern for the tenant management site and the other family developments in the PHA, except in the case of two high-rise projects reputed to be problem ridden, where vacancy rates were higher.

Thus, where reasonable judgments can be made, there is little reason to attribute improvements in vacancy rates to the demonstration or to tenant management per se. Forces affecting the PHA as a whole in Louisville and New Haven and the condition of the local private housing market in New Orleans provide more likely explanations for those changes in vacancies. Further support for the absence of a demonstration impact on vacancy comes from comparing the gain scores of the tenant management sites with those of the control sites (1979 minus 1976 vacancy rate). There was no significant difference between them.[13]

---

13. Suzanne B. Loux and Robert Sadacca, "Analysis of Changes at Tenant Management Demonstration Projects," Working Paper #1335 (Washington, D.C.: Urban Institute, 1980). For vacancy rate, the gain score for the tenant management sites was 0 and that for the control sites was −.01; the difference (.01) was not significant at the .10 level.

Vacant Unit Preparation. Vacant unit preparation is closely linked to vacancy rate and rental income. When vacancies occur, some decision must be made as to whether—and how quickly—the vacated unit will be prepared for occupancy. In most instances, this requires scarce resources. If there is an available pool of applicants, prompt vacancy preparation means that the unit will be ready for occupancy and begin to generate income sooner. If no pool of applicants exists, however, prompt vacancy preparation, unless coupled with security procedures, may result in vandalism and be more costly than would have been the case had the unit not been prepared. At the tenant management sites, there was usually an available pool of applicants, so prompt vacancy preparation became an important factor in the financial state of the development.

At A. Harry Moore in Jersey City, Louisville, New Orleans, and Rochester, there was a significant improvement in the vacant unit preparation rate (Table 7-6). Louisville is an interesting case in point because of the fluctuations that occurred there. Although on balance there was a significant increase in the rate, for the period April 1977 through September 1978 there was a precipitous drop (from 27 to 5 percent), after which the rate climbed again. In Louisville, as well as at A. Harry Moore in Jersey City and in Rochester, increases in the vacant unit preparation rate were significantly greater after transfer of management responsibility to the TMC than had been the case in the precontract period (Table 7-6 and Figure 7-6).

In New Haven, a PHA-wide situation clearly hindered vacant unit preparation performance. Aggravation of the housing authority's financial position and a PHA-wide cutback in the maintenance work force beginning in the third quarter of 1978 considerably reduced the resources available for vacancy preparation work. This situation resulted in an overall worsening of the vacant unit preparation rate over the course of the demonstration, despite a pattern of increase in the six quarters before the third quarter of 1978. No change in the vacant unit preparation rate was detected at Curries Woods in Jersey City.

On balance, the majority of tenant management sites improved vacant preparation performance, and most of these experienced greater success after the transfer of management responsibility to the tenant management corporation. However, this improved performance cannot be clearly attributed to the effectiveness of tenants as managers.

PERFORMANCE INDICATORS IN THE TENANT MANAGEMENT DEMONSTRATION BY SITE AND CALENDAR QUARTER

Figure 7-6   **VACANCY UNIT PREPARATION RATE (%)**

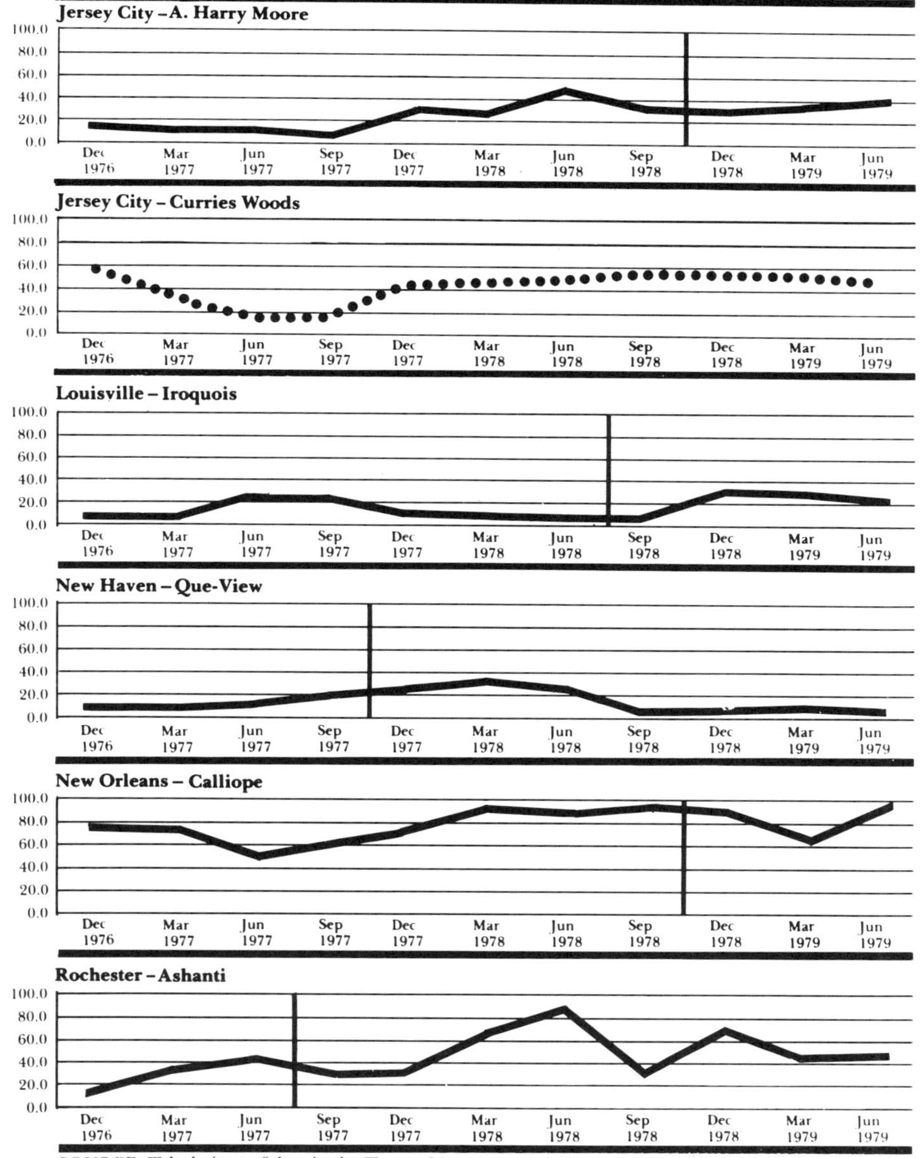

SOURCE: Tabulations of data in the Tenant Management Information System.

NOTES: Solid line graphs represent trends which are significant at the 0.10 level or above. Dotted line graphs represent trends which are not significant at the 0.10 level. Vertical line indicates the boundary between the pre- and post-contract periods.

Table 7-6. Performance Indicators in the Tenant Management Demonstration by Site and Calendar Quarter, Vacant Unit Preparation Rate (*percent*).[a]

	Monthly Average in Quarter Ending					
Site	Dec. 1976	March 1977	June 1977	Sept. 1977	Dec. 1977	March 1978
Jersey City A. Harry Moore	17.7	11.1	12.7	6.8	24.6	22.1
Jersey City Curries Woods	57.5	32.9	17.0	19.2	43.3	46.5
Louisville Iroquois Home	6.7	6.7	27.3	25.8	12.7	8.9
New Haven Que-View	7.4	7.0	13.9	20.5	25.4	37.9
New Orleans Calliope	78.5	74.1	50.2	62.2	76.6	94.4
Rochester Ashanti	15.5	36.6	46.4	31.9	35.0	70.8

a. Vacant unit preparation rate is defined as the proportion of unprepared vacant unit workload prepared in the month.

b. Estimate of the probability that changes in vacant unit preparation rate over the course of the demonstration are attributable to chance. This estimate takes into account the differences in vacant unit preparation rate from quarter to quarter for each of the eleven quarters of the demonstration.

c. Estimate of the probability that changes in vacant unit preparation rate between the precontract and postcontract periods are attributable to chance. This estimate contrasts the vacant unit preparation rate for the entire period prior to contract signing with vacant unit preparation rate for the entire period subsequent to contract signing. The numbers of quarters in the pre- and postcontract periods vary by site.

d. Significant at the .10 level or above.

N/AP—Not applicable.

—Indicates the boundary line between the pre- and postcontract periods.

Source: Tabulation of data in the Tenant Management Information System.

Table 7-6.   continued

| Monthly Average in Quarter Ending | | | | | | |
June 1978	Sept. 1978	Dec. 1978	March 1979	June 1979	Demo. P Value[b]	Pre vs. Post P Value[c]
47.2	35.5	28.4	33.5	40.2	0.02[d]	0.07[d]
49.8	57.8	57.3	54.9	53.6	0.23	N/AP
6.5	5.2	27.0	30.7	22.8	0.000[d]	0.05[d]
27.0	6.7	10.3	9.8	5.0	0.07[d]	0.34
91.1	96.3	70.6	69.3	91.9	0.01[d]	0.93
88.9	36.1	63.9	42.9	50.0	0.000[d]	0.03[d]

First, at several sites—for example, Louisville and Rochester—extraordinary efforts were exerted on the part of the PHA in cooperation with the tenant management corporation to reduce the vacant unit preparation workload as a condition of the TMC's acceptance of management responsibility. Although their success in increasing the vacant unit preparation rate may not have occurred in the absence of the demonstration, certainly one cannot attribute it to tenant management alone. Moreover, in comparison with their control counterparts, the tenant management sites did no better (or worse) in improving vacant unit preparation.[14]

14. Suzanne B. Loux and Robert Sadacca, "Analysis of Changes at Tenant Management Demonstration Projects," Working Paper #1335 (Washington, D.C.: Urban Institute, 1980). For the "number of days to prepare a vacant apartment for a new tenant," the tenant management sites showed a gain score of 1 and the control sites, a gain score of −9.3; the difference (10.3) was not significant at the .10 level.

Maintenance

Maintenance of a housing development—the routine completion of repair work and similar jobs—has the most direct relationship to the day-to-day comfort and convenience of the tenants themselves. Responsiveness to their requests is an ongoing and very visible function of management to which tenants can readily react, and it substantially affects the quality of life in the project from the tenants' perspective. Tenants are concerned that their maintenance requests are completed within a reasonable amount of time and that the quality of work done is high. Although the tenant management sites did experience some difficulty in this area when compared to their control counterparts, there was no statistically significant difference.

Routine Job Completion. The data available to assess the level of routine job completion were limited at three of the six tenant management sites. No information was available for New Haven, and in the case of the Jersey City sites, data were available only for the last five of the eleven quarters of the demonstration. Despite these limitations, some trends were discernible.

Overall, the completion rate for routine maintenance requests from tenants worsened over the course of the demonstration (Table 7-7 and Figure 7-7). In both Jersey City sites and in New Orleans this was clearly the case, as indicated by significant decreases in the routine job completion rate. In New Orleans there was improvement followed by a steady decline, in spite of the fact that the average number of work order requests decreased significantly. At the other two sites, there was no significant change in work order requests. In the case of A. Harry Moore and New Orleans, the decrease was even more significant after the transfer of management. Only in Rochester was a clear pattern of significant improvement evident in the routine job completion rate. It increased 46 percent over the course of the demonstration, with most of this improvement occurring in the postcontract period, when improvement was significantly greater than during the precontract phase. This improvement in performance was accompanied by significant decreases in the number of service requests both over the course of the demonstration and between pre- and postcontract periods. The routine job completion rate changed significantly in Louisville, but although the overall trend is toward

PERFORMANCE INDICATORS IN THE TENANT MANAGEMENT DEMONSTRATION BY SITE AND CALENDAR QUARTER

Figure 7-7 ROUTINE MAINTENANCE JOB COMPLETION RATE (%)

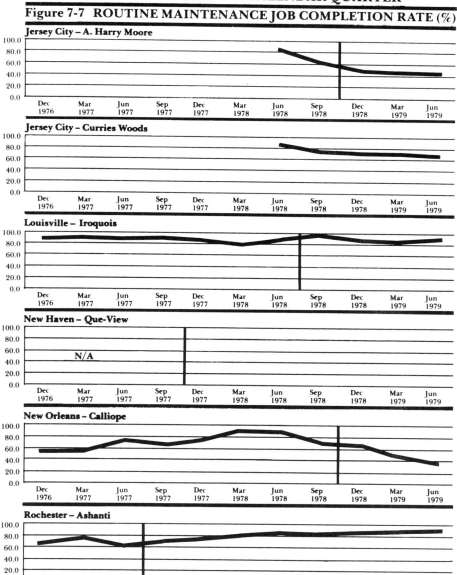

SOURCE: Tabulations of data in the Tenant Management Information System.

NOTES: Solid line graphs represent trends which are significant at the 0.10 level or above. Dotted line graphs represent trends which are not significant at the 0.10 level. Vertical line indicates the boundary between the pre- and post-contract periods.

Table 7-7.   Performance Indicators in the Tenant Management Demonstration by Site and Calendar Quarter, Routine Job Completion Rate (*percent*).[a]

	Monthly Average in Quarter Ending					
Site	Dec. 1976	March 1977	June 1977	Sept. 1977	Dec. 1977	March 1978
Jersey City A. Harry Moore	N/A	N/A	N/A	N/A	N/A	N/A
Jersey City Curries Woods	N/A	N/A	N/A	N/A	N/A	N/A
Louisville Iroquois Home	87.9	92.1	87.2	91.1	81.4	79.7
New Haven Que-View	N/A	N/A	N/A	N/A	N/A	N/A
New Orleans Calliope	57.5	57.0	70.9	68.2	74.3	92.7
Rochester Ashanti	62.5	78.7	61.3	68.2	74.0	82.6

a. Routine job completion rate is defined as the proportion of the total job workload completed per month.

b. Estimate of the probability that changes in routine job completion rate over the course of the demonstration are attributable to chance. This estimate takes into account the differences in routine job completion rate from quarter to quarter for each of the eleven quarters of the demonstration.

c. Estimate of the probability that changes in routine job completion rate between the precontract and postcontract periods are attributable to chance. This estimate contrasts the routine job completion rate for the entire period prior to contract signing with routine job completion rate for the entire period subsequent to contract signing. The numbers of quarters in the pre- and postcontract periods vary by site.

d. Based on one month's data.

e. The value for this quarter adds to more than 100 percent because recalculation of the workload identified several jobs completed but not previously included in the completion rate calculation.

f. Significant at the .10 level or above.

N/AP—Not applicable.

N/A—Not available.

—Indicates the boundary line between pre- and postcontract periods.

Source: Tabulation of data in the Tenant Management Information System.

Table 7-7.   continued

| Monthly Average in Quarter Ending | | | | | | |
June 1978	Sept. 1978	Dec. 1978	March 1979	June 1979	Demo. P Value[b]	Pre vs. Post P Value[c]
82.9[d]	59.4	47.4	45.4	42.4	0.004[f]	0.002[f]
85.5[d]	77.0	70.9	70.6	65.4	0.08[f]	N/AP
89.5	102.6[e]	88.6	80.6	93.7	0.09[f]	0.48
N/A	N/A	N/A	N/A	N/A	N/A	N/A
90.6	74.8	64.1	49.3	37.4	0.000[f]	0.000[f]
86.3	83.4	85.7	90.8	91.1	0.000[f]	0.000[f]

improvement, it included several fluctuations, with low points in the December 1977 and March 1978 quarters in the precontract period, and in the March 1979 quarter in the postcontract period. No significant change occurred between the pre- and postcontract phases.[15]

The generally poor maintenance performance of the tenant management sites is corroborated by other data. In 1979, tenants at the sites reported significantly longer periods for management to respond to routine job requests than in 1976.[16] However, on balance, the ten-

15. During the precontract period there was a decrease in the average number of requests and an increase during the postcontract period.

16. Suzanne B. Loux and Robert Saddaca, "Analysis of Changes at Tenant Management Demonstration Projects," Working Paper #1335 (Washington, D.C.: Urban Institute, 1980). For routine maintenance, tenants reported, on the average, 27 more days than in 1976 to respond (significantly different from zero at .10 level); the calculation of this number included several outlying values and obscures the fact that the median number of days in 1979 was 6.5 days to respond to a request.

ant management sites did not seem to fare any worse than the control projects in terms of routine maintenance performance. There was no significant difference between the two in the number of days it took to respond to routine maintenance requests.[17]

Summary

A wide array of management performance indicators were monitored over the course of the demonstration. Those selected for discussion were chosen because of factors such as whether what occurred added important knowledge, whether the findings were comprehensible, and whether the data on which the findings were based were reliable.

The indicators selected provided 42 cases (seven variables for six sites). In two cases, data could not be analyzed.[18] An examination of the remaining 40 cases (displayed in Table 7-8) indicates that improvement in management performance definitely occurred at the tenant management sites over the course of the demonstration. In 23 cases (58 percent) there was improvement, and 13 cases (32 percent) showed greater improvement after the transfer of full management responsibility to the tenant management corporation (during the postcontract period). Some improvement occurred at all sites, and at three (A. Harry Moore in Jersey City, Louisville, and Rochester), improvement occurred on at least five of the seven management performance indicators. In nine cases (23 percent) there was no change, and in another eight cases, three of which were in New Haven, there was a decline in management performance. Improvement was most often shown in terms of vacancy rate and vacant unit preparation rate.

In assessing the meaning of these findings, an attempt must be made to evaluate circumstances outside tenant management that might account for their occurrence. There does seem to be some evidence that at half the sites, tenant management had a positive effect on the average monthly rent due, which in turn led to an increase in average monthly rent collected. The improvement in vacancy rate

17. Suzanne B. Loux and Robert Sadacca, "Analysis of Changes at Tenant Management Demonstration Projects," Working Paper #1335 (Washington, D.C.: Urban Institute, 1980). The gain score for the tenant management sites was 27.2 days and for the control sites 6.1 days; their difference of 21.1 was not significant at the .10 level.

18. In one case, the data were unavailable, and in the second, it was impossible to determine what the trend was.

and vacant unit preparation, on the other hand, seems to be associated with PHA commitment in terms of staff and resources, and the improvement that occurred at the tenant management sites was not significantly different from that experienced by the control sites.

The major finding on management performance is perhaps overshadowed by the several caveats related to the improvement that did occur. In comparison with their conventionally managed counterparts, the tenant management sites performed as well in all management areas. In essence, the weight of the evidence seems to indicate that public housing residents are fully capable of performing "hard" management tasks—the nuts and bolts of real estate management—at a level that seems comparable to that of conventional public housing managers.

PHYSICAL IMPROVEMENTS

Fifteen million dollars in Modernization Program (MOD) funds and additional monies under the Target Projects Program (TPP) were designated for physical improvements at the demonstration sites. While none of the program's predecessors in the predemonstration period had received such funds as part of the introduction of tenant management, the demonstration's sponsors felt that the infusion of funds for physical improvement was needed to provide an incentive for participation and to give the program a fair test.

Rationale for Modernization Funding

The provision of MOD funds was a direct response to the tenant management experience in St. Louis. As a prime example of aging public housing stock, the St. Louis tenant management developments suffered from a myriad of problems associated with physical deterioration. This deterioration was a constant visible reminder of the ills of public housing both to the fledgling tenant management corporations and to the tenants at large. As such, it overshadowed any positive steps toward more efficient and sensitive management taken by the tenant management corporations, and their inability to reverse it threatened tenant management:

> It is very hard for a [TMC] to keep credibility with its community if it can't deliver on broken pipes or grounds that don't have a blade of grass. . . . The

Table 7–8. Summary of Management Performance Measures by Site.

Performance Measures	Overall Performance[a]	Site			
		Jersey City A. Harry Moore	Jersey City Curries Wood	Louisville	New Haven
Average monthly rent due per unit ($)	+	improved[c]	worsened	worsened[c]	improved[c]
Average monthly rent collected ($)	0	no change	no change	no change	improved[c]
Rent collection rate (%)	+	improved	no change	improved[c]	worsened[c]
Units owing more than one month's rent (%)	0	improved	no change	improved	worsened[c]
Vacancy rate (%)	+	improved[c]	improved	improved	improved[c]
Vacant unit preparation rate (%)	+	improved[c]	no change	improved[c]	worsened
Routine job completion rate (%)	-	worsened[c]	worsened	improved	N/A

		Site		Rival Hypotheses[b]		
Performance Measures	Overall Performance[a]	New Orleans	Rochester	PHA	Housing Market	Control Group
Average monthly rent due per unit ($)	+ 0	improved[c]	no change	–	–	no
Average monthly rent collected ($)	+ 0	improved[c]	improved	–	–	–
Rent collection rate (%)	+ 0	no change	no change	–	–	–
Units owing more than one month's rent (%)	+ 0	unable to determine	improved	–	–	yes
Vacancy rate (%)	+	improved	improved[c]	yes	yes	yes
Vacant unit preparation rate (%)	+	improved	improved[c]	yes	–	yes
Routine job completion rate (%)	–	worsened[c]	improved	–	–	yes

a. + = improvement; – = worsening; $\dagger$ = mixed pattern; 0 = little or no change. The assessment of overall change was based on whether the postcontract period showed greater improvement than the precontract period.

b. (–) indicates that rival hypotheses of this type were not examined.

c. Pre-post contract difference significant at the .10 level.

N/A – Not available.

Source: Summary drawn from Tenant Management Information System.

incinerators were in violation of the code and . . . were spewing all kinds of debris on the people and the ground. . . . The tenants had to be given the tools they needed to give the demonstration an honest test.[19]

The two initial TMCs did not receive TPP funds until their second year of existence, in 1974, nor MOD monies until even later. Although they managed to survive without the extra money, program observers and participants felt that when the funds did become available, they helped the new tenant management corporations solidify their management positions. A major implication of the St. Louis experience was that additional funds were needed for visible physical improvements to encourage tenant support of the tenant management corporation. In essence, improvements realized under MOD would increase the developments' safety, comfort, and attractiveness and thereby earn tenant support for the tenant management corporations as sponsors of such improvements.

In selecting sites for the national demonstration, planners tried to strike a balance between, on the one hand, sites that were so dilapidated that the dim prospects for making any progress would frustrate and detract from any successful effort to stage the program and, on the other hand, sites needing only minor repairs that would not be noticeable enough to bring credit and support to the TMC. However, physical condition was not the only criterion for site selection; resident interest and PHA support were also crucial, as was the case in Rochester, a relatively new development where the offer of MOD funds was not the overriding factor in favor of participation. For other, older sites, the guarantee of MOD funds would be a major inducement for involvement, and improvements realized as a result would contribute to their ability to operate efficiently.

Finally, MOD was seen as an important factor in achieving the goals of the demonstration. It was anticipated that these improvements would make the sites attractive enough to draw tenants with higher incomes, whose rents would boost site revenues and perhaps facilitate better management performance. It was also hoped that improvements in the safety, comfort, and attractiveness of the developments would increase resident satisfaction with their community and heighten residents' pride so they would cooperate more fully in upkeep efforts. In addition, MOD projects were viewed as

19. Allan R. Talbot, *The Evolution of the National Tenant Management Demonstration Program* (New York: The Ford Foundation, February 1977), p. 8.

a vehicle for increasing resident employment, a third goal of the demonstration.

Modernization Activity: Process and Outcomes

Since its inception in 1968, the MOD program has sought to include tenant input in local activities and to increase tenant employment. In reality, tenant involvement very often was little more than the expression of minor preferences after major decisions had already been made. There were some notable exceptions to this practice—for example, in St. Louis, where tenant organizations' input was solicited for the MOD program, which predated tenant management, and where decisions on MOD allocations among the PHA developments were made by the Tenant Affairs Board (TAB) in cooperation with the PHA.

The MOD process is protracted and complicated and involves considerable technical expertise. Aside from the potentially cumbersome process of getting residents to agree on needed improvements and to select among alternatives, it involves a series of bureaucratic approvals and a long sequence of designing, estimating, bidding, and contracting activities. Following these tasks, the actual work must be monitored. And over time, inflation may undermine the best laid plans.

Residents began participating in MOD decisions during the planning phase of the demonstration, since a request for funds for specific modernization plans were part of each site's initial proposal. These MOD activities were usually discussed and negotiated between the housing authority, tenant representatives, and MDRC—subject to further modification as subsequent events occurred.

One of the first tasks facing TMC board members was to review the modernization priorities and modify them in light of resident preference or according to their understanding of how MOD funds could be used to further the goals of the tenant management corporation. These modifications usually included completing more visible site improvements or renovating individual units first in an attempt to gain resident support for the tenant management corporation early in the demonstration. Sometimes the tenant management corporation's modifications were in response to a poll of resident preferences or to budget constraints. In Rochester, for example, a tenant survey indicated that the planned daycare center would be under-utilized and funds would be better spent for a community center. On other occasions in the demonstration, changes in MOD plans originated with the PHA; these revisions often stemmed from unanticipated needs for major emergency repair work, as in Jersey City's Curries Woods, where emergency replacement of a boiler took priority over previously scheduled improvements.

The $15 million in MOD funds set aside for the demonstration was allocated among seven sites; allocation was based primarily on the size of site, with some consideration given to the site's condition and whether or not it had previously received MOD funding.[20] In Louisville and New Orleans, portions of the TPP allocations were also used for physical improvements.[21] Tables 7-9 and 7-10 provide an overview of activities made possible by Modernization Program funds.[22] These can be grouped into several categories. Physical safety was an issue important to all tenants, and sizable amounts of money were allocated to enhance safety and security, including installation of exterior lighting, deadbolt locks and doors, and hallway fire doors. Other physical improvements were geared to enhancing residents' comfort, such as electrical rewiring in New Orleans and Louisville, to permit the installation of air conditioners, and the installation of storm windows in Rochester. Proposed projects also included improvements to individual units such as bathroom and kitchen renovation as well as aesthetic improvements to the developments as a whole, including graffiti removal and grounds improvements. In four

20. With the dropping of Oklahoma City in 1978, this amount became $13,993,000; the amount was increased by $19,480 from other funds, such as predemonstration PHA MOD monies, bringing the total allocation to $14,012,480. This latter figure is the one used in computations performed for Tables 7-9 and 7-10.

21. Eight hundred seventy-five thousand dollars of the TPP allocation for New Orleans (Calliope) was designated for proposed physical improvements, as was $24,000 of the TPP allocation for Louisville (Iroquois). The projects for which TPP funds were used in New Orleans included repair and replacement of drainspouts and gutters, painting of public halls, termite proofing of buildings, replacement and/or repair of screen doors, removal of graffiti, new refrigerators and ranges, subsidence and drainage, sewer machines, bathroom fixtures, exterior and cycle painting, stairway pans, purchase of an electric truckster, two pick-up trucks, various maintenance machines, and tree trimming. For Louisville, the projects were a self-help paint program, grounds improvement and landscaping, and purchase of a passenger van.

22. Information in Tables 7-9 and 7-10 is limited to projects supported by MOD funds; projects for which TPP funds were used are not included in the disussion, nor is Oklahoma City included.

sites, construction or major renovation was proposed—a community center in Rochester, New Orleans, and New Haven and a daycare center in Louisville.

An assessment of the demonstration's MOD efforts will be approached from several perspectives, including the percentage of proposed projects completed, the percentage of allocated funds expended, tenants' assessment of the tenant management corporation's ability to accomplish physical improvements, and the quality of the work done. The assessment of the quality of the work is provided in the discussion of the tenant management corporation board's monitoring of workmanship.

Tables 7–9 and 7–10 indicate that the sites varied considerably in the extent to which MOD work had been completed at the close of the demonstration. Overall, 57 percent of the total projects planned had been completed by June 30, 1979, with a range from 28 percent in New Haven to 93 percent in Rochester. At A. Harry Moore and Curries Woods in Jersey City and at Que-View in New Haven, less than 50 percent of the projects had been completed. However, it should be borne in mind that failure to complete MOD projects on schedule is not an uncommon phenomenon. The majority (73 percent) of the top priority projects had been completed or substantially completed by the demonstration's end.

The fact that the overall completion rate of 57 percent represented only 45 percent of the total MOD allocation indicates that some of the more expensive projects had not been completed. New Orleans is the prime example of this situation. Sixty percent of the MOD projects had been completed, but they represented only 25 percent of the total MOD allocation. Work had not begun on the community-administrative building or on electrical rewiring; exterior and interior lighting had not been completed. The allocation for these items was $3.9 million of a total MOD allocation of $6.5 million. Projects on which virtually no work had been done ("no work begun" and "architect's design phase" in Table 7–10) represent 20 percent of the total projects of all sites. On a site-by-site basis, the percentage of projects not yet begun ranged from 7 percent in Rochester and Curries Woods to 47 percent in New Haven, with the figures for four of the six sites below 20 percent. Overall, however, 60 percent of the total allocation had been spent by the demonstration's end, ranging from 94 percent in Rochester to 42 percent in New Orleans.

Table 7-9. Modernization Projects and Status of Activities at the Tenant Management Sites.

Site	Total Number of Dwelling Units	Total Demonstration MOD Allocation[a] ($)	Specific Modernization Activities		Percent Completed on 6/30/79[c]
			Activity	Status on 6/30/79[b]	
Jersey City: A. Harry Moore	664	997	*Fire standpipe refurbishment	Substantially completed	46
			*Hallway fire doors	No work begun	
			*Compactor renovation	Substantially completed	
			*Kitchen modernization	Completed	
			*Replacement stoves and refrigerators	Completed	
			*Refurbishment of vacant apartments	Completed	
			Installation of gas-burning incinerator system	Work begun	
			Elevator modernization	Completed	
			Exterior of buildings (masonry)	No work begun	
			Heating system refurbishment	Completed	
			Tile installation	Work begun	
			Painting and cleaning stairwells	Completed	
			*Bathroom modernization	Substantially completed	
Jersey City: Curries Woods	712	1,015	*Grounds improvement	Work begun	38
			*Electrical system rehabilitation	Substantially completed	
			*Lexan glass installation	Completed	
			*Elevator modernization	Completed	
			*Installation of gas-burning incinerator system	Work begun	
			Bathroom modernization	Substantially completed	
			Kitchen modernization	Completed	

*denotes those items considered to be top priority in the sites' application to HUD.

Site				Item	Status
	854	$3,500,000	80	Boiler system replacement	Completed
				Hallway painting	Work begun
				Hallway tile installation	Work begun
				Exterior of buildings (masonry)	No work begun
				Stairwell painting	Work begun
				Apartment painting	Ongoing
Louisville: Iroquois Homes RMC				*Construction of daycare center	Completed
				*Repair of roofs, gutters, and downspouts	Completed
				*Repair and replacement of boiler systems, gaslines, heating systems	Completed
				*Electrical rewiring	Completed
				Replacement of doors and installation of deadlocks	Completed
				Purchase of van	Completed
				Replacement of stoves	Completed
				Renovation of units for the handicapped	Work begun
				Sidewalk and structural repairs	No work begun
				Graffiti removal	Completed
New Haven: Que–View	260	1,650	28	*Thermal windows	Substantially completed
				*Grounds improvement	Consultant design phase
				*Renovation of community center	Architect design phase
				*New entry design	Work begun
				Bathroom renovation	Completed

*denotes those items considered to be top priority in the sites' application to HUD.

(Table 7–9. continued overleaf)

Table 7-9. continued

Site	Total Number of Dwelling Units	Total Demonstration MOD Allocation[a] ($)	Specific Modernization Activities		Percent Completed
			Activity	Status on 6/30/79[b]	
New Haven: Que–View (continued)			Storm windows, doors, and locks	Work begun	
			Repairs to building exterior	Ongoing	
			Heating system repairs	Ongoing	
			Apartment interiors	Completed	
			Laundry room renovations	No work begun	
			Daycare center renovation	Architect design phase[d]	
			Master TV antenna system	No work begun	
			Plumbing system repairs	No work begun	
			Basement cleanout	No work begun	
			Kitchen exhaust fans	No work begun	
New Orleans: Calliope	1,550	6,524	*Plumbing renovation	Completed	60
			*Bathroom tile	Completed	
			*Renovation of administration building[e]	Architect design phase	
			*Security hardware (steel locks/do and doors)	Completed	
			*Electrical rewiring	No work begun	
			*Kitchen renovation	Architect design phase	
			*Space heaters	Completed	
			Purchase of truck	Completed	
			Purchase of office furniture and equipment	Completed	
			Interior and exterior lighting	Substantially completed	

*denotes those items considered to be top priority in the sites' application to HUD.

Rochester: Ashanti	221	307	93
*Landscaping			Completed
*Purchase of recreation equipment			Completed
*Purchase of automotive equipment			Completed
*Storm windows			Completed
*Basement remodeling			Completed
Fascia and gutters			Completed
Community building renovation			Completed
Concrete stoops			Completed
Purchase of office furniture and equipment			Completed
Telephone equipment			Completed
Window repair			Completed
Heating system renovation			Completed
Linoleum stair treads			No work begun

a. Actual monies designated for the MOD projects listed in the table actually totaled $14,012,480.

b. The following statuses are identified:

No work begun

Architect design phase—projects that were still in the planning stage

Work begun—projects in which plans have been drawn up and work had started, but was not near completion

Substantially completed—projects in which the great majority of work had been done and funds expended

Completed

Ongoing projects—those undertaken as the need arose

*denotes those items considered to be top priority in the sites' application to HUD.

c. "Completed" and "ongoing" used in the computation of "percent completed on 6/30/79."

d. It was decided not to build the planned daycare center. $1,450 was spent before deciding not to build the facility.

e. Plans to renovate the administration building were stopped when the housing authority decided to build a new structure.

Note: Oklahoma City is not included in this table; the total MOD allocation to that site was $1,007,000, and the site included 537 units.

Source: Quarterly MOD reports submitted by the sites and PHA Staff.

Table 7–10. Modernization Projects: Summary of Activity at End of Demonstration.

Site[a]	Actual Funds Allocated to MOD Projects ($)	Funds Spent as of 6/30/79		Items Completed as of 6/30/79		Items not Begun or in Architect's Design Phase as of 6/30/79	
		Amount ($)	Percentage of Allocation	Percentage of Total Projects	Percentage of Total Allocation	Percentage of Total Projects	Percentage of Total Allocation
Jersey City: A. Harry Moore	966,734	675,030	68	46	46	15	10
Jersey City: Curries Woods	1,015,266	751,004	74	38	43	7	7
Louisville: Iroquois	3,500,000	3,254,837	93	80	91	10	6
New Haven: Que–View	1,669,800	690,059	44	28	13	47	39
New Orleans: Calliope	6,524,000	2,738,123	42	60	25	30	46
Rochester: Ashanti	306,680	287,006	94	93	94	7	6
All sites	14,012,480	8,395,059	60	57	45	20	29

a. Oklahoma City not included; total MOD allocation was $1,007,000.
Source: Quarterly MOD reports submitted by the sites and PHA staff.

As the discussion of the status of MOD items strongly implies, the pace of the work varied widely among the sites. In Rochester, the work rate was exceptionally rapid; virtually all projects undertaken had been executed by mid–1978. Modernization in New Haven got off to a good start, but progress was derailed by a nine-month strike of housing authority electricians. At Calliope in New Orleans and at the Jersey City sites, modernization work proceeded at a faltering pace.

Encouraged to take a substantial role in both determining which activities would be undertaken and monitoring their implementation, tenant management corporations at the demonstration sites experienced both the benefits and the problems associated with the MOD process. The tenants' new role was a limited one. Though the TMC had power of oversight regarding MOD work, they had little actual control when work did not go according to plan. Thus, the tenant management corporation could communicate its concerns to the housing authority over delays in scheduling and poor quality work, but only the housing authority could deny a contract, withhold a payment until satisfactory completion of work, or take other action.

Delays in the completion of MOD work proved to be a major problem for the tenant management corporations; they were the rule rather than the exception. It is difficult to ascertain to what extent the delays resulted from business as usual or from the involvement of the tenant management corporations in the MOD process. The considerable lead time required for drawing up plans, consulting architects and engineers, and letting the projects out for bid was a source of delay at all sites. Some additional causes of delay included union problems and strikes that held up repairs and construction. This dilemma plagued all housing authority developments in New Haven and Jersey City, as did misunderstandings with local HUD officials in Louisville.

Other sources of delay may be attributed to tenant management corporation involvement in monitoring the MOD process. The encroachment of novice tenant management corporation board and staff members onto the purview of the housing authority's modernization department engendered resistance at all sites and may have complicated normal procedures. At one site, for example, the PHA modernization department failed to invite the TMC board members to preconstruction conferences on MOD projects, and the PHA staff often treated board members in an abusive manner. At another site, the PHA department failed to follow plans jointly made with the TMC in the installation of new door locks.

Apart from the physical improvements made possible by the infusion of funds, the MOD experience had other consequences, both positive and negative, for the demonstration participants. PHA staff, for instance, tended to view tenant management corporation involvement as a mixed blessing. On the one hand, tenants were seen as novices, untutored in the technical nature of MOD work and causing delay and disruption of the process as a result. On the other hand, the tenant management corporation was seen as encouraging progress by arranging for contractors to gain access to individual apartments. At one site, problems with the PHA regarding MOD proved to be a catalyst in uniting the board against questionable practices in the PHA modernization department. MOD not only provided a focus around which the tenant management board coalesced and took decisive action but also served to rectify some undesirable conditions within the PHA. A positive consequence of tenant management corporation involvement in monitoring the implementation of MOD work, where it occurred, was the tenants' careful examination of ongoing and completed work to ensure its quality. Their vigilance in this effort and their insistence that shoddy work not be paid for were of obvious benefit to both the PHA and their fellow residents.

Negative reactions from the tenants at large were also a consequence of the MOD experience. In its role as liaison with the tenant community, the TMC was the entity that was most exposed to both the heightened expectations of the community and the frustration and blame when improvements did not materialize. At one of the southern sites, for instance, a high priority MOD expenditure was to be rewiring of the site's electrical system to support such apartment appliances as air conditioners. Serious delays occurred when the tenant management corporation board discovered that the plans drawn up by the PHA engineer placed the air conditioners in bedroom windows that also provided the only access to each apartment's fire escape. This discovery necessitated a complete redesign of the wiring plans and resulted in residents spending another summer without air conditioning. Residents accused the TMC of not producing the promised improvements, yet it was never really in the power of the tenant management corporation to deliver on many of these MOD promises, and in fact, in this particular instance it was the tenant management corporation's discovery that probably prevented an even more serious problem.

In spite of the difficulties that this situation imposed, delays in completion of MOD work do not seem to have seriously undercut the viability of tenant management at any of the sites. Residents in the wider community seemed, in fact, not to have measured tenant management corporation success in terms of MOD achievements; less than 1 percent of the tenants surveyed by the Urban Institute indicated physical improvements as the most important purpose of the tenant management corporation. Among tenants surveyed, physical improvements were most frequently mentioned as an area in which the tenant management corporation was able to get things done.[23] When MOD improvements did not materialize, TMC board and staff members reported that residents became angry and expressed that anger, yet they did not seem to withdraw their support from the tenant management corporation and its general purposes. It appears that residents judged the tenant management corporation no different from the housing authority overall—no better, but no worse. Only 6 percent of the residents who felt that the tenant management corporation did a better job than the PHA in managing the development mentioned physical improvements as an example,[24] and only 3 percent of those who said the TMC was doing a worse job mentioned this area.

On balance, perhaps the most important positive consequence of MOD funds was largely unanticipated. They provided a focus around which the tenant management corporation boards could make concrete decisions and, in the process, build organizational strength. At some sites, the board members' sense of their own powers was augmented through negotiations with housing authority staff concerning MOD issues. Whereas the managerial policies implemented by the tenant management corporation seemed to be more stringent than those of the housing authority—tenants were pressed to pay their rents on time and were responsible for hallway clean-ups—the introduction of physical improvements to the sites allowed board mem-

23. Suzanne B. Loux and Robert Sadacca, "Analysis of Changes in Tenant Management Demonstration Projects," Working Paper #1335 (Washington, D.C.: Urban Institute, 1980). Among the tenants who knew about the TMC, 47 percent ($N = 62$) felt that the organization was able to get things done. Of these 37 percent ($N = 23$) mentioned "physical improvements" as an area in which this was the case; physical improvements were also mentioned more than any other area of activity. Among the tenants who felt that the TMC was not able to get things done (33 percent, $N = 43$), only 12 percent ($N = 5$) mentioned physical improvements as an example.

24. Ibid. Twenty-seven percent of the tenants felt that the PHA did a better job than the TMC; 34 percent, the same; 22 percent, worse; and 27 percent did not know.

25. See the section of this chapter on tenant employment.

bers to feel like benefactors rather than policemen. MOD monies thus provided board members with the capacity to do for their fellow residents, rather than merely to them.

Is MOD Necessary to Tenant Management?

The demonstration's planners felt that the infusion of large doses of MOD funds was a necessary ingredient of the program. It was thought that the monies would encourage PHAs and tenants to participate in the demonstration, improve the deteriorated physical condition of public housing, enhance the credibility of the tenant management corporation, and finally, facilitate the achievement of some of the demonstration's goals.

Based on program findings, the assessment of MOD's importance to tenant management is mixed. Certainly MOD monies served as incentive to PHAs to participate in the demonstration; this is evident from the executive directors' comments in interviews. Substantial improvements in the physical condition of the developments were realized despite significant delays and other aggravations faced by the tenant management corporation board and staff. These aggravations included complaints from fellow tenants as the TMC became the whipping boy for residents' frustration over the delays. In some instances, MOD efforts may have even temporarily damaged or undermined a tenant management corporation's credibility rather than heightened it. Moreover, housing experts have suggested that physical improvements to the sites are not a very satisfactory means of gaining resident support for tenant management because tenants feel that living in clean, safe, and attractive housing is a right, not a privilege, and because improvements are not unique to tenant management but have been or may be made under the aegis of the housing authority.

With regard to the demonstration's goals, modernization funds did not have their anticipated impact of increasing resident employment. Relatively few site residents were employed in MOD activities.[25] With regard to a second demonstration goal related to MOD—attracting higher income tenants—it is difficult to ascertain whether there was any success. Data suggest that some higher income tenants did become residents at the tenant management projects during the dem-

25. See the section of this chapter on tenant employment.

onstration,[26] but it is difficult to link this to MOD improvements, especially in view of the slow pace at which they occurred.

MOD funds did, on the other hand, have some important and positive unanticipated consequences. These funds provided a focus around which the tenant management corporation boards made decisions and, in the process, built organizational strength. Moreover, the funds provided the opportunity for board members to feel that they were doing something for their fellow residents rather than just acting as strict managers. Finally, the participation of TMC members in monitoring workmanship resulted in the identification of shoddy work and its correction.

The conclusion most readily suggested when looking at the demonstration experience and those of predemonstration tenant management programs is that MOD funds are not a necessary ingredient for an incipient tenant management program. What seems more important is that the TMCs have control over site improvements whenever they occur. At the first two nondemonstration tenant management sites still in existence (St. Louis and Boston), MOD funds were available to the tenant management corporation only after several years of operation. When MOD funds did become available, they were seen as helping the TMCs solidify and strengthen their position with the resident community.

During the demonstration, where MOD monies were initially a part of the tenant management package, drawbacks were evident—namely, universal delays in implementing MOD and perhaps additional ones occasioned by the involvement of fledgling tenant management corporation boards; poor performance in terms of generating tenant employment; and complaints associated with MOD that a novice tenant management corporation is especially likely to experience. These experiences suggest that MOD funds may not contribute significantly to enhancing the credibility of the young TMC through early visible improvements to the site or through increased tenant employment. Moreover, the overall conditions surrounding the utilization of these monies did not contribute in a major way to the instruction of the demonstration board and staff members, since they were more immediately concerned with achieving stability in their new management roles. Consequently, such funds may not be that beneficial during the first year or so of tenant management.

26. See the section of this chapter on real estate management.

What all this suggests is not that MOD funds are unimportant to tenant management but that their availability may not be indispensable to mounting a successful tenant management program or to tenant management per se. It may be preferable, then, to postpone major MOD activities until the tenant management corporation has achieved some stability in its new management role and gained the confidence of tenants and can better deal with a possibly reluctant housing authority modernization department.

TENANT EMPLOYMENT

Increasing the level and affecting the patterns of employment for the residents of public housing were seen as important potential benefits of the demonstration from its inception. Whether viewed as central to the demonstration's purposes or a natural consequence, there were a number of ways in which the demonstration could have an impact in the employment area. The most direct way in which tenant management could improve employment levels was through the creation of tenant management corporation staff positions. Not only were these positions restricted to residents but, by design, the program increased the number of employees comprising the on-site management staff. The availability of supervisory types of positions within the tenant management corporation could be viewed not only within its job creation context, but also as a means of upgrading the skills and longer term employment potential for the residents who secured such positions.

It was hoped, in addition, that the tenant management corporation would be able to increase tenant employment through a number of indirect mechanisms. For example, in its role as developer and coordinator of on-site social services, the TMC could ensure that such programs gave priority to residents in its hiring. The tenant management corporation could also exert influence in obtaining priority consideration for residents when housing authority positions became available, especially on-site positions in conventional areas such as maintenance and clerical work.

In addition, it was felt that the TMC could be instrumental in increasing resident employment in Modernization Program projects directed at physical improvements to the sites—a function strongly supported by HUD regulations, which stipulate that residents be given preference in hiring for MOD work to the extent feasible. In each case, however, the tenant management corporation's potential influence would be limited by union and/or civil service requirements concerning prequalifications and seniority. Finally, the tenant management corporation could serve as the on-site coordination or management mechanism for federally funded programs having job creation potential for residents, especially the Comprehensive Employment and Training Act (CETA). The tenant management corporations would not only manage the funds and allocate jobs to residents, but also increase the level of such resources flowing into the TMC community.

This section explores these tenant employment issues during the demonstration at the six sites participating in the program for its full term.[27] The primary discussion centers on the levels of employment and job development efforts, with less attention to the types of individuals employed and their job experience. The limited data that are available on the latter topics come from a questionnaire administered to a subsample of employed tenants.[28]

Tenant Employment: An Overview

Over the life of the demonstration, at least 425 tenants were employed at various times and in various on-site jobs at the tenant management projects.[29] This number includes tenants employed on the TMC basic management staff; in clerical, maintenance, and security positions; in jobs as aides, assistants, and other ancillary staff; in physical improvements projects; and in summer programs. Table 7–11 indicates that tenant employment levels increased steadily during the program with some minor fluctuations.[30] For all sites com-

27. Oklahoma City is not included in the discussion.

28. The primary sources of data used in this section are the Tenant Management Information System (TMIS), Tenant Employment Survey, and the TMC Staff Questionnaire.

29. This number includes employed tenants tracked by the Tenant Management Information System (TMIS) ($N = 279$) and tenants listed in the Tenant Employment Survey compiled by the TMC manager but not in the TMIS ($N = 146$). The number is probably somewhat understated, because New Haven did not complete a survey form and Oklahoma City was not included in the analysis. The best information available on Oklahoma City indicates very limited resident employment, however.

30. Table 7–11 includes only tenants tracked in the TMIS. For the most part, the TMIS included the tenant management staff, clerical, security, and some maintenance employees.

Table 7–11.   Tenant Employment During the Tenant Management
Demonstration by Site and Calendar Quarter.

Site	Category	Quarter Ending		
		Dec. 1976	March 1977	June 1977
Jersey City A. Harry Moore	Number of Tenant Employees[a]	19	27	[b] 25
	Total Number of Project Employees[a]	54	60	57
	Percent Tenants of Total Employees	35.2	45.0	43.9
Jersey City Curries Woods	Number of Tenant Employees[a]	14	15	18
	Total Number of Project Employees[a]	32	31	32
	Percent Tenants of Total Employees	43.7	48.4	56.3
Louisville Iroquois Home	Number of Tenant Employees[a]	5.5	6.3	6.5
	Total Number of Project Employees[a]	30.0	32.1	32.5
	Percent Tenants of Total Employees	18.3	19.6	20.0
New Haven Que–View	Number of Tenant Employees[a]	0	0	[b] 2.0
	Total Number of Project Employees[a]	1.35	1.35	5.35
	Percent Tenants of Total Employees	0.0	0.0	37.4
New Orleans Calliope	Number of Tenant Employees[a]	2	2	5
	Total Number of Project Employees[a]	57	52	67
	Percent Tenants of Total Employees	3.5	3.8	7.5
Rochester Ashanti	Number of Tenant Employees[a]	1	[b] 18	17
	Total Number of Project Employees[a]	7	24	23
	Percent Tenants of Total Employees	14.3	75.0	73.9
All Sites	Percent Tenants of Total Employees	22.0	34.1	33.9

a. Expressed as full-time equivalents and include only workers employed at the site.

b. Quarter in which TMC management staff hiring was begun.

Table 7–11. continued

Quarter Ending (continued)							
Sept. 1977	Dec. 1977	March 1978	June 1978	Sept. 1978	Dec. 1978	March 1979	June 1979
29	31	26	16	18	24	25	19
58	62	58	37	38	45	50	43
50.0	50.0	44.8	43.2	47.4	53.3	50.0	44.2
15	17	16	b 25	25	22	24	22
31	32	44	44	44	43	44	46
48.4	53.1	36.4	56.8	56.8	51.2	54.5	47.8
5.5	b 20.5	20	17	20	16	18	20
29.3	50.5	38.5	35.5	35.0	37	39	45
18.8	40.6	51.9	47.9	57.1	43.2	46.2	44.4
2.0	4.2	3.5	3	2	3	2.5	3.75
6.5	8.45	7.75	9.35	5.6	8	7.5	9.75
30.8	49.7	45.2	32.1	35.7	37.5	33.3	38.5
22	b 25	18	21	21	26	24	21
93	107	89	73	72	64	60	55
23.7	23.4	20.2	28.8	29.2	40.6	40.0	38.2
21	19	20	20	15	18	18	16
27	24	26	25	19	21	22	20
77.8	79.2	76.9	80.0	78.9	85.7	81.8	80.0
38.6	41.8	40.1	45.6	47.3	50.0	50.1	46.5

Source: Tenant Management Information System.

bined, the level of tenant employment rose from an average of slightly under 23 percent of all employees at the housing developments during the first year to over 48 percent during the final year.

Most tenant employment at the start of the demonstration was accounted for by the two Jersey City sites, which had a fairly well-established history of hiring tenants prior to the demonstration. Over 80 percent of such employment was in maintenance jobs, with the rest scattered among clerical and aide positions. From the quarter ending December 1976, when 45 positions were filled by tenants, to the quarter preceeding the hiring of TMC management staff (which varied by site), tenant employment rate increased to 87 positions filled by tenants. Tenant employment as a percentage of total employment thus increased to about 30 percent (an increase of about 45 percent). The major change occurred in New Orleans, where over 20 maintenance personnel were hired from among the residents, but smaller increases occurred at most other sites as well, primarily in the hiring of clerical aides and maintenance personnel.

Once TMC management staff came on board at the sites, total site employment increased, and the proportion of residents to total personnel also increased. From then on, the percentage of tenants employed fluctuated between 40 and 50 percent, depending on circumstances at particular sites. There was a measurable decline in tenant employment in the last quarter as the sites began cutting staff sizes in anticipation of reduced tenant management funding.

It is clear that tenant employment increased over the course of the demonstration at all sites as compared with the levels at the beginning. In addition, with the exception of the Jersey City sites where the HUD-recommended level of 25 percent had already been reached before or early in the demonstration, all sites surpassed that benchmark over the course of the program.[31]

The Jobs and the Target Population

Positions. The exact positions held by tenants varied widely among the tenant management sites. The array of jobs, however, can be grouped into five principal categories—core TMC management,

31. HUD encourages PHAs to hire tenants for available positions. It is considered desirable to have PHA tenants comprise at least 25 percent of the total PHA work force. See U.S. Department of Housing and Urban Development, "Upward Mobility of Low-Rent Public Housing Residents," Notice No. HM73-28 (LHA), November 28, 1973.

Table 7–12.   Distribution of Employment Categories by Tenant Management Site.

Employment Category	Jersey City A. Harry Moore	Jersey City Curries Woods	Louisville Iroquois	New Haven Que-View	New Orleans Calliope	Rochester Ashanti
			Sites			
Core TMC management[a]	x	x	x	x	x	x
Social service, recreational, educational, and other aides and assistants[b]	x	x	x	x	x	x
Clerical[c]	x	x	x	x	x	x
Security[d]	x	x	x	x	x	x
Maintenance[e]	x	x	x	x	x	x
Miscellaneous summer employment	x	x	x	x	x	x

a. Includes manager, assistant manager, lane or building managers, social service coordinator.
b. Includes housing assistant, social service aides and advisors, recreational aides, education assistants, youth coordinators, senior citizen coordinator, special program coordinators, laundry attendants, daycare workers, paint coordinator, TMC MOD liaison, MOD inspector, community activity workers, teacher aides, parent-child coordinator, mailroom aide.
c. Includes account clerk, clerk-typists, and desk clerks.
d. Includes security officers and aides.
e. Includes building maintenance workers, janitors, laborers, maintenance repairmen, firemen.
Source: Tenant Management Information System, Tenant Employment Survey, and MDRC files.

Table 7–13. Parameters of Tenant Employment.

Employment Category[a]	Number of Slots	Employees Number	Employees Percentage	Salary Range	Source of Funds for Salaries
Core TMC management	46	58	18	$5400–16,500	Demo. TPP, PHA
Social service, recreational, educational, and other assistants and aides	42	63	20	$2318– 8,800	Demo. TPP, Demo. MOD, CETA, non-Demo. TPP
Clerical	15	24	8	$5400– 9,775	PHA, CETA, non-Demo. TPP
Security	31	40	13	$6552– 8,920	Demo. TPP, CETA
Maintenance and construction[b]	74	128	41	$6772–16,429	PHA, Demo. TPP, Demo, MOD, CETA
Total	208	313	100	N/AP	N/AP

a. See notes to Table 7–12.
b. Includes tenants who were employed in connection with physical improvements to the sites.
N/AP – Not applicable.
Source: Tenant Management Information System and Tenant Employment Survey.

social services (recreational and educational aides) and other aides and assistants, clerical, security, and maintenance (see Tables 7–12 and 7–13).[32] With the exception of maintenance jobs in New Haven and security jobs in New Haven and New Orleans, tenants were found in every employment category at all sites.

Table 7–13 briefly summarizes the major parameters of tenant employment by job category during the demonstration. Of the 313 tenants employed, excluding tenants employed in the summer only, the largest percentage of tenants were employed in the maintenance category (41 percent). During the program, however, tenant employment in other job categories increased to the extent that, overall, the majority of tenants were employed in nonmaintenance areas, including 18 percent as core management staff and 20 percent as aides and assistants of some kind. Sixty-two percent of all jobs held by tenants were created during the demonstration period. The total number of job slots available was 208.

Salaries for the jobs held by tenants covered a very broad range — from an average annual salary of $16,000 for top management and maintenance positions to $2,000 for part-time aide and assistant positions of various types. Sources of funds for tenant salaries varied. Demonstration funding was used to support 56 percent of all tenants' salaries, with 85 percent of this coming from TPP monies and the remainder from MOD funds. Regular PHA funds were used to cover about 30 percent of salary costs, with CETA and miscellaneous other sources[33] each accounting for about 7 percent.

Employees. To assess the demographic characteristics of those residents securing jobs through tenant management, a questionnaire was administered to core TMC staff in the spring of 1979. Thirty-seven persons were interviewed out of the 58 who had ever held such positions. Because this small subsample represents only about 12 percent of all tenants employed at tenant management sites during the demonstration, it must be judged as more typical of tenants who responded to tenant management jobs per se than of all tenants who

32. Tables 7–12 and 7–13 do not include miscellaneous summer employment. All told, 112 tenants were included as summer employees. This group primarily included youths employed with CETA funding.

33. Some positions were funded by more than one source during the demonstration; the figures include these instances of multiple funding sources. Summer CETA employees are not included in these figures. "Miscellaneous and other sources" include nondemonstration TPP and MOD, Title XX, and other sources.

held any on-site job. Nevertheless, the survey does provide a profile of an important segment of resident employees.[34]

The profile of core TMC staff members revealed them to be females (89 percent), between 21 and 44 years of age (81 percent), heads of households (81 percent) with at least one child (89 percent), and high school graduates (84 percent). With regard to employment history, almost 60 percent had not had a regular job in the two years prior to employment, and 70 percent had received some of their income in the prior year from welfare benefits. The majority who reported holding regular jobs had been marginally employed and had received welfare and other income transfer benefits as supplements to their wages. In virtually every instance, accepting employment with the tenant management corporation represented an increase in salary for these residents. Given this fact, it is not surprising that many had left other jobs in order to accept employment with the tenant management corporation. Although increase in salary was undoubtedly a reason for doing so, these residents cited other factors such as reduced transportation costs, the ability to be near their families during the day, and the opportunity to perform work that would benefit their communities as important in their decision. In taking tenant management corporation jobs, these residents voluntarily assumed the risk that the program would be discontinued once the demonstration was over. Employment in tenant management markedly improved the situation of tenants surveyed. Only 22 percent reported receiving welfare benefits as additional income once they became employed.

Job Experience: Tenure, Turnover, and Post–Tenant Management Employment

Since resident employment at the tenant management sites was to some extent a temporary situation whose duration was dependent on the availability of funding, there was no real job security for employees. The overall turnover rate during the demonstration was 68 percent,[35] and among the TMC core management staff, the turnover

34. Excluding tenants in summer employment.
35. Summer employment excluded.

rate was 43 percent. It is difficult to put these rates in perspective, however, because an appropriate comparison is lacking, especially with turnover among regular public housing authority employees.

It was anticipated that the work experience gained by resident employees at the site during the demonstration could be a stepping stone to longer term work situations, but since a large percentage of employed tenants were still on the job at the demonstration's end, it was not possible to estimate this potential benefit. Information on a sample of 32 employees representing 16 percent of those who no longer held their original positions indicated that about two-thirds were still employed in some other position at the tenant management corporation site or elsewhere.

Tenant Management and Job Development

Tenant management can be viewed as a job development vehicle to counter some of the results of structural unemployment so evident in urban low-income communities. In this section, attention is therefore focused on the job development activities undertaken during the demonstration.

Job Creation. Of the 208 new positions that tenants filled during the demonstration, the majority fell in the categories of core TMC management, aides and assistants, and security. With minor exceptions, each site created a core tenant management staff of manager, assistant manager, building or lane managers, and a social services coordinator.[36]

The level of job creation varied among the TMC sites, however, with some, but not all, sites emphasizing the job creation potential of tenant management and using it as an opportunity to get as many residents as possible on the payroll. In doing so, while understanding that it might be difficult to sustain a relatively large work force once funds were exhausted, they seemed genuinely to have believed that

---

36. Except in New Haven, the tenant management corporation manager was not a created position, but one in which a tenant was substituted. New Haven also did not create a social services position. Although Louisville created four assistant manager positions, it did not add any lane managers or a social services coordinator; it chose instead to incorporate the responsibilities of these positions into the assistant manager's duties. In New Orleans, there was an assistant manager as well as a manager prior to the demonstration.

savings realized from improved management, when combined with outside funding, could sustain a large number of these jobs.

Rochester provides one example of a site where significant job creation took place in the core TMC management and security areas. Throughout most of the demonstration, Rochester's staff complement fluctuated between 16 and 22 full-time employees, although the site was the smallest in the demonstration. This is scarcely smaller than the staff of 21 fielded in New Orleans which, at 1,500 units, was the largest site. The size of Rochester's staff was large relative to that of New Orleans and other tenant management corporations primarily because of its substantial tenant security force (eight full-time members). Other sites either have not fielded a security force (New Haven and New Orleans) or have hired a combination of residents and nonresidents (A. Harry Moore and Curries Woods in Jersey City and Iroquois Homes in Louisville).

Job creation efforts in the two Jersey City sites and Louisville included jobs generated through the operation of an expanded social services program (reflected in the aides and assistants employment category). In Jersey City, it was understood that some positions were created to provide resident employment as much as to render services to the wider tenant community. Accordingly, the tenant management corporations at the Jersey City sites hired and supervised several tenant employees responsible for providing recreational, tutorial, and senior citizens' programs for their communities for the relatively short period that these programs operated. Although these employees were largely hourly workers at or near the minimum wage level and although their continued employment was dependent on uncertain funding, the created positions nevertheless provided some degree of financial support for the residents who were employed. In Louisville, an expansion of social services in the form of a new daycare facility provided the TMC with an opportunity to fill five full-time jobs as daycare workers. Each available position was filled by a tenant.

During the demonstration, most of the job creation efforts were supported by demonstration funds (TPP and MOD), although CETA funds supported some positions. It is desirable for the housing authorities to absorb the salary costs of created jobs into their regular operating budgets to the extent possible; it ensures the continuation of such jobs when special funds have been exhausted. This occurred to a limited extent. For example, in Rochester, the PHA absorbed into its regular operating budget the assistant manager, two lane managers, the social services director, and three of the eight security positions over the course of the demonstration. Similarly, the PHA in New Haven assumed a portion of the costs of the newly created manager and assistant manager positions. In New Orleans, the PHA absorbed the salary of the social services coordinator beginning in the last quarter of 1978. In Jersey City and in Louisville, none of the salary costs of TMC–created positions were incorporated in the PHA's operating budget during the demonstration. CETA funds were used largely to pay for summer jobs, primarily for youths (see Table 7–12). Other CETA positions (23 in all) provided employment for maintenance, security, and clerical workers, but all indications are that these jobs would have been available whether tenant management existed or not.

Postdemonstration support of created positions is an important issue if any sustained impact is to be realized from job creation efforts during the demonstration. The continuation of those jobs with some potential for permanence (mostly in the TMC core management, clerical, and security areas) requires alternative sources of funding once demonstration funds are exhausted. Options include increased operating receipts, absorption into the PHA operating budget, private monies, and possibly ongoing federal employment and training programs (CETA). Increased operating receipts are an unlikely prospect, especially in light of the concomitant decrease in federal subsidy that would take place pursuant to the dictates of the Performance Funding System. In some cases, the PHA can absorb some of the salaries for the created positions, but there is a limit to this given the precarious financial condition of many large urban PHAs. Private funds raised in Rochester did support one position during a part of the demonstration and are likely to continue after it ends, but although the other sites had several additional efforts underway to secure funds from private sources, none had been committed by the end of the demonstration.

Given the socioeconomic characteristics of the individuals who held these positions and the entrylevel nature of the positions and salaries (ranging from $2,318 part-time to $9,000 for the most part), public service employment under CETA (Title II(D) and VI) would seem the most logical source of support. During the demonstration period, however, little use was made of this potential funding source.[37]

Use of MOD Funds in Job Development. As Table 7–14 indicates, relatively few (28) tenants realized jobs as a consequence of the millions of dollars in MOD funds used for physical improvements at the sites. In fact, only seven or eight of these tenants worked directly on physical improvements; the remainder had jobs in the security, maintenance, and aides and assistants categories. For those who did work on MOD projects (in Louisville and New Orleans), the periods of employment ranged from 3 to 12 months. Louisville was most successful in this respect. For four workers who were hired by contractors doing on-site work, jobs lasted as long as a year while the replacement of roofs was being completed. There is no readily apparent reason for the underutilization of MOD projects as a source of tenant employment. Perhaps, however, the TMC was too busy with other problems surrounding MOD work to prevail upon contractors to hire tenants at least for laborer positions.

Overall Changes in Employment Patterns

The Urban Institute survey looked at the question of resident employment during the demonstration in a broader context, measuring the working status of residents overall. Between 1976 and 1979, there was a significant decrease at the tenant management sites in percentage of nonretired individuals in nonworking statuses. In addition, the percentage decrease was significantly greater at the tenant management sites than at the control projects.[38] Significantly larger

37. In Oklahoma City an agreement was reached between the TMC and the CETA prime sponsor to fund several positions using this mechanism, but the housing authority refused to allow it.

38. For, "% non-retired households who do not work, attend school or job-training," the gain score (1979 minus 1976) for the tenant management sites was significantly different from zero at the .10 level. For this same variable, the gain score for the tenant management sites was −12.6 (a decline) and the one for the control sites, 01.1; the difference (13.7) was significant at the .10 level. The significant differences emerged even though 80 percent of the tenants surveyed had lived at the tenant management sites at least two years. This fact suggests that although some of the difference may be accounted for by newer, higher income, better educated, and more skilled tenants, some of the change is also due to improvements among the longer term residents.

percentages of tenants were working in 1979 than in 1976, and the statistically significant improvement was maintained when demonstration sites were compared to the control projects.[39] Between 1976 and 1979 there was also a significant gain in average annual income at the tenant management sites ($1,239), but while a difference in gains was maintained between tenant management sites and control sites ($838), it was not statistically significant. Although it is not possible to attribute this change in employment patterns solely to the presence of tenant management, the TMC's role in job creation is responsible for at least a portion of this gain.

Summary

The demonstration was successful in increasing tenant employment levels beyond those in existence at the beginning of the program and exceeded the HUD recommendation regarding resident employment. The extent to which increased employment occurred varied with the particular job development strategy adopted by the sites.

The greatest job creation potential was realized in terms of the TMC core staff, which was the source of more job creation than any other employment category. In its expansion of on-site social services, the TMCs did succeed in providing employment for many residents, but many of these positions were short lived. Maintenance remained the most usual employment category for tenants, although the numbers of tenants employed in maintenance jobs decreased in proportion to other categories over the course of the demonstration.

The demonstration was successful in reaching its target population. Most of the subsample of tenant employees examined in this respect had not worked at a regular job in the two years prior to their TMC job and had been receiving welfare during the previous year. Success was also realized in the demonstration's impact on the

---

39. The gain score (1979 minus 1976) for tenant management sites for the percentage of tenants working either full-time or part-time was significantly different from zero at the .10 level. For this same variable, the gain score for the tenant management sites was .22, and the one for the control projects, −.01; the difference (.23) was significant at the .10 level. Although the changes were not statistically different, there were decreases at the tenant management sites between 1976 and 1979 in "average number of adults usually home between 9:00 A.M. and 6:00 P.M." and the "% households receiving income from welfare." The decreases were greater at the tenant management sites than at the control projects, although not significantly so.

Table 7–14. Tenant Employment: Utilization of MOD and CETA.

| | Funding Source | | | | | |
| | MOD | | | CETA | | |
Site	Number of Tenants	Employment Area/Position	Duration	Number of Tenants	Employment Area/Positions	Duration
Jersey City: A. Harry Moore	13	Security	1–2 mos.	95	Maintenance and recreation aides	Summer
Jersey City: Curries Woods	1	Laborer	20 mos.	2	Maintenance	N/A
Louisville: Iroquois	9	Laborers	3–12 mos.	5	Beautification program	Summer
	2	Community workers	N/A	8	Security	2–13 mos.
				2	Clerical	14 mos.
				1	Social service advisor	N/A
				1	MOD inspector	N/A
Total	11			17		

Table 7–14. continued

New Haven: Que-View	1	TMC MOD liaison	N/A	0	N/AP	N/AP
New Orleans: Calliope	2	Laborers	N/A	8	Beautification program	Summer
				2	Community workers	2–15 mos.
Total	2			10		
Rochester: Ashanti				4	Maintenance	Summer
				7	Maintenance	4–12 mos.
Total	0	N/AP	N/AP	11		
Total Tenants	28			135[a]		

a. Excluding tenants in summer employment programs, the total tenants employed using CETA funds is 23.

N/A – Not available.

N/AP – Not applicable.

Source: Tenant Employment Survey and Tenant Management Information System.

employment status of tenants with related reductions in the receipt of welfare. It is difficult to assess the extent to which employment during the demonstration eased the transition of former employees at the tenant management sites into the wider labor market because very limited information was available.

Little success was realized in generating resident employment through MOD projects. With regard to CETA, the TMCs largely played a deployment role.

During the demonstration, the securing of more stable funding sources for created jobs was limited. At three sites, the PHA supported wholly or in part some of the created positions during the latter part of the demonstration, and CETA funds were used at four of the sites (excluding summer employment). Private funds supported one position at one site.

On balance, the sites fared reasonably well in the amount of tenant employment that occurred during the demonstration. The real challenge that remains is sustaining those jobs still in existence at the end of the demonstration and ensuring that tenants continue to occupy those conventional PHA on-site jobs that were obtained during the program.

TENANTS' SATISFACTION AND ASSESSMENT: TENANT MANAGEMENT AND THE RESIDENT COMMUNITY

The concept of tenant management and the goals of the demonstration are inextricably linked to the resident community, and tenant management was seen as having a variety of purposes with regard to this constituency. Through the performance of management functions, the tenant management board and staff were to deliver appropriate services in an efficient manner to ensure that their fellow tenants were provided with decent, safe, and sanitary housing. The TMC was also seen as a vehicle for soliciting and interjecting residents' input on matters of importance to the housing community, as well as gaining their cooperation in achieving and maintaining improvements that would enhance the vitality of the community physically, socially, and economically. Finally, for some, the TMC was seen as a more effective representative of the tenant body in dealing with the PHA.

Any discussion of tenant management must include efforts directed by the TMC toward its constituency, the resident community. Although indicators of good performance such as rent collection rate and tenant employment may improve, a dissatisfied constituency can threaten the consolidation of such gains. At least on a conceptual level, any efforts by the TMC to improve project conditions and maintain that improvement must be met with a positive or, at minimum, a neutral response from the community. In this section, tenant management community relations efforts and other tenants' experiences with, perceptions of, and assessments of the TMC are discussed.[40]

Tenants' Experience with and Response to Tenant Management: Experiences and Perceptions

A part of the rationale for tenant management included the expectation that somehow it would differ from PHA management because of the tenant status of the TMC board and staff members. In addition, as previously noted, the management policies implemented by the TMC and the management style adopted by it were much more vigilant than the PHA management. Interviews with tenants at the tenant management projects and their control counterparts have borne this out in a rather cogent fashion, as Table 7–15 indicates.

The TMC's vigilance in preventing apartment abuse and maintaining appliances and other aspects of individual units in good repair is suggested by the statistically significant differences between the tenant management sites and their counterparts in the first two items in Table 7–15. In comparison to tenants at the control sites, tenant management residents reported a significant increase in apartment inspections by management; in addition, significantly more residents of the demonstration sites in 1979 than in 1976 reported that man-

40. Information in this section is primarily based on tenant surveys conducted by the Urban Institute in 1976 (baseline) and in 1979 (follow-up). One hundred and eighty-one randomly selected residents were interviewed at the six tenant management projects, plus 395 residents at 18 control projects. Comparisons between the tenant management group and the control group were made using gain scores—that is, the difference between the absolute value of a variable in 1976 and 1979. A .10 percent level of significance is used throughout the discussion as the statistical criterion against which to determine whether change occurred and whether there was a difference between the tenant management and control sites. For further details on the Urban Institute surveys, see Appendix A.

Table 7–15. Residents' Experiences and Perceptions of Management.

Residents' Experiences and Perceptions	Average Gain Scores (1979 minus 1976)			Average Actual Scores (1976)	
	Tenant Management	Control	Tenant Management-Control Difference	Tenant Management	Control
Percentage of residents reporting someone from management showed them how things worked when they moved in	19.10[c]	2.70	16.40[d]	51.6	67.7
Number of times project manager or staff inspects apartment[a]	0.30	−0.20	0.50[d]	0.6	0.8
Residents' perception of how strictly management enforces rent collection rules[b]	0.12	−0.10	0.22[d]	0.69	0.85
Residents' perception of the strictness of management[b]	0.09[c]	−0.02	0.11[d]	0.33	0.40
Percentage of residents believing management or management's staff is the best contact to get some action on a complaint	−4.30	−13.20	8.90	69.50	80.40
Percentage of households knowing the name of the management person to contact in case there is a complaint	−0.90	−8.40	7.50	60.70	65.00

a. Average number of times per year.
b. 1 = strict; 0 = not strict.
c. Difference between 1979 and 1976 scores significantly different from zero at the .10 level.
d. Significant at the .10 level.

Source: Suzanne B. Loux and Robert Sadacca, "Analysis of Changes at Tenant Management Demonstration Projects." Working Paper no. 1335 (Washington, D.C.: Urban Institute, 1980).

agement had showed them how things worked when they moved into their apartments. Moreover, both of these increases were significantly greater than that at the nondemonstration sites. The firmer hand of the TMC is illustrated by the tenant management residents' perception of greater strictness on the part of management. In analyses of public housing data collected by the Urban Institute in 1973, 1974, 1976, and 1977, the variable measuring residents' perception of management strictness has consistently shown a strong positive relationship to management performance.

Not only did the tenant management projects report a significant increase in strictness between 1976 and 1979, but their gain scores in 1979 were significantly greater than that of the control sites.[41] In fact, while the tenant management sites showed an increase in strictness, the controls showed a decrease. The tenant management sites' positive showing on this indicator may very well be a prelude to better performance than that evidenced within the short time frame of the demonstration.

Compared to these positive indications of the way in which residents view TMC management, the TMC seems to have experienced less success in making management more accessible and responsive to the tenants at large. There were no significant differences between 1976 and 1979 at the tenant management sites or between the tenant management and control sites in terms of tenants' believing that project management staff were the best people to contact to get action on a complaint or knowing the name of the management person to contact in case there was a complaint.[42]

Perceptions of Improvements in Management Functions.   An important related question is whether the TMC's more vigilant and stringent style was accompanied by improvements in the performance of management functions as perceived by the tenants. Tenants at both the tenant management sites and the control projects were asked in 1979 whether any change had occurred over the last two years in the

41. Strictness was in terms of management generally (1976 versus 1979 and TMC versus controls) and rent collection rules specifically (TMC versus controls).

42. Interestingly enough, there was also no statistically significant difference between the tenant management project managers and the control project managers in the increase in the number of households they knew by name and sight, but there was a larger increase (nonsignificant) at the tenant management sites than at the control sites between 1976 and 1979.

performance of selected management functions. Tenants at the demonstration sites were then asked how much of the change was due to tenants taking over management.

As Table 7-16 indicates, tenant management residents perceived little change over the two-year period and little, if any, change attributable to the tenant management corporation. In addition, the amount of change perceived did not differ from that seen at the control sites. However, if the analysis is limited to the four tenant management sites that most closely approximated the demonstration model (A. Harry Moore in Jersey City, Louisville, New Orleans, and Rochester), a somewhat more positive picture emerges. Tenants at these four sites reported significant improvements in social services and management–tenant relations, and when these sites were compared to their control counterparts, the demonstration sites fared significantly better in the area of security. At the four tenant management sites, the residents reported no improvement in security, while tenants at their control counterparts viewed security as worsening over the past two years. This indicates that in the absence of the demonstration, conditions might also have deteriorated at the tenant management sites.[43] Relevant experiences were in line with the perception of no change at the tenant management sites, with no significant changes perceived in vandalism, burglary, personal victimization, or the addition of security devices to apartments by tenants.[44]

Satisfaction with Project Conditions. Perhaps the acid test of tenant management from the tenants' perspective is their satisfaction with project conditions regardless of what they feel about management style or performance. This perception of the importance of tenant satisfaction was shared by the demonstration's sponsors, who saw as one of the program's major purposes the evaluation of tenant man-

43. Suzanne B. Loux and Robert Sadacca, "Analysis of Changes at Tenant Management Demonstration Projects," Working Paper #1335 (Washington, D.C.: Urban Institute, 1980). For the four tenant management sites, the "improvement score" for security was 0, while for their 16 controls it was −.2 (a difference of .2, significant at the .10 level).

44. No significant differences in estimate of annual cost of vandalism per unit; percent of apartments broken into, vandalized, or with personal victimization; or percent of households that have added special locks and alarms when tenant management sites' improvement scores are compared to zero or when tenant management sites' scores are compared to controls.

Table 7–16.   Tenants' Perception of Improvement in the Performance of Management Functions.

Management Function	Improvement Score[a]			
	Tenant Management	Control	Tenant Management-Control[b] Difference	Change Due[c] To TMC
Management	.06	.01	.05	.06
Maintenance	.04	–.11	.15	–.01
Security	–.06	–.21	.15	.00
Social services	.02	.00	.02	.02
Tenant–management relations	.07	–.02	.09	.01
Tenant selection	–.15	–.15	.00	–.07

a. Tenants were asked whether performance in six management areas ("management functions") had gotten better, stayed about the same, or gotten worse during the two preceding years; 1 = better; 0 = same; –1 = worse (the original scores were: 2 = better, 1 = same, 0 = worse, but were changed to reflect negative (i.e. losses) scores).

b. TM minus control: The control projects' improvement score mean was subtracted from the Tenant Management projects' improvement score mean. A positive result indicates that the Tenant Management projects improved more (or declined less) than did the control projects. The extreme and midpoint scores are +2.00 = TM projects' improvement score averaged +1.00 (all better), and the control projects' improvement score averaged –1.00 (all worse); 0.00 = no difference between TM and Control project improvement scores; –2.00 = TM projects' improvement score averaged –1.00 (all worse), and the control projects' improvement score averaged +1.00 (all better).

c. Tenants were asked whether they thought the change (better or worse) was due to the tenants taking over management; +1.00 = change was for the better and attributed to TMC; 0.00 = no change, or change was not attributed to TMC; –1.00 = change was for the worse and attributed to TMC.

Source: Suzanne B. Loux and Robert Sadacca, "Analysis of Changes at Tenant Management Demonstration Projects," Working Paper #1335 (Washington, D.C.: Urban Institute, 1980).

agement as a means of increasing residents' satisfaction with their housing.

There were consistent positive trends at the tenant management sites in all areas of tenant satisfaction when 1976 scores were compared to 1979 scores and when the tenant management projects were compared to the controls (Table 7–17). That is, there were increases in satisfaction between 1976 and 1979 at the tenant management sites and greater increases than there were at the control projects. In four areas (condition of units, management, maintenance, and safety and security), the 1979 scores at the tenant management sites were significantly better than the 1976 scores. Despite these positive indications, in only two of seven areas of project conditions (management and recreational facilities) did the difference between the tenant management and control project gain scores reach statistical significance.

These positive trends have appeared in spite of the perception at all six tenant management sites that there had been little change in the performance of important management functions over the two-year period. Additional analyses using composite gain scores of satisfaction with project conditions in general yielded findings that tenant satisfaction increased more at the tenant management projects than at the control projects. An average of the first six variables in Table 7–17 indicated a significantly greater increase in the level of satisfaction at the tenant management sites.[45]

Community Relations

The TMCs used a variety of techniques to solicit their constituencies' support and cooperation, to gain input concerning residents' desires and attitudes, and to inform tenants about the TMC and its decisions. These techniques included meetings for the entire resident community or some geographical portion of it, newsletters, flyers, home visits, and more informal encounters with tenants by TMC board and staff members in the course of going about their daily business. Surveys were also used occasionally to obtain information. For example, it was through a survey that the Rochester TMC learned

45. See Suzanne B. Loux and Robert Sadacca, "Analysis of Changes at Tenant Management Demonstration Projects, Working Paper #1335 (Washington, D.C.: Urban Institute, 1980).

Table 7–17. Resident Satisfaction with Project Conditions.

Area of Project Conditions	Average Gain Scores (1979 minus 1976)			Average Actual Scores (1976)	
	Tenant Management	Control	Tenant Management–Control Difference	Tenant Management	Control
Satisfaction with neighbors[a]	.05	−.01	.06	.59	.62
Evaluation of condition of units[b]	.08[c]	.00	.08	.68	.74
Satisfaction with management[a]	.06[c]	−.04	.10[d]	.53	.65
Satisfaction with maintenance[a]	.03	−.03	.06	.59	.66
Satisfaction with cleanliness of buildings and grounds[a]	.05	−.06	.11	.43	.57
Satisfaction with safety and security[a]	.08[c]	.00	.08	.35	.44
Satisfaction with project recreational facilities[a]	.12	−.03	.15[d]	.20	.30

a. 1 = satisfied; 0 = not satisfied.

b. 1 = good; 0 = poor.

c. Difference between 1979 and 1976 scores significantly different from zero at the .10 level.

d. Significant at the .10 level.

Source: Suzanne B. Loux and Robert Sadacca, "Analysis of Changes at Tenant Management Demonstration Projects," Working Paper #1335 (Washington, D.C.: Urban Institute, 1980).

that a proposed daycare center would be underutilized and that funds would be better spent for the construction of a community center.

Social, recreational, educational, and special events provided vehicles for publicizing the TMCs, gaining resident support, meeting community needs, and raising money. The sites sponsored such activities as parties, dances, fairs, bingo evenings, flea markets, a celebration of Black History Week, outings for children, and Thanksgiving dinners for the elderly. Most of the TMCs organized at least one sitewide clean-up day and launched other programs to improve the physical appearance of the development, such as beautification campaigns. In addition, the TMCs at several of the sites ran health, recreational, consumer, and tutorial programs.

Knowledge of the TMC. The tenant management demonstration brought a much greater awareness of site activities among residents than was in evidence at the control sites. Almost 75 percent of the tenants surveyed at the demonstration sites knew of the existence of a tenant organization at their development. Of those, 86 percent knew the TMC by name, and 30 percent knew the name of the chairperson. By contrast, at the control sites, only 32 percent of the residents surveyed knew of the existence of a tenant organization, and of those, 30 percent knew the name of the chairperson of that organization.

Participation in tenant-organization-sponsored events was considerably greater at the demonstration sites because of this increased awareness. For example, 36 percent of the residents at the tenant management sites had attended a TMC meeting. At the control sites, on the other hand, only 15 percent had attended any meetings at all. For nonmeeting events such as social gatherings, fairs, or what one board member characterized as "giveaways," 37 percent of the residents surveyed at the demonstration sites said they had attended, while only 9 percent of the control sites' tenants reported attending such events.

When asked about the tenant organization's responsibilities, the tenant management site residents most frequently mentioned managing the project (33 percent), taking care of maintenance (39 percent), and handling complaints (30 percent). There was less familiarity with many of the specific aspects of the TMC's management role such as setting project rules and regulations, hiring project employees, selecting new tenants, handling rent delinquencies, and eviction of tenants. Awareness of these responsibilities ranged from 15 to 5 percent.[46]

In spite of the substantial difference between involvement by tenants at the demonstration sites as compared to the control sites, board and staff members still felt that the community was not sufficiently active or, when active, was negative. A few TMC board and staff members mentioned the lack of visible improvements at the sites and the residents' suspicion that meetings would be "all talk and no action" as possible reasons for this.

Evaluation of the TMC

According to the documentation interviews, most board and staff members felt that the attitudes of other tenants toward tenant management were mixed, ranging from active support through neutrality and indifference to active opposition. They did not consider the latter to be a widespread problem, but rather a specific reaction to the increased strictness of tenant management by residents who were violating project rules and fearful of being discovered—for example, in housing a person not listed on the lease.

However, opposition with accompanying hostility also occurred in situations other than those involving a single rule-breaking tenant. At all sites, the TMCs encountered dissident factions who sought to mobilize other tenants against the TMC and to contest the TMC's authority through appeals to the PHA and, at least in one case, to HUD officials. Over time, most of the TMC boards managed to isolate and counter the dissidents and in the process to establish their own legitimacy and become stronger, more effective groups. However, at one site, dissident residents were instrumental in toppling the first TMC board and continued to attack the subsequent board for the remainder of the demonstration.

In general, the Urban Institute survey reports that residents of the demonstration sites were satisfied with tenant management. Table 7–18 summarizes findings in this regard. Forty-seven percent of the tenants who knew about the TMC felt that it was able to get things done, while 33 percent thought it did not. Fifty percent felt that the

---

46. Percentages based on a total number of tenants who knew of a tenant organization ($N = 132$), which includes 32 percent of the respondents who did not know what the TMC did.

Table 7-18. TMC Tenants' Evaluation of the TMC.[a]

Tenant's Evaluations	Average or Percentage of Respondents	Number of Respondents
Overall		
Residents believing TMC is able to get things done		
Yes	47.0	(62)
No	32.6	(43)
Don't know	20.4	(27)
Total	100.0	(132)
Residents believing TMC has made things better for		
Most of the tenants	26.5	(35)
Some of the tenants	23.5	(31)
Few of the tenants	23.5	(31)
None of the tenants	9.8	(13)
Don't know	16.7	(22)
Total	100.0	(132)
TMC versus Old Tenant Organization		
Residents believing TMC represents the tenants		
Better than old tenant organization	28.0	(37)
Same as old tenant organization	27.3	(36)
Worse than old tenant organization	18.1	(24)
Don't know	26.5	(35)
Total	100.0	(132)
Average Score[b]	1.13	(97)
TMC versus PHA		
Residents who believe TMC is managing project		
Better than PHA	26.5	(35)
Same as PHA	34.1	(45)
Worse than PHA	22.0	(29)
Don't know	17.4	(23)
Total	100.0	(132)
Average Score[b]	1.06	(109)

a. Limited to respondents who knew there was a TMC/tenant organization (N–132).

b. 2 = better; 1 = same; 0 = worse.

Source: Suzanne B. Loux and Robert Sadacca, "Analysis of Changes at Tenant Management Demonstration Projects," Working Paper #1335 (Washington, D.C.: Urban Institute, 1980).

TMC had made things better for at least some of the tenants, while 10 percent felt that no tenants had benefited. The majority also felt that the TMC was doing as well or better than former tenant organizations in representing tenants (55 percent) and the PHA in managing the project (61 percent). Moreover, on the average, the tenants felt that the TMC did a slightly better job (1.13) of representing the tenants than the former tenant organization and a slightly better job (1.06) than the PHA in managing the project.[47]

Summary

A generally positive picture of the TMC emerges from an examination of its performance from the tenants' perspective. Although little improvement in the performance of specific management functions was perceived, the increase in satisfaction with overall management was significantly greater for tenant management residents than for their control counterparts. Moreover, management at the demonstration sites was seen as having become stricter, a characteristic strongly and positively correlated with improved management performance — a good omen for the future. Tenants at the demonstration sites were much more aware of the tenant organization's existence, and the level of their participation was greater than at the control sites. Evaluation of the TMC produced a fairly positive assessment of it — approximately half of the tenants felt that it was able to get things done, and on the average, it was rated as doing a somewhat better job than the previous tenant organization and the PHA.

47. Refers to the "average score" where 2 = better and 1 = same.

8 COSTS OF TENANT MANAGEMENT

The experience of the National Tenant Management Demonstration, like that of its precursors, indicates that tenant management is more expensive than conventional housing management. Increased budgetary outlays at all of the demonstration sites are due primarily to increased site personnel. Whereas before the demonstration the typical staff at a given site consisted of a project manager plus a secretary, the tenant management corporation buttressed this administrative core with an assistant manager and lane managers and often added social services staff and security officers as well. The salaries and fringe benefits paid to these employees, along with the cost of technical assistance, account for most of the incremental cost of the program.

This chapter analyzes the costs of tenant management at each of the demonstration sites. Two sets of data are presented. The first of these compares the actual expenditures for each site throughout the three-year demonstration with an estimate of the costs that would have been incurred over the period had the housing authority continued to provide its former level of management services. The actual costs include heavy start-up expenses associated with technical assistance and board and staff training. This first comparison, then, shows the incremental cost of establishing and operating a tenant management corporation.

The second data set shows the actual cost of operating the three functioning tenant management corporations for which data were available (Ashanti in Rochester, Calliope in New Orleans, and A. Harry Moore in Jersey City) for a year-long period after the signing of the management contracts, along with an estimate of the costs the housing authorities would have incurred during the same time period for the pre–tenant management level of services.[1] By excluding start-up expenses, this comparison gives a more accurate picture of the additional annual cost of operating an ongoing tenant management corporation.

The analysis does not deal with the benefits of tenant management at any length, although increases in revenue beyond those that would be expected as a result of inflation are discussed insofar as they offset increased costs. A thorough cost–benefit analysis was not planned primarily because of the difficulty of measuring and assigning monetary value to such important benefits as increased resident employment, greater tenant satisfaction, and improved monitoring of MOD contracts.

The chapter opens with a discussion of the methodology used in the analysis. Then the costs of tenant management are presented for each site to identify the items that accounted for increased or reduced costs to the housing authority and the uses to which special demonstration funds (HUD TPP monies and Ford Foundation grants) were put. The chapter ends with some cross-site comparisons about the costs of the program.

THE METHODOLOGY OF THE COST ANALYSIS

As noted above, the analysis compares the actual costs of tenant management with the estimated costs that would have been incurred had the housing authority continued to provide management at the predemonstration service level. Two major tasks, then, were to arrive at reasonable costs projections and to determine what actual costs were.

---

1. Because the Housing Authority of Louisville failed to establish project-based budgeting during the course of the demonstration, the expenditures reported for Iroquois represent a proration of all housing authority costs, based on the fact that Iroquois' 584 units make up 14 percent of all units under HAL's aegis.

Estimating the Cost of Continued PHA Management

Before the demonstration began, the accounting system used by the participating housing authorities reported revenues and expenditures for the housing authority as a whole, rather than on a site-by-site basis. It was therefore necessary to find a method of determining what proportion of total housing authority expenditures the demonstration site accounted for over time as well as at the outset of the demonstration. Because there was no easy alternative available, PHA personnel suggested using a proration based on number of units. That is, the number of units in the demonstration development was divided by the total number of units under housing authority management; the resulting percentage, applied to total housing authority expenditures during the 12-month base period, yielded the base period dollar expenditures attributable to the demonstration site.[2]

This procedure has clear deficiencies: it does not take into account such crucial factors as the age and type of the development, its state of repair, or the nature of the resident population (a family development is expected to incur more "wear and tear" and higher costs than projects for the elderly). On the other hand, use of the proration procedure was recommended by its conceptual clarity, as well as by the fact that four of the six housing authorities had not developed alternative proration formulas by the end of the three-year period. Because the Jersey City and Rochester housing authorities devised their own methods for allocating total expenditures to individual projects, those procedures were adopted for the cost analysis in the cases of the A. Harry Moore, Curries Woods, and Ashanti TMCs.

Once an allocation method had been devised, it was necessary to develop a means of projecting base costs using a reasonable set of inflation factors. An investigation of possible methods was undertaken, and the inflation factors decided on are those used in HUD's Performance Funding System (PFS) to determine operating subsidy allocations for local housing authorities.[3] Computed each

2. The base period was the most recent 12-month period prior to (or, in the case of New Haven, overlapping) the demonstration period for which the housing authority reported annual costs. Base periods, therefore, varied depending on when the housing authorities began their fiscal years.

3. U.S. Department of Housing and Urban Development, *Low-Income Housing Program—PHA Owned Rental Housing, Performance Funding System* (Washington, D.C. HUD-52723D, annual), Appendix 13, Table 4.

year for metropolitan areas and counties, they are based on U.S. Census Bureau surveys of local government salaries (excluding teachers' salaries).

These inflation factors were applied to all housing authority line items except utilities and nonroutine expenditures. Because of exceptional inflation in the utilities costs and the unpredictable nature of nonroutine expenditures, actual, rather than projected, costs for utilities were figured into the total estimate. By definition, nonroutine expenditures (such as the emergency purchase of a new boiler) could not be projected with much accuracy; nonroutine expenses of $250,000 one year could shrink to a fraction of that amount the next. Here, too, actual costs, not projections, were used.

Determining Actual Costs

Monies available to the sites during the demonstration came from three funding sources—the housing authority operating budget; the special demonstration allocation, which came from HUD TPP funds;[4] and small supplementary amounts made available from foundation funds.[5] Expenditures charged to the PHA's operating budget were drawn from quarterly data reports submitted by the sites as part of the Tenant Management Information System. The data submitted were verified for accuracy and adjusted where appropriate.[6]

Demonstration monies received through TPP were to be spent for activities that would improve the economic and social conditions of

4. The award of TPP monies to housing authorities is a part of the basic HUD appropriations process. These funds are not allocated automatically by formula; instead, they go to specially selected sites, including those chosen for participation in the National Tenant Management Demonstration.

5. Modernization expenditures are excluded from this analysis. Although these represent costs incurred during the demonstration, they are not costs of tenant management as such. The use of MOD monies is discussed in some detail in Chapter 7.

6. MDRC fiscal and information systems staff visited Jersey City, New Orleans, and Rochester and compared in some detail financial and management performance data for the four tenant management sites with underlying books of accounts; internal housing authority fiscal reports; and monthly occupancy, vacancy, and rent records. In general, the information reported to MDRC was found to be fairly accurate; where there were errors, these were verified with the responsible housing authority official, and appropriate changes were made in the tables used for this chapter. In addition, data for Louisville and New Haven were spot tested in house using previously published reports as a reference. No data verification were undertaken for Oklahoma City.

the developments, such as special social services and tenant education programs, and for the salaries of tenant management staff. Special demonstration expenditures were reported in requisitions for additional funds that the sites submitted quarterly through MDRC to the HUD offices. The categories for reporting these expenditures were somewhat different than the categories used by the housing authorities in their budget reports. One task of the analysis was to fit special demonstration budget line items into the housing authority classifications in order to give a clearer picture of the ways in which these monies were used in conjunction with housing authority funds. With the exception of expenditures for technical assistance, this could generally be done with little difficulty.

The sites were required to turn over 30 percent of their special demonstration allocations to MDRC. These funds were used primarily to pay for the costs of technical assistance and training provided at the sites. Most of this cost was contracted by MDRC to individual consultants or to McCormack, Baron and Associates, but some technical assistance and training was provided by MDRC field staff. To a lesser extent, these funds also went toward the cost of monitoring, research, and administration. In this chapter the special demonstration costs that are reported include the funds kept by the sites plus the portion of the funds received by MDRC for technical assistance and training.

MDRC made about $90,000 of its grant from the Ford Foundation available to the sites for expenses that could not be paid for by the housing authorities and were probably not reimbursable under HUD funding regulations. These funds covered such items as stipends for board members, babysitters' fees, reimbursement for telephone calls, and social activities. The demonstration projects used these funds in fairly similar ways, and variations by site are not discussed. In the accompanying tables, these are labeled administrative costs and are added in with the demonstration expenditures from TPP funds.

Some of these expenses could probably be dispensed with in a "no frills" tenant management budget. But others were important morale boosters and eased the financial burden that participation in tenant management would otherwise have imposed on people with limited discretionary income. In any event, expenditures charged to this grant constituted a minuscule fraction—no more than 2.5 percent—of total incremental costs at any site.

THE INCREMENTAL COST OF ESTABLISHING THE TMC

A. Harry Moore (Jersey City)

The Jersey City Housing Authority has developed a method for allocating total housing authority costs to specific sites. According to the housing authority's formula, different allocation proportions are used for different line items, with such factors as the development's age, the total number of units, the number of bedrooms, and the number of children in the resident population taken into account.

By this reckoning, A. Harry Moore, a 25-year-old, high-rise development with (as of September 30, 1977) almost 1,300 children among its 600 households, accounted for 18 percent of all housing authority expenditures in the fiscal year ending March 31, 1976. These base costs were then inflated by the HUD–approved factors— 8 percent for the 1976–1977 fiscal year (6.4 multiplied by 1.25 to cover the three months between the end of the housing authority's fiscal year and the beginning of the demonstration); 7.1 percent for the 1977–1978 fiscal year; and 6.1 percent for the 1978–1979 fiscal year. The cost of continued housing authority management at the predemonstration level of services is thus projected at $4,156,000 for the three-year demonstration period, as seen in the first column of Table 8–1.

Housing Authority Funds. The second column of the table shows that the Jersey City Housing Authority reported its actual expenditures for A. Harry Moore at $4,807,000 over the same three years. Hence, under tenant management, the housing authority spent about $651,000 or 16 percent more than it would have had it continued to manage the site at the same level of service provision. Increases over projected levels were marked in most line item categories, especially administration and general expenses. The percentage increase over the model is highest for tenant services because at the beginning of the demonstration the housing authority decided to grant developments the full amount of HUD tenant services dollars to which they were entitled, rather than only a part of that amount. The bulk of this increment in housing authority costs was borne during the second two years of the demonstration.

Table 8-1. Comparison of Estimated Cost of PHA Management and Actual Cost of Tenant Management, July 1, 1976–June 30, 1979, Jersey City—A. Harry Moore.

Expense Item	Projected PHA Cost, Pre–TM Services ($000)	Actual Tenant Management Costs			Total Incremental Cost ($000)	Percentage Increase (Decrease)
		PHA Funds ($000)	Special Demonstration/ TPP Funds ($000)	Total ($000)		
Administration	508	769	275	1,044	536	105.5
General expenses	286	468	19	487	201	70.3
Tenant service	3	21	9	30	27	900.0
Utilities	2,268	2,268	0	2,268	0	0
Maintenance	1,075	1,265	0	1,265	190	17.7
Protection	0	0	48	48	48	N/AP
Total routine expenses	4,140	4,791	351	5,142	1,002	24.2
Technical assistance	0	0	94	94	94	N/AP
Other nonroutine expenses	16	16	1	17	1	6.3
Total operating expenses	4,156	4,807	446[a]	5,253	1,097	26.4
Total rental income	1,776	1,760	N/AP	1,760	16	
Net operating expenses	2,300	3,047	446	3,493	1,112	

a. Includes $15,000 in discretionary funds made available by MDRC for otherwise uncovered expenditures.

N/AP—not applicable.

Source: Quarterly Tenant Management Information System reports and TPP fund requests.

Special Demonstration Expenditures. Of the $431,000 in special demonstration funds out of TPP that went for program operations, over two-thirds went to pay the salaries of tenants employed by the tenant management corporation on its administrative, social services, and security staffs and to subsidize the salaries of a number of central office housing authority employees who spent time on the program.[7] Technical assistance costs at A. Harry Moore were relatively low because the housing authority liaison to the tenant management corporation performed these duties throughout the demonstration. Thus, the $94,000 reported in technical assistance costs covers a partial allocation of the time of MDRC field representatives, along with the fees paid to McCormack, Baron and Associates, who provided ongoing training throughout the demonstration.

Total Incremental Cost. The fourth and fifth columns of Table 8–1 show that the total cost of operations at A. Harry Moore came to $5,253,000 and that the total incremental cost of operations at the site was $1,097,000. Well over half this cost went for personnel, both central office and on site. The proportion of incremental costs allocated to technical assistance, 8.6 percent, was the lowest of all the demonstration sites. The additional costs represent an increase of 26.4 percent over the entire three years of the demonstration.

Rental Income and Net Operating Expenses. Expenditures cover one side of the cost ledger; revenues fill the other. The latter, and their impact on net incremental operating expenses, are reported below the double line in Table 8–1.

Inflation can be expected to result in increases in rental income as well as in expenditures. As tenants receive salary and wage hikes, or cost of living increases in their welfare grants, these are reflected in higher rents. The projection assumed that rent revenues would rise at the same rate as costs, and the same HUD inflation factors were applied to the base rent. By these means, it was estimated that A. Harry Moore would generate $1,776,000 in rents over the three-year period. The actual rent collected—$1,760,000—fell slightly short of that mark. This shortfall of $16,000 should be factored in when calculating the net incremental cost of the demonstra-

---

7. In addition, $15,000 in monies made available to the site by MDRC were spent for administrative purposes. See earlier discussions.

tion. When this is done, the net cost of operations at the site is $1,112,000.[8]

Curries Woods (Jersey City)

As might be expected, analysis of costs at the Curries Woods TMC yields results similar to those at A. Harry Moore. There are two chief differences: Curries Woods incurred higher technical assistance costs, and it was less successful than its sister site in generating rental income.

Curries Woods is five years younger than A. Harry Moore and larger by some 50 units. Using the same base period as for A. Harry Moore (the fiscal year ending March 31, 1976), and inflating line item expenditures by the same HUD–approved factors, the projected cost of continued housing authority management at Curries Woods over the three years of the demonstration was $4,185,000—about $30,000 more than the comparable estimate for A. Harry Moore (see Table 8–2).

---

8. Several alternative methods for estimating inflation-related increases in tenants' incomes were tested. HUD, in a computer model used to determine the size of requests for congressional allocations, assumes that, nationwide, tenants' incomes will rise by 6 percent per year (personal communication, HUD staff member, 5/6/80). If this assumption is followed, then rental income at A. Harry Moore can be projected at $1,748,000, and the net incremental cost of operations drops to $1,085,000, or 2.5 percent below the $1,112,000 shown in the table.

Increases in the OMB poverty guidelines for a nonfarm family of four were also employed as a gauge of inflation. The rates of increase were 6.4 percent for the period 1976–1977; 6 percent for 1977–1978; and 8.1 percent for 1978–1979 (MDRC calculations based on OMB figures). Using these indexes, the projected rental income at A. Harry Moore would be $1,789,000, and the net incremental cost of operations would be $1,789,000 or 1.3 percent more than the net incremental cost obtained by using PFS inflation rates.

The decision to use PFS inflation factors to project increases in rental incomes as well as costs was based on the fact that these more accurately reflect local variations in the cost of living than do the other indicators examined. Appendix Table B–1 shows the projected rental income and the net incremental cost of operations obtained by using PFS inflation factors and the two sets of alternative assumptions. With the exception of Calliope, the net incremental costs obtained under the other two sets of assumptions fall between −3.7 and +1.3 percent of the costs reported in this chapter. The Calliope case can be explained by a set of unusual circumstances—the low total operating expenses incurred by the site, its success in securing rent revenues, and the fact that PFS inflation factors for New Orleans are higher than the alternative measures of inflation.

Table 8-2.   Comparison of Estimated Cost of PHA Management and Actual Cost of Tenant Management, July 1, 1976–June 30, 1979, Jersey City—Curries Woods.

Expense Item	Projected PHA Cost, Pre-TM Services ($000)	Actual Tenant Management Costs			Total Incremental Cost ($000)	Percentage Increase (Decrease)
		PHA Funds ($000)	Special Demonstration/ TPP Funds ($000)	Total ($000)		
Administration	545	821	212	1,033	488	89.5
General expenses	308	642	6	648	340	110.4
Tenant service	3	19	5	24	21	700.0
Utilities	2,253	2,252	0	2,252	0	0
Maintenance	1,053	1,181	0	1,181	128	12.2
Protection	0	0	47	47	47	N/AP
Total routine expenses	4,161	4,915	270	5,185	1,024	24.6
Technical assistance	0	0	133	133	133	N/AP
Other nonroutine expenses	24	24	2	26	2	8.3
Total operating expenses	4,185	4,939	405[a]	5,344	1,159	27.7
Total rental income	1,905	1,817	N/AP	1,817	88	
Net operating expenses	2,280	3,122	405	3,527	1,247	

a. Includes $12,000 in discretionary funds made available by MDRC for otherwise uncovered expenditures.

N/AP—not applicable.

Source: Quarterly Tenant Management Information System reports and TPP fund requests.

Housing Authority Funds. The housing authority reported its total management expenditures at the site as $4,939,000. Again, the preponderance of the $754,000 or 18 percent, increase is accounted for by administrative costs and general expenses; again, too, the housing authority sustained the largest part of this increase in the second and third years of the demonstration, rather than at the outset.

Special Demonstration Expenditures. Special demonstration funds were spent in similar ways at Curries Woods and A. Harry Moore, with the largest part of the allocation going toward housing authority and tenant management staff salaries. However, technical assistance costs at Curries Woods were a good deal higher than those at its companion site. Although at the outset of the demonstration the housing authority liaison functioned as technical assistant, this arrangement proved unsatisfactory, and thereafter, MDRC contracted with two successive individuals to provide technical assistance to the ailing tenant management corporation on a part-time or full-time basis. The $133,000 in technical assistance expenditures shown in Table 8–2 includes their fees, along with part of the costs of MDRC field representatives' time. In addition, McCormack, Baron and Associates assisted at the site initially and later returned to train the tenant management staff.

Total Incremental Cost. The actual cost of operations at Curries Woods came to $1,159,000 more than would have been the case had the housing authority continued to provide services at the predemonstration level. Personnel costs constituted 42 percent of this increase.

Rental Income and Net Operating Expenses. The troubled experience of the tenant management corporation and the disfavor in which it was held by many of the site's residents may be partially reflected in the fact that rental income collected at Curries Woods fell short of the projected amount by $88,000. When this difference is taken into consideration, net operating expenses rise to $1,247,000—more than would have been spent had the Jersey City Housing Authority continued to manage the site at the same level of services.

Ashanti (Rochester)

The Rochester Housing Authority had begun to plan for site-specific budgeting before the demonstration began. Although Ashanti, with 211 units, represents only 11 percent of the units under housing authority management, as a family development it could be expected to incur higher costs than a project for the elderly. In fact, the budget devised by the Rochester Housing Authority for the fiscal year beginning October 1, 1975, allocated 15 percent of the total housing authority budget to Ashanti, although this proportion varied by line item. Base costs were calculated by applying the percentages of costs allocated to Ashanti to total expenditures, by line item, for the October 1, 1974–September 30, 1975 period. These base costs were then multiplied by the HUD–approved annual inflation factors—6.5 percent for the period through June 30, 1977 (increased by 5 percent (.75 × 6.5) to cover the nine months from October 1, 1975 through the beginning of the demonstration in July 1976); 6.9 percent for the period from July 1, 1977, through June 30, 1978; and 6.0 percent for the period from July 1, 1978, through the end of the demonstration in June 30, 1979. The estimated cost of continued housing authority management at Ashanti over the three years was thus projected at $1,134,000 (see Table 8–3).

Housing Authority Funds. The table also shows that actual housing authority expenditures for Ashanti totaled nearly $1.4 million for the three-year period.[9] Incremental costs to the housing authority can therefore be calculated at $265,000. Costs increased in all budget categories except tenant services, a category that includes salaries paid to the social coordinator and others charged with the delivery of social and recreational services.

It appears that social services functions previously performed by the housing authority were taken over by the tenant management corporation and paid for out of special demonstration monies. Increases in maintenance costs (a category covering salaries of maintenance workers and costs of materials) may be associated with sig-

---

9. This figure includes an estimate for the quarter from July 1, 1976, through September 30, 1976, for which no quarterly information report was available. Costs for that period were estimated using an average of costs for the succeeding three quarters.

Table 8-3. Comparison of Estimated Cost of PHA Management and Actual Cost of Tenant Management, July 1, 1976–June 30, 1979, Rochester–Ashanti.

Expense Item	Projected PHA Cost, Pre-TM Services ($000)	Actual Tenant Management Costs			Total Incremental Cost ($000)	Percentage Increase (Decrease)
		PHA Funds ($000)	Special Demonstration/ TPP Funds ($000)	Total ($000)		
Administration	284	315	115	430	146	51.4
General expenses	211	312	39	351	140	66.3
Tenant service	32	24	9	33	1	3.1
Utilities	198	198	0	198	0	0
Maintenance	349	443	0	443	94	26.9
Protection	20	67	75	142	122	610.0
Total routine expenses	1,094	1,359	238	1,597	503	46.0
Technical assistance	0	0	198	198	198	N/AP
Other nonroutine expenses	40	40	0	40	0	0
Total operating expenses	1,134	1,399	436[a]	1,835	701	61.8
Total rental income	313	490	N/AP	490	(177)	
Net operating expenses	821	909	436	1,345	524	

a. Includes $14,000 in discretionary funds made available by MDRC for otherwise uncovered expenditures.

N/AP—not applicable.

Source: Quarterly Tenant Management Information System reports and TPP fund requests.

nificant increases in the vacant unit preparation rate and in the maintenance request completion rate during the postcontract period. There was an unexpectedly large increase in costs of protection, a category covering both the salaries of security personnel and security hardware. This increase is probably due to the Rochester Housing Authority's funding of 5 of the 14 security guards at Ashanti (positions that had never before existed).

The incremental cost to the housing authority was spread fairly evenly over the three years of the demonstration. This was true in part because the shift of three of the four tenant management staff positions (the manager, assistant manager, one lane manager, and the social services coordinator) from special demonstration funding onto the housing authority payroll occurred relatively early in the demonstration, in December 1977.

Special Demonstration Expenditures. Ashanti spent $422,000 in special demonstration funds out of TPP for on-site program operations. Outside of technical assistance expenses, the major part of these monies went to pay the salaries of tenant management employees. The special demonstration allocation initially funded the employment of the core management staff, including the housing manager, assistant manager, and three of the four lane managers, along with the salaries of the recreation and social services director and her assistant (shown in Table 8–3 under tenant services) and 9 of the 14 security patrol members (shown under protection). As noted above, several of these positions had been transferred to the housing authority payroll by the end of the demonstration.

Ashanti received more technical assistance—$198,000—than any other site in the demonstration. This sum paid for the services of McCormack, Baron and Associates during the training period, the full-time employment of a technical assistant throughout most of the three years of the demonstration, and that portion of the MDRC field representative's responsibilities that involved technical assistance rather than monitoring.

Total Incremental Cost. The fifth column of Table 8–3 shows that the total incremental cost of operations at Ashanti during the demonstration period came to $701,000. Three areas of expenditures accounted for most of this increase—salaries paid to tenant management corporation employees, general expenses, and technical assistance. Indeed, because the amount expended was so high, technical assistance made up a larger proportion of the total incremental cost of Ashanti than at any other site—nearly 30 percent.

Rental Income and Net Incremental Operating Expenses. The Rochester Housing Authority, in budgeting for the 1976 fiscal year, calculated that Ashanti could be expected to supply 8 percent of the housing authority's total rental income; the base rent for Ashanti was then computed by multiplying the total actual rental income for the fiscal year 1975 by this proportion. Applying the HUD inflation factors to the base rent, it was estimated that Ashanti would generate $313,000 in rental income over the demonstration period. In fact, almost half a million dollars ($490,000) in rent was collected. This difference of $177,000 offset the additional cost of tenant management to the housing authority, so that incremental net operating expenses drop to $524,000.

Que-View (New Haven)

The 260 units in the Quinnipiac and Riverview housing projects account for 7 percent of the federally assisted units under the management of the New Haven Housing Authority. To arrive at site-specific expenditures, this proportion was applied to total reported housing authority costs for the 12 months ending September 30, 1976. Although this period overlaps the first quarter of the demonstration, it was selected because it provided the most reliable cost information. Consequently, it was necessary to deflate the HUD-approved inflation rate to 5.25 percent (.75 × 7) for the fiscal year ending June 30, 1977, to account for the fact that only nine months of that period were covered. The inflation factor used in the second year of the demonstration was 7.1 percent, and in the third year, 6.5 percent. Thus the estimated total cost of providing management at the predemonstration level of service was $1,909,000 for the three-year period.

Housing Authority Funds. As Table 8–4 shows, the total incremental cost to the housing authority of management at Que-View came to $78,000, the lowest dollar amount for any of the tenant management sites. Additional administrative costs were low, espe-

Table 8-4. Comparison of Estimated Cost of PHA Management and Actual Cost of Tenant Management, July 1, 1976–June 30, 1979, New Haven–Que–View.

Expense Item	Projected PHA Cost, Pre–TM Services ($000)	Actual Tenant Management Costs			Total Incremental Cost ($000)	Percentage Increase (Decrease)
		PHA Funds ($000)	Special Demonstration/TPP Funds ($000)	Total ($000)		
Administration	216	220	197	417	201	93.9
General expenses	195	212	56	268	73	37.4
Tenant service	5	5	0	5	0	0
Utilities	943	943	0	943	0	0
Maintenance	415	509	6	515	100	24.1
Protection	118	81	8	89	(29)	(24.5)
Total routine expenses	1,892	1,970	267	2,237	345	18.2
Technical assistance	0	0	87	87	87	N/AP
Other nonroutine expenses	17	17	0	17	0	0
Total operating expenses	1,909	1,987	354[a]	2,341	432	22.6
Total rental income	673	684	N/AP	684	(11)	
Net operating expenses	1,236	1,303	354	1,657	421	

a. Includes $10,000 in discretionary funds made available by MDRC for otherwise uncovered expenditures.
N/AP–not applicable.
Source: Quarterly Tenant Management Information System reports and TPP fund requests.

cially compared with those incurred at other sites, probably because of high turnover and attrition among those New Haven Housing Authority staff members who had been concerned with tenant management. Protection costs dropped below projected levels because the financially pressed housing authority substantially reduced its expenditures for this purpose. On the other hand, actual expenditures exceeded projected costs in the area of maintenance because several maintenance workers were stationed at the site itself, rather than assigned to a general geographic area. In addition, because of tighter management supervision, more maintenance tasks may have been completed, although as noted in Chapter 7, TMIS data bearing on this issue are not available.

Special Demonstration Expenditures. Technical assistance and personnel costs accounted for most of the special demonstration funds that Que-View spent on program operations. Technical assistance was provided by the MDRC field representative, as well as by a number of part-time technical assistants whom MDRC hired in an effort to build organizational strength among tenant management board members. In addition, McCormack, Baron and Associates initiated training at the outset of the demonstration. The majority of special funds was spent in the first two years of the demonstration.

Total Incremental Cost. The total cost of operations at Que-View came to $432,000 above the model. Personnel costs, paid primarily through special demonstration monies, accounted for 47 percent of this increase, with maintenance and technical assistance costs responsible for most of the remainder.

Rental Income and Net Operating Expenses. Despite the site's many problems, the actual rent collected at Que-View exceeded the amount projected by $11,000. When this amount is subtracted from total costs, net incremental operating expenditures decline to $421,000. To some degree, this relatively low amount reflects high turnover among those central office staff who were familiar with the demonstration, along with the inability of the housing authority to maintain its previous level of service.

Calliope (New Orleans)

Calliope, with 1,500 units, was the largest in the demonstration, and the development accounted for 12.6 percent of all units under the management of the Housing Authority of New Orleans. To arrive at base period costs, this proportion was applied to expenses incurred by the housing authority during the fiscal year ending September 30, 1975. The resulting figures were then adjusted by the HUD-approved factors—14 percent (8 × 1.75) for the period between September 30, 1975, and June 30, 1977; 8.6 percent for the year ending June 30, 1978; and 8 percent for the year ending June 30, 1979. In this way, the costs of operations at Calliope at the same level of services as existed prior to the demonstration was projected at $3,954,000 (see Table 8–5).

Housing Authority Funds. Actual reported housing authority expenditures for Calliope during the demonstration came to $4,065,-000, or $111,000 above the projected figure. This increment of less than 4 percent represents the lowest percentage increase of any site in the demonstration. Housing authority expenditures increased in the residual category of general expenses and in the area of tenant services. The explanation for the latter increase is the same as at the Jersey City sites: the housing authority granted the development of full funding for tenant services to which it was entitled.

Savings occurred on three line items — administration, maintenance, and protection. Savings in administrative costs probably resulted from the decision to transfer special demonstration funding to budget the salaries of some tenant management personnel who had previously been paid out of housing authority funds (the tenant management coordinator is a case in point). Similarly, special funds paid for some maintenance projects that might otherwise have been charged to the housing authority and for the salaries of two maintenance supervisors and several maintenance workers. By contrast, in December 1978, the manager, assistant manager, and social services coordinator, whose salaries had previously been paid for by special demonstration monies, were placed on the housing authority budget.

Special Demonstration Expenditures. Because of the large number of physical improvements required at the site, Calliope received per-

Table 8-5. Comparison of Estimated Cost of PHA Management and Actual Cost of Tenant Management, July 1, 1976–June 30, 1979, New Orleans—Calliope.

Expense Item	Projected PHA Cost, Pre-TM Services ($000)	Actual Tenant Management Costs			Total Incremental Cost ($000)	Percentage Increase (Decrease)
		PHA Funds ($000)	Special Demonstration/ TPP Funds ($000)	Total ($000)		
Administration	203	188	266	414	211	103.9
General expenses	541	633	0	663	122	22.6
Tenant service	48	199	31	230	182	379.0
Utilities	1,951	1,951	0	1,951	0	0
Maintenance	1,079	959	37	996	(83)	(7.7)
Protection	27	0	0	0	(27)	(100.0)
Total routine expenses	3,849	3,960	294	4,254	405	10.5
Technical assistance	0	0	127	127	127	N/AP
Other nonroutine expenses	105	105	0	105	0	0
Total operating expenses	3,954	4,065	421[a]	4,486	532	13.5
Total rental income	2,120	2,411	N/AP	2,411	(291)	
Net operating expenses	1,834	1,654	421	2,075	241	

a. Includes $15,000 in discretionary funds by MDRC for otherwise uncovered expenditures; excludes $875,000 in TPP monies used for physical improvement projects.

N/AP—not applicable.

Source: Quarterly Tenant Management Information System reports and TPP fund requests.

mission to use some of its special demonstration allocation out of TPP for that purpose. About $875,000 in these funds went for projects such as termite proofing, the replacement of gutters and downspouts, electrical rewiring, and the purchase of new stoves and refrigerators. Since these expenditures are incidental to the establishment of the tenant management corporation, they are excluded from Table 8–5. The remainder of special funds were spent on salaries for Calliope's large on-site staff and for central office personnel and on technical assistance. At Calliope, the latter included part of the salaries of MDRC field representatives, a special consultant to the site hired by MDRC and local technical assistants.

Total Incremental Cost. Total operating expenses at the site over the three years exceeded the projection by $532,000. Personnel costs, reported on both the administration and tenant services budget lines, were responsible for the major share of the increase. Costs of both maintenance and protection dropped below projected levels.

Rental Income and Net Operating Expenses. While the model suggested that $2.12 million in rents would be collected during the demonstration period, the actual rental income of $2,411,000 exceeded that amount by $291,000. The latter figure, applied to total incremental costs, yields net operating expenses of $241,000, the smallest of any site in the demonstration.

Iroquois Homes (Louisville)

As noted above, the Housing Authority of Louisville had not developed a site-specific budgeting system by the end of the demonstration. The costs it reported to MDRC as actual management expenditures for Iroquois represent a proration of total housing authority costs for each line item. It is therefore impossible to assess increased costs for Iroquois in particular rather than for the housing authority as a whole, and in addition, the information in Table 8–6 covers only the final two years of the demonstration.

Over the years, $424,000 in special demonstration funds out of TPP were expended for site operations. As at most other demonstration sites, the majority of this sum went to pay tenant management staff salaries. The site received $118,000 in technical assistance,

July 1, 1976–June 30, 1979, Louisville–Iroquois Homes.

Expense Item	Projected PHA Cost, Pre-TM Services ($000)	Actual Tenant Management Costs[a]			Total Incremental Cost ($000)	Percentage Increase (Decrease)
		PHA Funds ($000)	Special Demonstration/ TPP Funds ($000)	Total ($000)		
Administration	N/AP	407	190	597	N/AP	N/AP
General expenses	N/AP	398	0	398	N/AP	N/AP
Tenant service	N/AP	33	56	89	N/AP	N/AP
Utilities	N/AP	799	0	799	N/AP	N/AP
Maintenance	N/AP	611	0	611	N/AP	N/AP
Protection	N/AP	47	15	62	N/AP	N/AP
Total routine expenses	N/AP	2,295	261	2,556	N/AP	N/AP
Technical assistance	N/AP	0	84	84	N/AP	N/AP
Other nonroutine expenses	N/AP	25	0	25	N/AP	N/AP
Total operating expenses	N/AP	2,320	345[b]	2,665	N/AP	N/AP
Total rental income	N/AP	858	N/AP	858	N/AP	N/AP
Net operating expenses	N/AP	1,462	345	1,807	N/AP	N/AP

a. Expenditures represent a proration of total housing authority costs, so that the figures shown here cannot be considered as funds expended for tenant management per se.

b. Includes $12,000 in discretionary funds made available by MDRC for otherwise uncovered expenditures; excludes $20,000 in TPP monies used for physical improvement projects.

N/AP—not applicable.

Source: Quarterly Tenant Management Information System reports and TPP fund requests.

which paid for a special consultant hired to help organize the tenant management board, a part of MDRC field costs, and two local technical assistants hired during the first two years of the demonstration. Special demonstration costs were spread fairly evenly over the three-year period.

Sunrise Acres (Oklahoma City)

The Sunrise Acres Tenant Management Corporation was dropped from the national demonstration in mid-1978, as it never approached the level of self-sufficiency required for true tenant management. The costs incurred by the site are shown in Table 8-7 only to present a complete picture of the costs of the National Tenant Management Demonstration. Because it is not meaningful to consider incremental tenant management costs at this site, no detailed cost analysis was undertaken.

Actual costs were derived from quarterly reports submitted by the housing authority from July 1, 1976, through March 31, 1978. Over the 21 months covered, the housing authority reported spending $890,000 at the site. An additional $213,000 was incurred in special demonstration out of TPP expenditures. The largest portion of this allocation went for salaries and for technical assistance in a vain effort to keep the tenant management corporation afloat.

THE ANNUAL INCREMENTAL COST OF AN OPERATING TENANT MANAGEMENT CORPORATION

Along with determining actual expenditures during the three-year demonstration period, the analysis sought to establish what an effectively operating tenant management corporation would cost annually. For this purpose, the cost of a year of full-fledged tenant management operations was calculated for three of the four[10] tenant management corporations judged to be viable and closest to the demonstration model. This annual cost was computed by determining

---

10. For reasons discussed earlier in this chapter, it was not possible to include Louisville in this analysis.

Table 8-7. Comparison of Estimated Cost of PHA Management and Actual Cost of Tenant Management, July 1, 1976–May 31, 1978, Oklahoma City–Sunrise Acres.

Expense Item	Projected PHA Cost, Pre-TM Services ($000)	Actual Tenant Management Costs			Total Incremental Cost ($000)	Percentage Increase (Decrease)
		PHA Funds ($000)	Special Demonstration/ TPP Funds ($000)	Total ($000)		
Administration	N/AP	236	104	330	N/AP	N/AP
General expenses	N/AP	126	3	129	N/AP	N/AP
Tenant service	N/AP	12	15	27	N/AP	N/AP
Utilities	N/AP	100	0	100	N/AP	N/AP
Maintenance	N/AP	361	0	361	N/AP	N/AP
Protection	N/AP	38	39	77	N/AP	N/AP
Total routine expenses	N/AP	873	151	1,024	N/AP	N/AP
Technical assistance	N/AP	0	62	62	N/AP	N/AP
Other nonroutine expenses	N/AP	17	0	17	N/AP	N/AP
Total operating expenses	N/AP	890	223[a]	1,103	N/AP	N/AP
Total rental income	N/AP	392	N/AP	392	N/AP	N/AP
Net operating expenses	N/AP	498	223	711	N/AP	N/AP

a. Includes $10,000 in discretionary funds made available by MDRC for otherwise uncovered expenditures.

N/AP—not applicable.

Source: Quarterly Tenant Management Information System reports and TPP fund requests.

total costs for the period under the management contract and arriving at an annualized figure.

Ashanti in Rochester was the only one of the tenant management corporations that functioned under the contract for at least a full year—24 months, in fact—so that the yearly operating cost for this site is a true average of costs incurred during the postcontract period. For the other sites, the annual cost represents a projection arrived at by extrapolation. Tables 8-8, 8-9, and 8-10 show the results. The tables largely replicate the earlier analysis, but cover only the period following the signing of the management contract.

A. Harry Moore (Jersey City)

Table 8-8 indicates that during the nine-month contract period, the increment in net operating expenses at A. Harry Moore totaled $283,000; annualized, the amount comes to $364,000. A comparison of Tables 8-8 and 8-1 yields several points. First, the data suggest that the incremental cost of operations at A. Harry Moore was spread remarkably evenly over the three years of the demonstration; the annualized increment in the net cost of operations under the contract, $364,000, is 32.7 percent of the entire increment in net operating cost of $1,112,000. This appears to be the case because as start-up costs declined (e.g., those associated with technical assistance) costs of tenant management personnel increased.

Over the course of the demonstration, the tenant management corporation became considerably more effective in collecting rents, while over the three-year period the site experienced a $16,000 shortfall in rental income. In the last nine months it collected a "surplus" of $82,000 over the projected amount. Overall then, while operating costs at A. Harry Moore did not decline over time, operations themselves became more efficient—a good omen for future success.

Ashanti (Rochester)

As at A. Harry Moore, the incremental cost of operations at Ashanti was evenly spread over the demonstration period. The $171,000 increment in net operating expenditures during the contract period

Table 8-8. Comparison of Estimated Cost of PHA Management and Actual Cost of Tenant Management, Contract Period Annualized, Jersey City – A. Harry Moore (Contract Period 9/20/78–6/30/79).

| Expense Item | Projected PHA Cost, Pre–TM Services ($000) | Actual Tenant Management Costs | | | Total Incremental Cost ($000) | Percentage Increase (Decrease) | Annualized Increment ($000) |
		PHA Funds ($000)	Special Demonstration/ TPP Funds ($000)	Total ($000)			
Administration	140	281	64	345	205	146.5	264
General expenses	79	72	3	75	(4)	(5.1)	(5)
Tenant services	1	15	3	18	17	1700.0	22
Utilities	696	696	0	696	0	0	0
Maintenance	296	409	113	409	113	38.2	145
Protection	0	0	15	15	15	N/AP	19
Total routine expenses	1,212	1,473	85	1,558	346	28.5	445
Technical assistance	0	0	19	19	19	N/AP	24
Other nonroutine expenses	4	4	0	4	0	0	0
Total operating expenses	1,216	1,477	104	1,581	365	30.0	469
Total rental income	489	571	N/AP	571	(82)		(105)
Net operating expenses	727	906	104	1,010	283		364

N/AP—not applicable.

Source: Quarterly Tenant Management Information System reports and TPP fund requests.

comprised 32.6 percent of the $524,000 total for the demonstration period as a whole (see Table 8-9). While expenditures for technical assistance declined with time, expenses in other cost categories increased.

Calliope (New Orleans)

At $241,000, the increment in net operating expenses was lower at Calliope than at any other site, and for the period under the management contract, that increment shrunk still further to $37,000, annualized to $46,000. This sum represents only 19 percent of the total, indicating that while the site incurred heavy expenses during the first two years, these had declined considerably by the third year. As at A. Harry Moore, rent collections were substantially higher than they had been earlier (see Table 8-10).

Summary

Table 8-11 recaps the data on incremental costs and also displays these costs on a per unit basis. The table makes it clear that the cost of implementing tenant management varied widely across the sites.

Over the course of the demonstration, Ashanti in Rochester was most expensive on both a percentage increase (61.8 percent) and per unit ($2,483) basis. Although Ashanti is a small development, numbering only 211 units, the tenant management corporation fielded a sizable staff of management and security personnel; the development also incurred high technical assistance costs. At the other end of the spectrum, the cost of establishing tenant management at Calliope in New Orleans exceeded the cost of continued management at the pre-demonstration level by only 13.5 percent; per unit, the net operating cost was only $155 more over the three years. Calliope's incremental costs were held down by the fact that rent revenues exceeded projections by almost $290,000. Also, unit costs are low in part because they are spread over Calliope's 1,550 units. On a per unit basis, the other sites were in the middle of these extremes, clustering between $1,600 and $1,750.

The same range is evident when the incremental cost of operating the tenant management corporation for a year under the manage-

Table 8-9. Comparison of Estimated Cost of PHA Management and Actual Cost of Tenant Management, Contract Period Annualized, Rochester—Ashanti (Contract Period 6/19/77–6/30/79).

Expense Item	Projected PHA Cost, Pre–TM Services ($000)	Actual Tenant Management Costs			Total Incremental Cost ($000)	Percentage Increase (Decrease)	Annualized Increment ($000)
		PHA Funds ($000)	Special Demonstration/ TPP Funds ($000)	Total ($000)			
Administration	200	220	77	297	97	48.5	47
General expenses	149	217	39	256	107	71.8	52
Tenant services	23	20	6	26	3	13.0	1
Utilities	115	115	0	115	0	0	0
Maintenance	246	314	0	314	68	27.6	33
Protection	14	47	65	112	98	700.0	48
Total routine expenses	747	933	178	1,111	373	49.9	181
Technical assistance	0	0	109	109	109	N/AP	53
Other nonroutine expenses	28	28	0	28	0	0	0
Total operating expenses	775	961	287	1,248	482	62.2	234
Total rental income	220	349	N/AP	349	(129)		(63)
Net operating expenses	555	612	287	899	353		171

N/AP—not applicable.

Source: Quarterly Tenant Management Information System reports and TPP fund requests.

Table 8–10. Comparison of Estimated Cost of PHA Management and Actual Cost of Tenant Management, Contract Period Annualized, New Orleans—Calliope (Contract Period 9/10/78–6/30/79).

Expense Item	Projected PHA Cost, Pre-TM Services ($000)	Actual Tenant Management Costs			Total Incremental Cost ($000)	Percentage Increase (Decrease)	Annualized Increment ($000)
		PHA Funds ($000)	Special Demonstration/ TPP Funds ($000)	Total ($000)			
Administration	59	51	78	129	70	118.6	87
General expenses	157	151	0	151	(6)	(3.8)	(7)
Tenant services	14	55	13	68	54	385.7	67
Utilities	563	563	0	563	0	0	0
Maintenance	313	304	11	315	2	(0.6)	2
Protection	8	0	0	0	(8)	(100.0)	(10)
Total routine expenses	1,114	1,124	102	1,226	112	10.0	139
Technical assistance	0	0	43	43	43	N/AP	53
Other nonroutine expenses	49	49	0	49	0	0	0
Total operating expenses	1,163	1,173	145	1,318	115	13.3	192
Total rental income	614	732	N/AP	732	(118)		(146)
Net operating expenses	549	441	145	586	37		46

N/AP not applicable.

Source: Quarterly Tenant Management Information System reports and TPP fund requests.

Table 8-11. Net Incremental Costs of Tenant Management.

| | Net Incremental Operating Expenses | | | | | |
| | Demonstration Period: 1976–1979 | | | Period Under Management Contract Annualized | | |
Tenant Management Site	Total ($)	Percentage Increase[a]	Cost per Unit ($)	Total ($)	Percentage Increase[a]	Cost per Unit ($)
Jersey City: A. Harry Moore (664 units)	1,112,000	26.4	1,676	364,000	30.0	548
Jersey City: Curries Woods (712 units)	1,247,000	27.7	1,751	N/AP	N/AP	N/AP
New Haven: Que-View (260 units)	421,000	22.6	1,619	N/AP	N/AP	N/AP
New Orleans: Calliope (1550 units)	241,000	13.5	155	46,000	13.3	30
Rochester: Ashanti (211 units)	524,000	61.8	2,483	171,000	62.2	810

a. Percentage increase of actual total operating expenses during the demonstration period, or during the period under the tenant management contract, over the projected operating expenses that would be incurred at the predemonstration service level.

N/AP—not applicable.

Source: Quarterly Tenant Management Information System reports and TPP fund requests.

ment contract is considered. Again, the per unit cost is lowest at Calliope ($30) and highest at Ashanti ($810). There is reason to assume that these costs will be lower in the future as the sites reduce their need for technical assistance and gain greater operating experience.

It is unlikely that many tenant management corporations can achieve the economies of scale and other savings that kept costs in New Orleans as low as they were. On the other hand, Ashanti's costs may have been unnecessarily high in terms of the results that were achieved. This analysis suggests the cost parameters within which tenant management can successfully be established.

CONCLUSION

The National Tenant Management Demonstration has shown that management by tenants is a feasible alternative to conventional public housing management under certain conditions. In the majority of the demonstration sites, the tenant participants—all long-time residents of low-income public housing, most unemployed, and the majority black female family heads—mastered in three years the skills necessary to assume management responsibility for the housing developments in which they lived. At least in the short period of the demonstration, however, the process was costly in terms of both the financial and the human resources needed to achieve stability.

The evaluation of tenant management on a series of measured standard performance indicators such as rent collection and the quality and timeliness of maintenance, shows that the residents were able to manage their developments as well as prior management had and, in so doing, to provide employment for some tenants and increase the overall satisfaction of the general resident population. Beyond these, perhaps equally important but less measurable indicators show that although participation in tenant management has demanded dedication and sacrifices of board and staff members, whatever the burdens of participation, most of those involved say that these have been outweighed by the benefits. Board and staff members report a number of positive personality changes—greater patience and ability to get along with people, mastery of shyness, pride in learning complex material, and greater confidence in their future. Participants take pride in what tenant management has accomplished for their developments, and feel—perhaps for the first time—power over their own lives and power to change their communities.

In citing its short-term achievements, it is well to remember that, in fact, tenant management did not do objectively better than conventional management, despite the considerable additional funds committed to the demonstration sites both for larger staffs and for long-term physical improvements. The time and energy devoted by key housing authority personnel and by the involved tenants are crucial, but could not guarantee a successful venture and must also be considered as a real but more intangible cost.

Tenant management cannot succeed without a cooperative housing authority. The executive director must firmly support the concept or at least be willing to give it a fair trial. While he or she need not devote a great deal of personal time and attention to the program, subordinate housing authority staff must be strongly encouraged to support the program. The director and the housing authority staff must also be willing to make changes in established procedures in order to accommodate tenant management needs.

Successful tenant management also depends on strong leadership within the resident community. Leadership potential probably exists in any tenant group, and normally, given sufficient time, resources, and housing authority support, those individuals who possess latent talents can be identified and their organizational skills developed. Thus, existing organized leadership was not a precondition of tenant management success, although its presence facilitated the early developmental process at three of the successful sites in Jersey City, Louisville, and Rochester. At these sites, the demonstration's electoral process produced boards that won the respect of the housing authority and the wider community. In the other instances, the first boards experienced considerable dissension, instability, and difficulty in making decisions, although initial board weakness was not necessarily a signal of permanent failure, as the experience of another successful site—New Orleans—indicates.

The experience of the demonstration suggests that no more than one forceful leader need emerge in order for the board as a whole to function successfully, although longer term continuity of the tenant management corporation would seem to require that other members acquire basic organizational knowledge. While turnover among board members has occurred at all the sites as a result of resignations or regular elections, most boards have retained a stable cadre of long-term members who have been able to assimilate newcomers and instruct them in the goals and techniques of the program.

One important task accomplished by all of the boards was the recruitment and hiring of a resident manager and subsequently, a tenant management staff. Again, as with the boards, turnover among staff occurred, but it was not a serious problem; in fact, in the early period following staff assumption of management responsibility, inadequate personnel were weeded out, and potential talent brought forth. Issues of supervision and the delegation of authority were more problematic. Some staff members had trouble giving orders to, or taking orders from, their fellow tenants, and technical assistance has been extremely valuable in dealing with the sensitive area of board-staff relations.

Where tenant management achieved stability, technical assistance was critical. The need for technical assistance was especially pronounced at the outset, because most board members lacked basic organizational skills such as group decisionmaking and conflict resolution, and throughout the demonstration, technical assistants helped the boards resolve internal conflicts and deal with both the housing authority and the resident community.

Although technical assistance is indispensable, it is not possible to generalize from the demonstration experience about how much or how little is required. That depends on the organizational sophistication of the tenant management board members and on the quality and quantity of resources that the housing authority commits to the program. Once again, the housing authority's attitude toward the program is crucial: if the housing authority endorses the program, then the technical assistant has a firm base on which to build the tenant management corporation's organizational competence. But the technical assistant's best efforts to build an effective board and staff will go for naught in an atmosphere of housing authority indifference or hostility.

Technical assistance functions can be divided among several people without impairing effectiveness, and given the difficulty of finding a single individual who can be all things to all parties, this is a reasonable course of action. Although all technical assistants need not be familiar with the details of housing management, at least one must be reasonably conversant with housing authority operations, so as to maintain the tenant management corporations' credibility as a management entity. Technical assistants who are independent of the housing authority will normally be essential to foster the TMC's independence, especially given the predictability of disagreements between the tenant management corporation and the housing authority. At Jersey City's A. Harry Moore site, however, a housing authority staff member effectively functioned as the technical assistant.

Training for board and staff is absolutely essential, but an exclusive training format is not required so long as there is a core program curriculum that stresses housing management issues and is flexible enough to accommodate local circumstances and varying rates of mastery. Outside trainers may well be unnecessary, and housing authority personnel can perform effectively as trainers if they see tenant management as an important priority for the housing authority as a whole.

These three crucial elements—housing authority cooperation, strong tenant leadership, and carefully administered technical assistance and training—work together to create the optimal conditions under which tenant management can flourish. By the end of the demonstration, most of these conditions had been met, and cooperative, if not always amicable, relations between the housing authority and the TMC had been established at four of the original sites—New Orleans, Louisville, Rochester, and Jersey City's A. Harry Moore. The executive directors of these four housing authorities reported that while participation in the demonstration taxed the time and resources of housing authority personnel, they would unequivocally opt to do it all over again. Their commitment to tenant management appeared to be grounded largely in the belief that residents of public housing should have a greater say in decisions that affect their lives.

At two of the sites that failed to either achieve or sustain tenant management—New Haven and Oklahoma City—difficulties were evident from the start, and to some extent, these outcomes could have been predicted by the relationships that existed between tenants and the housing authorities before the demonstration. Outcomes at the third unsuccessful site—Jersey City's Curries Woods—were less predictable, and perhaps the principal lesson to be drawn from that experience is that housing authority support and organized tenant leadership are necessary, but not always sufficient, conditions for the development of a positive relationship between the parties.

The judgments on the efficacy of tenant management within the context of the national demonstration were made within a fairly narrow framework of improving housing management. Essentially, the demonstration was not conceived as, nor was its time frame conducive to, an assessment of tenant management as a means to achieve broader social reform and improvement within a low-income community. This public housing community, with its high level of single parent welfare dependency and its high unemployment coupled with low educational and skill level attainment and patterns of social disorganization represents in many respects a microcosm of the urban decay that exists in so many of the nation's central cities. The more extensive experience of tenant management in St. Louis, which served as a model for the demonstration, indicates that as these fledgling tenant management corporations take hold, they have the potential for much broader impact on a variety of community development issues. By harnessing available resources for employment and training, education, and social services, as tenant management corporations in St. Louis have done, the process of increasing community blight may be effectively reversed. It seems axiomatic that such an achievement represents a far greater potential benefit than the need of tenant management to outperform conventional management on a much narrower set of indicators. Whether the more successful sites in the demonstration, having mastered the rudiments of property management, can move on to this higher level of community development is a question that merits the continuation of the sites and an ongoing assessment of their progress.

APPENDIXES

APPENDIX A

RESEARCH METHODOLOGY FOR THE NATIONAL TENANT MANAGEMENT DEMONSTRATION PROGRAM

This report capitalizes on the full scope of MDRC's involvement as manager of the demonstration. It is an institutional document rather than simply a research report on findings. As such it draws upon the perspectives, experiences, and efforts of the administrative, operations, and research staffs at MDRC. However, much of the information used in the report was collected and analyzed according to the research design for the evaluation of the demonstration. This appendix presents the major features of that design, including the primary areas of concern, the data sources utilized, and the analyses performed in the preparation of the report.

RESEARCH DESIGN

The substantive aspect of the research design was organized into four major components: (1) historical content of the demonstration, (2) documentation of the demonstration, (3) impact of the demonstration, and (4) cost of the demonstration.

- Historical context: Placed the demonstration in a comparative framework by examining other efforts at tenant management in public housing. The exploration of their forms, problems, successes, and failures provided some preliminary insights into the viability of tenant management as an option for public housing.

- Documentation: Focused on the development of the demonstration at the local level. Its descriptive and analytic account was guided by the following concerns—the effect of local factors and characteristics on the development of tenant management; the problems and issues typical of the various phases of site operations; the organization of the areas of management responsibility; and the relationships among the various participants in the TMC and between the TMC and other important groups such as the PHA.

- Impact: Assessment of the extent to which tenant management achieved the major goals of the demonstration and realized other consequences such as physical improvements.

- Cost: Focused on the incremental cost of establishing and operating a tenant management corporation. In addition, the analysis considered the additional cost of operating an ongoing tenant management corporation. On the benefit side, increases in revenue were discussed insofar as they affected increased costs.

The research for the historical context, documentation, and cost components was done wholly by MDRC staff, while the Urban Institute assisted MDRC in the collection and analysis of data for the impact component. The historical context component was the subject of another document and hence is not discussed further in this appendix.[1]

In designing the research, an attempt was made to be sensitive to both program outcomes and program features. The former would permit the drawing of inferences about the fact of success or failure at the demonstration sites; the latter would provide some sense of the process and substance of the program as a context in which to understand outcomes and to generate information needed for replication. The design effort was constrained by several factors in meeting its goals. These included the small number of sites (seven) participating in the demonstration and the variability in implementing the tenant management model and in local operating conditions.

---

1. William A. Diaz, *Tenant Management: An Historical and Analytical Overview* (New York: Manpower Demonstration Research Corporation, 1979).

The dearth of evaluation models on broad aim social programs such as the demonstration presented an additional challenge. Finally, the unanticipated length of time it took for most of the sites to establish fully functioning tenant management corporations severely limited the amount of program experience under tenant management available for analysis. This fact together with the demonstration time frame precluded the consideration of any long-term effects of the program.

DATA SOURCES

A variety of data sources was utilized in the demonstration research. Table A-1 provides a list of the major sources used for each of those components of the research discussed in the final report. Much overlap is apparent. In addition to those listed, other sources of information included archival materials, journal articles, books, and previous MDRC reports on the program. What follows is a brief description of the major sources of the data. MDRC staff was responsible for the collection and analysis of all the data from these resources with the exception of those from the Urban Institute survey.

MDRC Operations Staff Field Reports

MDRC field operations staff prepared monthly and quarterly written reports on each of the demonstration sites based on regular visits to the sites and reports submitted by local technical assistants. These reports detailed the process of program implementation and its problems, issues, and progress. They served as an ongoing record of the development of the demonstration at the local level.

Interviews

These interviews[2] were conducted by MDRC research staff, as opposed to those conducted as a part of the Urban Institute survey discussed below.

2. In addition to the MDRC interviews listed below, the technical assistants were also interviewed in 1978.

Table A-1.   Data Sources: Tenant Management Demonstration
Research.

Research Design Components	Major Data Sources
Documentation	• Interviews with TMC board and staff members, PHA executive directors and tenant management liaisons, and MDRC field representatives.
	• Questionnaires administered to TMC board and staff.
	• MDRC operations staff field reports.
Impact	• Interviews with TMC board and staff members.
	• Questionnaires administered to TMC board and staff.
	• Tenant Employment Survey.
	• Tenant Management Information System.
	• Urban Institute Survey (interviews and questionnaires).
	• Modernization Program (MOD) Quarterly Reports.
Cost	• Target Projects Program (TPP) Quarterly Requisitions.
	• Tenant Management Information System.

Source: MDRC files.

TMC Board Members. Interviews were conducted with selected TMC board members in 1978 and 1979. The board chairperson, another current member of the board, and the ex–board chairperson (if there was one) were interviewed at each site. Topics covered in the interview included board composition and functioning, board–staff relations, tenant management operations, the tenant management site community, TMC–PHA relationships, management performance, MDRC, perception of the board member's role, and overall perspectives on the TMC. A total number of 17 interviews with board members were conducted in 1978 and 15 in 1979.

TMC Staff Members. In 1979 the persons currently holding the positions of TMC manager and social services coordinator were interviewed at each site. In addition, one lane or building manager was interviewed, as was one ex-employee where this was possible. The TMC manager was asked to comment on TMC staff turnover, management procedures, board-staff relations, tenant management site community, management performance, perceptions of the TMC manager's role, and overall perspectives on tenant management. The lane or building manager and social coordinator's interviews focused on various aspects of their respective positions, with some additional attention to their perceptions about tenant management. A total of 17 interviews were conducted with current TMC staff, and five ex-employees were interviewed. In 1978, four TMC staff members were interviewed.[3]

PHA Executive Directors and Liaisons for Tenant Management. The PHA's executive director and its liaison for the tenant management program were interviewed in 1978 and 1979 (except in Oklahoma City). Topics covered included an assessment of TMC performance and its principal actors, TMC-PHA relationship, PHA efforts in establishing tenant management, management performance, and future PHA-wide and site plans with respect to tenant management.

MDRC Operations Staff. MDRC field operations staff provided the research staff with information on an ongoing basis throughout the demonstration. In addition, each staff member responsible at that time for monitoring a site was formally interviewed in 1979 as a part of the documentation component of the demonstration. These interviews focused on factual issues about the TMC board and staff members as well as the larger tenant community. They also included questions on the TMC-PHA relationship and such general issues as MDRC's role at the site, the adequacy of technical assistance, sources of nondemonstration funding, and postdemonstration plans for tenant management.

3. Management contracts existed at only two of the sites at the time.

Questionnaires

TMC Board and Staff. Current TMC board and staff members at all sites except Oklahoma City completed questionnaires prepared and administered by MDRC research staff in the spring of 1979. Both groups were asked questions about their personal background and their perceptions of TMC management performance. TMC board members were queried about their experience as such and asked to assess staff–board relations and staff performance. Staff were asked about their respective positions, training, supervisors, and board and staff relations. Owing to the unavailability of some participants at the time the questionnaires were administered, 27 of the intended 50 board members and 50 of the intended 58 staff members completed questionnaires.

Tenant Employment Survey. Each TMC manager was asked to complete a standard form on employment during the demonstration. Information requested on current and former TMC employees included name, title of position, hours worked per week, dates of employment, annual salary, and an evaluation of job performance. For current employees, job responsibilities were described. The reason for leaving his or her TMC position and current employment status were requested for former employees. In addition, information was requested on the extent of tenant employment in regular PHA positions, in temporary projects such as MOD, and in others using CETA funds. Tenant Employment Surveys were completed by five of the six TMC managers at sites remaining in the demonstration for its full duration.

Tenant Management Information System

The Tenant Management Information System (TMIS), consisting of Monthly Information Reports, Quarterly Information Reports, and a manual of instructions for their completion, was designed by MDRC to provide a major portion of the information used as the basis for assessing the impact and cost of the demonstration. The monthly reports provided information on occupancy, rent collection, response to tenants' maintenance service requests, reexaminations for continued occupancy and vacant unit preparation. The quarterly reports included information on expenditures and income, tenant employment, evictions, and moveouts. The reports were prepared by housing authority staff and submitted to MDRC, where they were checked for accuracy, consistency, and completeness. If errors or other problems were identified, they were discussed with the PHA in order to make the necessary adjustments. Other quality control techniques included a series of site visits by MDRC staff to compare the information provided in the reports with the records on which they were based.

Urban Institute Survey

A large-scale survey conducted by the Urban Institute[4] provided a significant segment of the information used in the chapter on the achievement of demonstration goals, especially in the areas of real estate management and tenants' satisfaction, and assessments of management performance and housing conditions. This survey is important in that it provided information not accessible from any of the data sources discussed above. First, the survey provided information on a set of sites not participating in the demonstration (controls) with which the tenant management sites were compared. Second, it provided the opinions, assessments, and perceptions of the constituencies of the various tenant management corporations—the resident community at the public housing developments participating in the demonstration.

The primary function of the Urban Institute comparison effort was to select a group of control sites and to collect and analyze data both from them and from participating sites before and after the implementation of tenant management at the demonstration sites. The Institute was selected because of its experience with public housing research and its extensive data base on a large number of public housing projects from which control sites could be selected. Moreover, the economies of scale realized in the collection of baseline ("before") data[5] and the methodology developed for the Institute's evaluation of the Housing Management Improvement Program made it a particularly suitable candidate to assist in the research effort.

4. A full report of the survey is contained in Suzanne B. Loux and Robert Sadacca, "Analysis of Changes at the Tenant Management Demonstration Projects," Working Paper 1335 (Washington, D.C.: The Urban Institute, 1980).

5. The Urban Institute concurrently collected data at 120 PHAs in spring 1976 when the baseline interviews were conducted at tht tenant management sites.

Baseline surveys were conducted in the spring of 1976, before the implementation of tenant management, and follow-up surveys were administered in the summer of 1979 at both demonstration and comparison sites. These surveys included interviews with a sample of public housing tenants, selected HUD field office personnel, PHA board of commissioners chairpersons, PHA executive directors, and other staff at the project level and questionnaires administered to PHA central office staff. The data used for the analysis in the report were based on the six tenant management sites remaining in the demonstration through its entirety and 18 comparison projects selected in 1979 from the Urban Institute's Standard Sample.[6] Table A-2 presents the sample sizes for each of the respondent groups. Survey data used in the final report came primarily from the analysis of the project residents' interviews. To a lesser extent, information from the project manager's interview was used.

Table A-2. Urban Institute Survey: Sample Sizes by Respondent Category.[a]

Respondent Category	Tenant Management		Control	
	1976	1979	1976	1979
Board chairman[b]	13	5	13	12
Executive director[b]	13	5	13	12
Central office staff[b]	99	96	262	258
Project manager	6	6	18	18
Project staff	30	30	70	71
Project residents	181	181	383	395

a. Excludes Oklahoma City.

b. The figures for board chairmen, executive director, and central office staff are included as part of the tenant management sample if any of their projects were in the demonstration. Jersey City, Louisville, and New Haven had both tenant management and control projects in the same PHA.

Source: Suzanne B. Loux and Robert Sadacca, "Analysis of Changes at Tenant Management Demonstration Projects," Working Paper #1335 (Washington, D.C.: Urban Institute, 1980).

6. The Standard Sample includes 120 PHAs (40 large, 40 medium sized, and 40 small) across the country. The 40 large PHAs were used as the pool from which the comparison (control) sites were selected; the 40 PHAs included a total of 170 randomly selected projects.

It was possible to select the 18 control sites subsequent to the 1976 baseline survey because all candidate projects for the match had been surveyed in 1976 as part of the Institute's follow-up survey for a large-scale HUD-sponsored housing management study on which the tenant management evaluation was piggybacked. More control or comparison than demonstration sites were included in response to problems of small sample sizes mentioned earlier. Since the number of tenant management sites could not be increased, enlarging the number of controls increased the likelihood of detecting statistically significant differences between the two groups.

After excluding projects with a predominantly elderly population from the Standard Sample projects, the tenant management projects were matched with a subset of the projects from the latter group using a computer matching process developed by the Urban Institute. An attempt was made to achieve a match that reflected similarity in the amount of TPP and MOD funds as well as on an array of variables that previous Urban Institute research had identified as important in an evaluation of performance. The matching procedure initially involved selecting a group of 16 controls for the four tenant management sites most closely approximating the demonstration model. Subsequently, the remaining two demonstration projects were each matched with a control site, bringing the total number of control projects to 18.

In their analyses, the Urban Institute aggregated the tenant management sites into one group and the control sites into another. It felt that this was superior to the alternate procedure (one tenant management site versus its controls) not only because of the increased power of the statistical tests, but also because, in reality, it is virtually impossible to find a "twin" project for each tenant management project. Two separate analyses were performed by the Institute, one using the four "purer" tenant management sites and another using all six sites. In the final report, only the latter analysis was used. Where the subgroup of four manifested a different pattern than the total of six, this fact was discussed in the text.

Interviews were conducted using prestructured questionnaires developed by the Urban Institute on the basis of its previous public housing surveys. Basically, the questions asked for facts, evaluations, amount of satisfaction, and opinions. In addition to the Institute's standard questions, others were added at MDRC's request to elicit more detailed information about tenant participation in management and tenant-management interaction. In 1979, respondents at the tenant management sites were also queried about the activities of the TMC and attitudes concerning tenant management.

Miscellaneous Other Sources

A variety of other data sources was used in the preparation of the report. Many were reports routinely prepared by sites pursuant to MOD and TPP funding. These included quarterly TPP requisitions prepared by the sites for approval by MDRC before submission to the HUD field offices for payment; MOD plans drawn up at the initiation of the demonstration and subsequent modifications; and MOD Quarterly Progress Reports (HUD Form 52995) submitted by the sites to the HUD field offices directly responsible for monitoring physical improvement activities.

DATA ANALYSIS

Aside from the first three introductory and status description chapters, the substance of the report focuses on the results from the documentation, impact, and cost components of the research design. Some of the data sources described above, such as the interviews with the principal tenant management participants at the sites and the Urban Institute survey, were used in several chapters; while others, such as the Tenant Employment Survey, were used in a more limited fashion.

The analysis done for the documentation, largely covered in Chapters 4, 5, and 6, relied primarily on interviews and questionnaires administered to the TMC board and staff, PHA staff, and MDRC field staff as well as on operations staff field reports. Data from these sources were compiled, ordered, and analyzed in order to reach valid conclusions regarding the major documentation concerns. Little statistical manipulation was undertaken in this analysis, except the preparation frequency distributions and some simple cross-tabulations.

The impact analysis, reported in Chapter 7, drew from a wide variety of data sources (see Table A–1) and utilized statistical analyses beyond the descriptive level in the discussions of management performance and tenant satisfaction and assessment.

The real estate management section relied primarily on (1) TMIS data for information on rent, occupancy, and maintenance available on a monthly basis throughout the demonstration; and (2) limited data from the Urban Institute surveys on these same topical areas. The TMIS data were more thorough and systematic in assessing the occurrence and pattern of change in performance over the course of the demonstration because of the frequency of reporting. They were also reported on a site-by-site basis. On the other hand, the Urban Institute data, aggregated for all sites, provided information at two time periods for the tenant management sites and provided comparable data on the control sites. In the analysis, the TMIS was examined initially to ascertain the fact of change and any patterns in it. Where they existed, similar variables for the Urban Institute survey were examined to further assess the significance of any change and to compare it with what occurred at the control sites. Essentially, the Urban Institute survey report was used as a source document to enlarge on MDRC's analysis based on the TMIS.

The analysis of variance with planned comparison was the strategy used in the assessment based on TMIS data. Concern was with the measurement of change over the course of the demonstration and a comparison of change between the pre- and postcontract periods on a site-by-site basis. The direction of change was determined by observation and an examination of the linear and quadratic terms of the analysis of variance.

The Urban Institute analysis on which MDRC drew was based on three sets of information—data measuring conditions in 1979, and data measuring change between 1976 and 1979 (the "change" or "gain" scores). Two major analyses were performed. First, to assess whether statistically significant change had occurred between 1976 and 1979 (i.e., the difference between the change score and zero), the t-test was used. In order to assess whether change that had occurred at the tenant management sites was significantly different from that occurring at the control sites during the same period, analysis of variance (F-test) tests were run. For certain groups of variables, only 1979 scores were used—tenants' perceptions of improvement in management functions (improvement variables and tenants' evaluation of the TMC). With regard to the improvement variables, average ratings were subjected to t-tests to ascertain if the perceived level of improvement was significantly different from zero (no perceived change). Subsequently, average ratings of the tenant management projects were compared with those of the control groups using an analysis of variance procedure to ascertain if there were any statistically significant differences. For tenants' evaluation of the TMC, simple frequency distributions were utilized in the analysis.

The physical improvements section of Chapter 7 relied largely on analysis of qualitative data from field reports and interviews and simple percentage distributions based on various reports submitted in connection with funding under the Modernization Program. In the tenant employment section, quarterly data from the TMIS were used as well as questionnaires completed by TMC board and staff and the Tenant Employment Survey completed by the TMC manager at each site. In assessing the extent of tenant employment, frequencies of the number of tenants employed by quarters were compared to total on-site employment, and change was assessed through observation of what occurred over time and through comparison with the HUD-suggested level of 25 percent. The analysis for the tenants' assessment and satisfaction relied basically on the Urban Institute analysis. Similar statistical analyses were performed for this section as for the analysis of management performance except only data from the tenant sample for the tenant management and control sites were used.

The cost section relied on data from the TMIS, TPP requisitions, and MDRC fiscal records. Raw data were on a quarterly basis. The analytic strategy initially involved the conversion of TPP reporting categories to PHA operating budget categories to provide a total cost picture (one including special demonstration funds and regular operating funds). Relevant quarters were then combined to arrive at total actual costs during the demonstration. Costs under conventional PHA management were estimated using the year before the demonstration as the base year and factoring in inflation for subsequent years to arrive at figures indicating what management would have cost in the absence of the demonstration. Simple numerical comparisons were then made between actual costs under the demonstration and the estimated cost in its absence. To assess what ongoing costs could be, available data on costs after the management contract was signed were annualized. This information was based on postcontract operating experience at three of the sites closely approximating the tenant management program model. At two sites, nine months' data were available for this purpose, and at one site, one year's data.

PROJECTED RENTAL INCOME AND NET INCREMENTAL OPERATING EXPENSES OF TENANT MANAGEMENT UNDER THREE ALTERNATIVE ASSUMPTIONS ABOUT INFLATION

Tenant Management Sites	PFS Inflation Factors[a]		HUD Projection Assumption[b]		OMB Poverty Guidelines[c]	
	Projected Rental Income ($000)	Net Incremental Operating Expenses ($000)	Projected Rental Income ($000)	Net Incremental Operating Expenses ($000)	Projected Rental Income ($000)	Net Incremental Operating Expenses ($000)
Jersey City: A. Harry Moore	1,776	1,112	1,748	1,085	1,789	1,126
Jersey City: Curries Woods	1,905	1,247	1,875	1,217	1,919	1,261
Rochester: Ashanti	313	524	309	520	315	526
New Haven: Que-View	673	421	658	406	670	418
New Orleans: Calliope	2,120	241	1,969	90	2,006	127

a. Inflation factors computed annually for metropolitan areas and counties; used in HUD's Performance Funding System (PFS).
b. Assumption that tenants' incomes will rise .06 per year; used by HUD to project budget requests.
c. Percentage increase Poverty Guideline for a nonfarm family of four.

MDRC DOCUMENTS ON
TENANT MANAGEMENT

PUBLISHED REPORTS

Diaz, William A. *Tenant Management: An Historical and Analytical Overview.* 1978.

Manpower Demonstration Research Corporation. *The First Annual Report on the National Tenant Management Demonstration.* 1977.

_____ . "Tenant Management." 1976. A descriptive brochure.

Motley, R. Susan (with the assistance of Donald Ridings and Angus Olson). *Tenant Management Operations Manual.* 1980.

Talbot, Allan R. *The Evolution of the National Tenant Management Demonstration Program.* New York: The Ford Foundation, 1977.

UNPUBLISHED WORKING PAPERS

Branch, Alvia. "The Tenant Management Demonstration Program: A Documentation of the First 18 Months of Program Implementation." February 1979.

Loux, Suzanne B., and Robert Sadacca. "Analysis of Changes at Tenant Management Demonstration Projects." July 1980.

Palmerio, Thelma. "Management and Other Characteristics of the Tenant Management Demonstration Program Sites: Year Ended September 30, 1977. June 1978.

Queeley, Mary A. "First Interim Report: Research on the National Tenant Management Demonstration Program." April 1977.

INDEX

A. Harry Moore Tenant Management
  Corporation (Jersey City): average
  monthly rent, 133, 134–136, 164;
  average monthly rent collected per
  unit, 138–141, 164; board of directors, 38–40, 58, 59, 62–63, 64–65,
  66–67; costs of demonstration,
  214–217, 232, 233; and Curries
  Woods TMC, 41; funding levels and
  sources, 28; employment of tenants,
  182–183, 184, 185, 190, 191, 194;
  and Jersey City Housing Authority,
  90, 95–96, 100–101, 104–105,
  106–107, 109; maintenance at,
  158–162, 164; profile of, 37–40;
  rent collection rate, 139, 142–143,
  164; staff, 72, 74, 81, 82; technical
  assistance at, 116, 121, 122, 216;
  tenants' perceptions of change, 200;
  training program, 116, 123; units
  owing more than one months' rent,
  143–146, 164; use of MOD funds,
  169, 170, 174, 175; vacancy rate,
  149–153, 164; vacant unit preparation, 154–157, 164
American Arbitration Association, 23
Annual Contributions Contract, 13
Ashanti Tenant Management Corporation (Rochester): average monthly
rent, 133, 134–136, 165; average
monthly rent collected per unit,
138–141, 165; board of directors,
54–55, 58, 62, 63, 66–67, 68; and
community, 202, 204; costs of demonstration, 220–223, 232, 234, 235;
employment of tenants, 182–183,
185, 190–191, 195; funding levels
and sources, 28; maintenance at,
158–162, 165; profile of, 53–55;
rent collection rate, 142–143, 165;
and Rochester Housing Authority,
90, 94, 98, 105–106, 107, 109,
110; staff, 73, 76–77, 81; technical
assistance at, 113, 120, 222; tenants'
perceptions of change, 200; training
program, 120, 123; units owing
more than one months' rent,
143–146, 165; use of MOD funds,
167–168, 169, 173, 174; vacancy
rate, 149–152, 165; vacant unit
preparation, 154–157, 165

Boston, 17
Boston Housing Authority, 17
Bromley-Heath Tenant Management
  Corporation, 17
Bronson Court, 53; *See also* Ashanti
  TMC

Budgeting, project based, 99; *See also* Costs of demonstration
Building managers, 22; *See also* Staff

Calliope Development Tenant Management Corporation (New Orleans): average monthly rent, 134–136, 165; average monthly rent collected per unit, 138–141, 165; board of directors, 48–50, 58, 59, 62, 63, 66–67; costs of demonstration, 226–228, 234, 236; employment of tenants, 182–185, 187, 190, 192, 195; funding levels and sources, 28; and Housing Authority of New Orleans, 90, 95–96, 104, 107, 109; maintenance at, 158–162, 165; profile of, 48–50; rent collection rate, 142–143, 165; staff, 72, 76, 81; technical assistance, 113, 118, 121; tenants' perceptions of change at, 200; training program, 118, 123; units owing more than one months' rent, 144–146, 165; use of MOD funds, 168–169, 172, 174, 175; vacancy rate, 149–153, 165; vacant unit preparation, 154–157, 165
Cambridge Housing Authority, 33
Capsule Dwellings, 53; *See also* Ashanti TMC
Carr Square Village, 18
CETA. *See* Comprehensive Employment and Training Act
Civil Rights movement, 15
Community; and tenant management, 202, 204–205
Community Action Programs, 15–16
Community Chest, Rochester, 55
Community Development Block Grant: to Iroquois Homes RMC, 46
Comprehensive Employment Training Act, 39, 181, 186, 187, 190–191, 194–195
Concerned Tenants Committee (Curries Woods), 41
Contract, management, 23, 101–103; delayed signing of, 128
Costs of demonstration, 209–210; A. Harry Moore TMC, 214–217, 232, 233; annual incremental costs of TMC, 230, 232; Ashanti TMC, 220–223, 232, 234, 235; Calliope TMC, 226–228, 234, 236; Curries

Woods TMC, 217–219; Iroquois Homes RMC, 228–230; methodology of analysis, 210–213; net incremental costs of tenant management, 237; Que-View TMC, 223–225; Sunrise Acres TMC, 230, 231
Crime, and public housing, 11, 13–14
Curries Woods Tenant Management Corporation (Jersey City): average monthly rent, 133, 134–136, 164; average monthly rent collected per unit, 138–141, 164; board of directors, 41–43, 60, 62, 63, 64–65, 67, 68; costs of demonstration, 217–219; employment for tenants, 182–183, 184, 185, 190, 191, 194; funding sources and levels, 28; and Jersey City Housing Authority, 90, 92, 100, 104–105, 107, 109–110; maintenance at, 158–162, 164; profile of, 41–43; rent collection rate, 142–143, 164; staff, 74, 81, 82; technical assistance, 116, 121, 219; training program, 116, 123; units owing more than one months' rent, 144–147, 164; use of MOD funds, 168, 169, 170–171, 174, 175; vacancy rate, 150–153, 164; vacant unit preparation, 154–157, 164

Dallas Housing Authority, 33
Darst, tenant association at, 18
Directors, TMC board of, 57; benefits of, 86–88; burdens of, 84–85; characteristics of, 60–62; continuity of membership, 63–69; development of, 62; interviews, 250; leaderships styles, 62–63, 64–67; and MOD funds, 167–168; patterns and problems of, 69–71; questionnaire, 252; recruitment of, 58–60; role perceptions, 85–86; and staff, 69–71, 72–73; training of, 111, 116–120, 122–125, 128; turnover, 68
Drug abuse in public housing, 11

Edith–Doran Townhouses, 53; *See also* Ashanti TMC
Education, 14
Employment, tenant, 180–181, 184; changes in employment patterns, 192–193; jobs, 184–187; job crea-

tion, 189–192; MOD funds in job development, 192; post-demonstration management employment, 189; by site, 182–183; target population, 187–188; tenure, 188–189; turnover, 188–189

Fairfield Villages, 53; *See also* Ashanti TMC
Ford Foundation, 18, 20, 26–29

Great Depression, 12
Grievances, HUD procedure, 14

Hawaii, tenant management program in, 17
Hawthorne effect, 129
Housing, public: cost of, 12; history of, 12–16; problems of, 11
Housing Act of 1937, 12–13; Brooke Amendments, 14
Housing Act of 1974, 15
Housing and Urban Development Act of 1965, 14
Housing Management Improvement Program (HMIP), 14–15
Housing manager, 78–79; *See also* Staff
HUD. *See* U.S. Department of Housing and Urban Development
Housing market: analysis of tenant management cities, 120; effect on demonstration, 129, 153, 165

Inflation, and cost analysis, 211–212, 260–261
Iroquois Resident Council, 44
Iroquois Homes Resident Management Corporation (Louisville): average monthly rent, 133, 134–136, 137, 164; average monthly rent collected per unit, 138–141, 164; board of directors, 44–46, 59, 63, 64–65, 71; costs of demonstration, 228–230; employment of tenants, 182–183, 185, 190, 191, 192, 194; funding levels and sources, 28; and Housing Authority of Louisville, 90, 95, 99, 100; maintenance at, 158–162, 164; profile of, 43–46; rent collection rate, 139, 142–143, 164; resident council, 59; staff, 73, 75, 81–82;

technical assistance, 117; tenants' perceptions of change, 200; training program, 117, 123–124; units owing more than one months' rent, 143–146, 164; use of MOD funds, 168–169, 171, 174, 175; vacancy rate, 149–153, 164; vacant unit preparation, 154–157, 164

Jersey City Housing Authority (New Jersey): and A. Harry Moore TMC, 38, 40, 59; cost analysis of A. Harry Moore TMC, 211, 214–215, 233; cost analysis of Curries Woods TMC, 211, 218, 219; and Curries Woods TMC, 42, 43; and McCormack, Baron and Associates, 116; and site selection, 34; technical assistance to TMCs, 121; and tenant management demonstration, 90–92, 95–97, 99–101, 104–110
Jersey City sites. *See* A. Harry Moore TMC; Curries Woods TMC
Jobs. *See* Employment, tenant

Korean War, 13

Labor practices, at A. Harry Moore TMC, 39
Lane managers, 22, 81–82
League of Women Voters, 23, 113
Lease, 14
Local Housing Authorities (LHAs), 12; *See also* Public Housing Authorities
Louisville, Housing Authority of (Kentucky): cost analysis of Iroquois Homes RMC, 228–230; and Iroquois Homes RMC, 44–46; and tenant management demonstration, 90, 93, 94, 95, 96–98, 99, 100, 103, 104, 106, 108, 109–110; site selection, 34
Louisville site. *See* Iroquois Homes Resident Management Corporation

McCormack, Baron and Associates, 29–30, 112; and A. Harry Moore TMC, 38–39; and Ashanti TMC, 120, 121, 222; and Calliope TMC, 118; cost analysis of TMCs, 213; costs of training at Que-View TMC, 225; and Curries Woods TMC, 42,

116, 121, 219; and Que-View TMC, 47, 117, 225; and Sunrise Acres TMC, 119; training program, 114, 123–125

Maintenance, 158–162, 164–165

Manpower Demonstration Research Corporation (MDRC): cost analysis of TMCs, 213; designated as program manager, 20; field representative, 29; organization of demonstration, 26; operations staff, 251; planning phase, 33–35; program operations, 29–30; research design, 30–32, 247–249; technical assistance at Curries Woods TMC, 219; technical assistance hired by, 112; and TMC staffs, 82; *See also* Tenant Management Information System

Modernization Program (MOD), 14–15; and A. Harry Moore TMC, 38, 40; and cost-benefit analysis of tenant management, 210; employment of tenants, 180–181, 187, 190, 194–195; funding levels, 28; funding rationale, 163, 166–167; importance to tenant management, 178–180; and organization of demonstration, 26; previous funding at Curries Woods TMC, 41; process, 167–169; program outcomes, 169–178; Public Housing Authority use of funds, 96; and St. Louis model, 19, 163, 166, 167; tenant input into, 16; and tenant participation in PHA affairs, 91–92; training program, 122

National Tenant Management Demonstration (NTMD): conclusions of, 239–243; data analysis, 256–258; data sources, 249–256; division of responsibility, 24; extension of tenant management, 108–110; funding, 28; major findings, 5–9; management of, 26–29; models for, 16–19, 21–25; organization of, 26–29; origins of, 11–16; predemonstration experiments, 16–19; process, 21–25; Public Housing Authority view of, 103–110; and real estate management, 127–131; research design, 30–32, 247–249; role of Manpower Demonstration Research Corporation, 29–35; site selection; *See also* Costs of demonstration; Tenant Management Corporations

National Tenants Organization (NTO), 15–16

National Welfare Rights Organization (NWRO), 15–16

Nepotism, in TMC hiring, 39, 72

Newark, New Jersey, 19

New Haven Housing Authority: cost analysis of Que-View TMC, 223, 224, 225; and Que-View TMC, 46–48; site selection, 33, 34; technical assistance to Que-View TMC, 121; and tenant management demonstration, 90, 92, 93, 94–95, 97, 99, 101–102, 104, 105, 108; and vacant unit preparation, 154

New Haven site. *See* Que-View TMC

New Orleans, Housing Authority of (HANO): and Calliope Development TMC, 49–50; cost analysis of Calliope TMC, 226–228; and tenant management demonstration, 90, 95–96, 97, 99, 104, 107, 108, 109, 110

New Orleans site. *See* Calliope Development TMC

New York State Equal Opportunity Commission, 55

Occupancy, 147–149, 164–165; and local private housing market, 129, 153, 165; vacancy rate, 149–153, 164–165; vacant unit preparation, 154–157, 164–165

Occupational counseling, 14

Oklahoma City Housing Authority, 33, 34; and Sunrise Acres TMC, 51–53; and tenant management demonstration, 90, 92, 96, 97–98; and technical assistance to Sunrise Acres TMC, 121

Oklahoma City site. *See* Sunrise Acres TMC

Olean Townhouses, 53; *See also* Ashanti TMC

Payment In Lieu of Taxes (PILOT), 13

Performance Funding System, 132, 191, 211–212

Physical improvements. *See* Modernization Program
PILOT, 13
Program Sequence Guide, 29–30; at A. Harry Moore TMC, 39; beginnings of, 112; at Que-View TMC, 47; and social services coordinator, 79; and training program, 122, 123–125
Project Review Committee, 26
Pruitt–Igoe development, 17–19
Public Housing Authorities: allocations based on rent income, 132; benefits of relationship with tenant management corporation, 105–108; Board of Commissioners, 97–98; contract with TMC, 23, 101–103; costs of continued management by, 211–212; demands of relationship with TMC, 104–105; and education, 14; Executive Director, 89, 93–97, 251; extension of tenant management, 108–110; financial problems of, 11; and Housing Management Improvement Program, 14–15; improvements to sites, 129; legislation to aid, 14; and MDRC field representative, 29; and Modernization Program, 14–15, 175–176; number of, 12; and occupational counseling, 14; and organization of demonstration, 26; predemonstration relationships with TMCs, 91–92; range of rents approach, 15; and rent reviews, 132; size of, 12; staff, 92, 98–101; and Target Projects Program, 14–15; and tenant employment, 187, 191, and Tenant Management Corporations, 89–91, 103–104; and Tenant Management Corporation staff, 22–23; and tenant participation, 14; Turnkey II program, 14–15; and vacant unit preparation, 154, 165
Public Housing Urban Initiatives, 46

Que-View Tenant Management Corporation (New Haven): average monthly rent, 134–136, 164; average monthly rent collected per unit, 138–141, 164; board of directors, 46–48, 60, 62, 63, 64–65, 67–68; costs of demonstration, 223–225; employment of tenants, 182–183,

185, 187, 194; funding levels and sources, 28; and housing authority, 90, 94–95, 97, 99, 102, 104, 105; maintenance at, 158–162, 164; profile of, 46–48; rent collection rate, 142–143, 164; staff, 75, 82, 83; technical assistance, 117, 121; training program, 117, 124; units owing more than one months' rent, 144–146, 164; use of MOD funds, 169, 171–172, 174, 175; vacancy rate, 149–153, 164; vacant unit preparation, 154–157, 164
Quinnipiac Terrace, 46; *See also* Que-View TMC

Ralston–Purina grant, 46
Real estate management by TMCs, 127–131, 162; maintenance, 158–162; occupancy, 147–149; rent collections, 137–143; rent delinquencies, 143–147; rents, 131–137; vacancies, 149–157
Rents: average monthly rent due, 133–137, 164–165; average rent collected per unit, 137–141, 164–165; collection rate, 139, 142–143, 164–165; and higher income tenants, 132; and Housing Act of 1937, 13; as inadequate to cover operations, 13; increasing rental income, 131–132; Performance Funding System, 132; range of rents approach, 15; rent reviews, 131–132; and tenant's employment status, 16; units owing more than one months' rent, 143–147, 164–165
Resident Management Corporation. *See* Iroquois Homes Resident Management Corporation; Tenant Management Corporations
Riverview Terrace, 46; *See also* Que-View TMC
Rochester Housing Authority (RHA): and Ashanti TMC, 53–55; cost analysis of Ashanti TMC, 211, 220, 221, 222, 223, 235; and tenant management demonstration, 90, 93, 94, 97, 98, 99, 101, 104, 105–106, 107, 110; site selection, 34

Rochester site. *See* Ashanti TMC
Rules and regulations, 22

St. Louis: as model for demonstration, 11–12; rent strikes, 18
St. Louis Housing Authority, 17–19, 89–90, 128, 167
71 Merritt Street Tenants Association (Curries Woods), 41
Sexism, 98
Social Services Coordinator, 79–81
Sooner Haven, 51; *See also* Sunrise Acres TMC
Staff: benefits of, 86–88; and board of directors, 69–71, 83–88; burdens of, 84–85; composition of, 73–78; and costs of tenant management, 209; housing manager, 78–79; interviews, 251; lane manager, 81–82; performance of, 82–83; questionnaire, 252; recruitment of, 72–73; role perceptions, 85–86; size of, 73–78; social services coordinator, 79–81; training of, 111, 116–120, 122–125, 128; *See also* Employment, tenant
Sunrise Acres Tenant Management Corporation (Oklahoma City): board of directors, 51–53, 58, 60, 66–67; costs of demonstration, 230–231; funding levels and sources, 28; and Oklahoma City Housing Authority, 60, 96, 110; profile of, 51–53; technical assistance to, 119, 121; training program, 119

Target Projects Program (TPP), 14–15; and A. Harry Moore TMC, 38; and cost analysis of TMCs, 212–213; funding levels, 28, 163, 166; and organization of demonstration, 26; Public Housing Authority use of funds, 96; support for St. Louis model, 18–19; and tenant employment, 187; and Tenant Manager Program, 17; and tenant participation in PHA affairs, 91–92; training program, 122
Taxes, property, 13
Technical assistance: at A. Harry Moore TMC, 116, 121, 122; at

Ashanti TMC, 120; at Calliope TMC, 118, 121; contribution of technical assistants, 115, 121–122; costs of, 216, 219, 222; at Curries Woods TMC, 116, 121; at Iroquois Homes RMC, 117; at Que-View TMC, 117; at Sunrise Acres TMC, 119; technical assistants, 112–113
Tenant Affairs Board (TAB), 18, 167
Tenant Associations, 91; leaders of, 58
Tenant Management Corporations: adversary relationships with Public Housing Authorities, 89; assistant manager, 22; benefits of relationship with PHA, 105–108; and community relations, 202–205; contract with PHA, 23, 101–103; demands of relationship with PHA, 104–105; and demonstration model, 21–23; developmental process, 23–25; evaluation of, 205–207; and extension of tenant management, 108–110; manager, 22; and MOD funds, 176–179; predemonstration relationships with PHAs, 91–92; and PHA Board of Commissioners, 97–98; and PHA executive director, 93–97; and PHA staff, 92, 98–101; recreation director and/or aides, 22; responsibilities of, 22; social services director and/or aides, 22; tenants' perceptions of, 197–202; *See also* Costs of demonstration; Directors, board of; Employment, tenant; Staff, *names of individual Tenant Management Corporations, e.g.*: Ashanti Tenant Management Corporation
Tenant Management Information System, 31, 32–33, 130, 252–253
Tenants' Representative Council (New Haven), 92
Tenants' Rights, 14
Training, of board and staff: at A. Harry Moore TMC, 116, 123; at Ashanti TMC, 120, 123; of board of directors, 128; at Calliope TMC, 118, 123; at Curries Woods TMC, 116, 123; at Iroquois Homes RMC, 117, 123–124; at Que-View TMC,

117, 124; of staff, 128; at Sunrise Acres TMC, 119
Turnkey II Program, 14–15

Unions, 39
United Community Council (Curries Woods), 41
U.S. Census Bureau, 212
U.S. Department of Housing and Urban Development (HUD): allocations for demonstration, 20; funding levels, 26–29; in Louisville, 175; Office of Policy Development and Research, 26; and organization of demonstration, 26; and St. Louis model, 18; and tenant employment, 180–181; and tenants' rights, 14; *See also names of specific HUD programs*
U.S. Office of Economic Opportunity, 15–16

U.S. Supreme Court, rulings of, 13, 14
United Way (Rochester), 55
Urban Institute: public housing data, 199; on rent collection, 147; research design, 32
Urban Institute survey, 70, 107–108, 120–121, 253–256; on employment, 192–193; on MOD funds, 177; on tenants' evaluation of TMCs, 205

Vacancy. *See* Occupancy
Vandalism, and public housing, 11, 13, 16, 38, 200
"Vertical slums," 13

Wagner–Steagall Act, 12; *See also* Housing Act of 1937
Washington, D.C., 17
World War II, 13